SHAPED BY STORIES

MARSHALL
GREGORY

SHAPED
BY
STORIES

The

Ethical Power

of Narratives

University of Notre Dame Press

Notre Dame, Indiana

Library of Congress Cataloging-in-Publication Data

Gregory, Marshall W., 1940–
Shaped by stories : the ethical power of narratives / Marshall Gregory.
p. cm.
Includes bibliographical references and index.
ISBN-13: 978-0-268-02974-6 (pbk. : alk. paper)
ISBN-10: 0-268-02974-1 (pbk. : alk. paper)
1. English literature—Study and teaching. 2. American literature—Study and
teaching. 3. Ethics in literature. 4. Literature and morals. I. Title.
PR35.G75 2009
820.9'353—dc22
2009027705

To Valiska,

the one and only

From the time we are born, the narrative cradle of story rocks us to the collective heartbeat of our species, ushering us across the threshold of consciousness and into the domain of humanity.

—CHAPTER 1

CONTENTS

꒰꒱꒰Ｘ꒱꒰

ACKNOWLEDGMENTS

I have always been struck by the poignancy of Samuel Johnson's sad words at the end of the preface to his great dictionary: "I have protracted my work till most of those whom I wished to please have sunk into the grave, and success and miscarriage are empty sounds." Having finished this book, what strikes me now with great force is the mixed gratitude and sadness I feel that fate has allowed me to escape Johnson's melancholy condition in some ways but not in others. To those living and dead whose instruction, kindness, and support over many years are woven into the views and attitudes that form this book, it gives me deep pleasure to acknowledge my gratitude and my indebtedness.

First I must acknowledge Wayne Booth, whose death in October 2005 was a great loss to the humanities in general, to the discipline of English in particular, and to me in a deeply personal way. Wayne, as he insisted on being called, was my teacher in graduate school at the University of Chicago and was a teacher to me in all the years of our relationship until his death. In addition, Wayne was always a profoundly companionable, charming, and affectionate friend; my coauthor on previous books; and a source of inspiration for keeping at my scholarship.

In addition to Wayne Booth, I must also acknowledge the assistance and support of Robert McCauley, a philosopher and friend from Emory University who over the years has demonstrated just how generous a deep friendship can be by not only critiquing my work intellectually, which has been immensely beneficial, but hammering at me personally to keep whacking away at a project that he has honored by insisting on its importance. If Wayne Booth played a major role in getting me started, Bob McCauley has played a major role in keeping me going. Bob perfectly illustrates Aristotle's claim that true friendship is the act of wishing good things for the friend rather than oneself.

I must also acknowledge the assistance of my many students. None of them were ever aware of helping me do my research, I'm sure, but as I have had occasion in class after class, and especially in the literary criticism course I teach every year, to touch on this book's issues, I found that the opportunity to explain literary and critical ideas to my students—just the pleasant duty of responding to their questions—has been important in fertilizing the intellectual soil out of which this project has grown. I have always followed the principle that if I could not make the most complicated ideas in this book clear to smart undergraduates, then those ideas probably were not yet clear in my own head.

Penultimately, I must thank both the Indiana Humanities Council and Butler University for giving me grants at different times to work on this book.

Finally, it gives me the greatest delight of all to acknowledge the unfailing support of Valiska Gregory, who, as a skillful intellectual, astute critic, gifted writer, and loving friend, has helped me in every conceivable way, not only in the writing of this book but in all the common (and sometimes nutty) projects we have undertaken ever since we met the first day of freshman orientation and fell in love as first-year college students. Valiska and our wonderful daughters, Melissa and Holly, have enriched the quality of my life and work beyond all calculation. I cannot imagine that doing anything creative would have seemed possible to me—or would have seemed worth doing even if possible—without them. To adapt to my ladies of beauty and talent what Shelley says of poetry, they are "the center and the circumference" of what I know and what I care about most deeply.

An earlier version of chapter 9 has appeared as "Ethical Engagements over Time: Reading and Rereading *David Copperfield* and *Wuthering Heights*," *Narrative* 12.3 (October 2004): 281–305. "The Grave" by Katherine Anne Porter from *The Leaning Tower and Other Stories*, copyright 1944, 1972 by Katherine Anne Porter, is reprinted by permission of Houghton Mifflin Harcourt Publishing Company and of Random House UK. "The Catbird Seat," originally published in book form by James Thurber, copyright © 1945, 1973 by Rosemary A. Thurber, is reprinted by arrangement with Rosemary A. Thurber and the Barbara Hogenson Agency, Inc.

PREFACE

The world is a story we tell ourselves about the world.
—Vikram Chandra

This book explores the ethical implication of the universal human obsession with stories. Sales of narratives—novels, biographies, autobiographies, histories, and so on—run into the millions every year. The average American watches six hours of TV every day, most of it stories. Parents read thousands of stories to their offspring, including the old legends, fairy tales, and myths that they themselves grew up with, and when parents aren't reading to their children, the kids are absorbing other stories from Saturday morning cartoons. A new blockbuster movie can earn $40 million in its opening weekend. Video rental stores and Netflix are growth industries. People now buy their favorite TV shows on DVDs and rewatch them without commercials. Ministers and teachers and motivational speakers and politicians exert their effects on audiences mainly through stories. Most TV commercials are miniature narratives, and even the oldest stories never disappear. The summer of 2004 saw yet two more movies based on Greek myths—*Troy* and *Alexander*—while 2005 gave us a new version of *Beowulf*, and both movie and dramatic productions of Shakespeare's plays go on endlessly. There was yet another movie version of *Beowulf* in 2008, employing some of the biggest names in Hollywood (Angelina Jolie, for example). YouTube, blogs, and online publishing open up more and more avenues of storytelling and story consuming almost daily. *Truly, as our bodies are surrounded by air so are our lives saturated by stories*. Both air and stories are so profoundly ubiquitous that we spend hardly any time thinking about how impossible or different our lives would be with them, but once we *do* start such a train of thought, an inquiry into how stories potentially influence ethos can no longer be viewed as a matter of narrow academic interest. It must be viewed as a matter of broad human interest.

While most people, on reflection, will probably accept my claim that human beings are obsessed with stories, many of these same people are likely to become queasy about my additional claim that this obsession exerts a potentially serious influence on their ethos: on the kinds of persons they turn out to be. "Ethos," the Greek word for character, refers to persons as ethical agents, as people who make decisions about good and bad and who decide their own conduct. Inquiry into the influences that make us the kind of agents we become—the influences that shape our character, or ethos—is called "ethical criticism," which, clearly enough, derives from the word "ethos" itself. Ethical criticism, then, examines the influences on us that shape our ethos.

To say, however, that I have written a book of *ethical* criticism is to begin a path of analysis that is slippery, controversial, and confusing. It is slippery because "ethical" is a term used in many different ways by many different people. It is controversial because "ethical" is a term that will always get someone's hackles up somewhere, somehow. And it is conceptually confusing because popular discourse about ethics in America—the references to ethics that typically crop up in newspapers, on TV, and in everyday conversation—is abominably inconsistent, often narrow and dogmatic, and sometimes just silly.

I would prefer to formulate my topic in a way that doesn't invite controversy and that doesn't get people's hackles up, but the truth is that "ethical criticism" says exactly what I mean and is therefore too useful a term for me to throw out in favor of a less accurate substitute designed with the futile hope of deflecting or avoiding criticism. In this book I inquire into the influences, especially from stories, that help shape ethos, and I do so because I think, frankly, that the inquiry into story as a possible influence on character has never been done as thoroughly as it needs to be. Even in the writings of the great canonical critics who have dealt with this issue—Plato, Horace, Cicero, Philip Sidney, Samuel Johnson,

Matthew Arnold, F. R. Leavis, and others—this issue has mostly been dealt with by assertions, slogans, and pre-cooked formulas, not analysis.

The reasons why ethical critics in past centuries seldom did real analysis of stories' ethical influence throw light on why this task remains to be done today. In the first place, during those many centuries in which there was no mass media, there was little need to develop hard arguments in defense of story because both story's intrinsic value and the value of studying it were mostly taken for granted. The few detractors of story who arose, like Plato in ancient Greece or the Puritans in the seventeenth century, were mostly dealt with by supercilious put-downs rather than by arguments. In the second place, during those long centuries when the value of story was taken for granted, certain texts—especially the Greek and Roman classics—were granted an almost religious status, a view that tends to produce more reverence than argument. In the third place, ethical criticism deals with stories' relations to life, and even though most people might concede that they don't have life completely figured out, this does not prevent them from having lots of opinions to which they feel emotionally committed. Because opinions about life are easy to come by—even the weakest thinkers among us have a lot of them—people often act as if ethical criticism is easy because it seems to invite the advancing of opinions rather than to require the making of arguments. In the fourth place, many ethical critics avoid the kind of arguments I engage in here, especially if they are literary critics or literary academics, because they have an intuitive aversion to being transformed into sociologists, political scientists, or psychologists. They want to talk about literature, not about sociology or psychology, and their descriptive eloquence about literary engagements—an eloquence that is often sweeping, sometimes profound, and emotionally compelling; one thinks of the descriptive eloquence of an Edmund Wilson or a Lionel Trilling—has tended to satisfy their sense of what kind of defense of literary study works.

As this book will clearly show, however, it *is* possible to do ethical criticism without becoming either a sociologist or a psychologist, but there is an additional, more important reason why I have written this book: the few—the very few—contemporary critics who have dealt with ethical criticism have written books addressed almost exclusively to other critics and academic professionals. This does not mean that these contemporary books are not good—a few of them in fact are brilliant—but they will never be read by a broad audience. I am convinced, however, that the influence of stories is of great importance to all citizens, not just to professional critics and academics, and I have written this book in a manner that is accessible to an audience as broad as the topic's importance. It is not limited in its address to other specialists. Of course I want my academic colleagues to read this book—it addresses issues of vital importance to the teaching and interpretation of stories of all kinds—but I do not use in this book professional or academic jargon. On the other hand, I have *not* dumbed down the book's ideas. It is simply the case that the issues I talk about do not require professional or academic jargon for their clear discussion.

In order to test the viability of my claims and arguments, my readers do not need to possess any particular set of intellectual or academic notions. They merely need to be willing to read closely, to be thoughtful, and to ask whether the things I say about stories map onto their own experience. My hope is that readers will discover that the experiences with stories I illuminate for them are experiences they will immediately recognize as theirs and as important, but ones they have not hitherto thought about reflectively or critically. If this book helps readers become more thoughtful and perceptive consumers of stories, it will have done its job.

Reading for Life

What's at Stake? A Story about Stories

Long ago, with elegant succinctness, Horace defined the educational transposition by which readers identify with narratives: "Change the name," he says, "and you are the subject of the story" (*Satires,* 1.1). From the time we are born, the narrative cradle of story rocks us to the collective heartbeat of our species, ushering us across the threshold of consciousness and into the domain of humanity. What's at stake in our lives and in this book is (1) the way stories embrace human existence in a narrative environment that is ubiquitous and inescapable, (2) the way stories construct pictures of the world's workings and interpretations of the world's events that are not only emotionally compelling but that we often treat as knowledge, (3) the way stories invite (and, to a surprising degree, control) responses of emotion, belief, and judgment that we hardly ever refuse to give, (4) and the way stories exert shaping pressure on our ethos because both the "knowledge" offered by stories and our seldom denied responses constitute kinds of practice, modes of clarification, and sets of habits for living that, once configured and repeatedly reinforced, accompany us into real-life situations day in and day out.

The overarching claim of this book is that stories are an important component of the ethical development that all human beings undergo because stories are an important component of every human being's education about the world. I will have much to say in this book about the benefits offered by our educational encounters with stories, but I will not be repeating the age-old claim so often advanced by Western humanists that, somehow, literary education automatically elevates and improves moral character. Just as the nutritionists' claim that "we are what we eat" does not entail a corollary belief that all foods are equally good for us, so my claim that stories are *important* for everyone is not the same thing as claiming that all stories are always *good* for everyone.

To give you a sense of the distance between the claims I make here and the extravagant claims often advanced throughout the history of literary education (at least in the West) by such humanists as Petrarch, Philip Sidney, Percy Shelley, Matthew Arnold, and others, listen here to Petrarch's glorification of the virtues that one acquires by reading classical works of literature (from a work in Latin written near the end of Petrarch's life in 1374):

> [These works, the *studia humanitatis*] stamp and drive deep into the heart the sharpest and most ardent stings of speech, by which the lazy are startled, the ailing kindled, and the sleepy aroused, the sick healed and prostrate raised and those who stick to the ground lifted up to the highest thoughts and to honest desire. Then earthly things become vile; the aspect of vice stirs up an enormous hatred of vicious life; virtue and "the shape, and as it were, the face of honesty," are beheld by the inmost eye "and inspire miraculous love" of wisdom and of themselves, as Plato says. (497)

Who knew that studying the classics could yield not only honest desires but heal the sick? More than two hundred years later, however, Philip Sidney's claims for benefits of a literary education are hardly less extravagant. Literary study produces automatic moral improvement, he says, by means of "this purifying of wit, this enriching of memory, enabling of judgment, and enlarging of conceit, which commonly we call learning, under what name so ever it come forth, or to what immediate end soever it be directed, the final end is, to lead and draw us to as high a perfection, as our degenerate souls made worse by their clay-lodgings, can be capable of. . . . Now therein of all Sciences . . . is our Poet the Monarch.

For he doth not only show the way, but giveth so sweet a prospect into the way, as will entice any man to enter into it" (163).

In the history of Western education, at least until late in the twentieth century, books on literary education have often taken this line of extravagant praise and pugnacious assertiveness about the "improving" effects of literary study—the implication is frequently made that such improvement occurs automatically and inevitably—but you will not find me repeating such claims in this book. In the first place, I don't believe them. Stories can only extend invitations, not coerce effects. In the second place, traditional encomiums in defense of literary education always ignore one crucial logical entailment of their praise, namely, that any kind of learning capable of producing powerful benefits *must* entail a corollary power to do harm. The traditional defenders of literary study have often operated like terrier defense attorneys eager to dig up every conceivable virtue that will make their gilt client (Lord Literature of Epic Hall located in the county of Nature and designed by that redoubtable architect Truth) look good in the eyes of the jury, while assiduously avoiding any reference to facts that might raise doubts about the value of some stories' effects. In the third place, traditional defenses of literary education have always focused not on narratives in general but on forms of art that authors and critics of canonical art usually call "great *literature*." Despite my profession as a teacher of traditional British literature, however, as well as my lifelong addiction to literary works (some of them great and some of them not) this book is *not* exclusively about literature. It is about *stories*—narratives in general—and the world of stories is much vaster than the world of literature. Only some of us are addicted to literature. All of us are addicted to stories. My claim is that exposure to stories is *educational* and therefore *formative*, and the appropriate follow-up to this claim is not a set of specific predictions about the inevitable outcomes of our formative experiences with stories but rather an analysis of why and how stories exert formative influence in the first place. Just an account of what "formative" might mean, for example, turns out to be a highly complex issue, an account that requires many books for its investigation, including this one. Let me begin my investigation into the influence of stories by telling a story—my own. How stories worked for me illustrates in a general way how stories work for us all.

The beginning of my story is that I was born into a highly dysfunctional family. My parents never managed to get their individual lives in order, and they found overwhelming the task of constructing a family life that might nourish the development of two children. Instead of being raised by my parents, I was mostly raised by the stories I read. Sometimes this was a good thing for me; sometimes it was not. The adventure stories, travel tales, and legends and fairy tales that I devoured in my childhood benefited the development of my language powers, imagination, and capacities for both introspection and empathy. But when at age thirteen I discovered my adolescent uncle's hidden cache of Mickey Spillane novels and eagerly devoured their salacious contents like a kid who had discovered a box of forbidden chocolates, I, who knew absolutely nothing about the forbidden sweetness of either women or sex, came in for some horrible lessons about both. I learned that real men spice sex with violence and that women like it that way, that real men are disposed to violence even when sex is not at stake, and that real men view women as commodities to be owned, mastered, and bullied, not treasured and not even respected. On the other hand, I was so ill-equipped to place Spillane's violent and sexist images into any social context or set of relations readily available either to my experience or to my imagination that his stories did me no lasting harm. This escape was mainly because of my ignorance, however, not because the stories themselves are harmless.

But the education that I gleaned from most of my youthful encounters with stories was profoundly useful to me. Because my parents didn't mind how much I read as long as I completed my chores and maintained the family fiction that I had no needs, reading stories was for me an escape. Stories also projected hope, a vision of different and better worlds, and they bestowed on me a blessed education about life that supplemented the meager instruction I received in the rural Indiana communities where I lived in the mid-fifties, communities where some of my classmates came to school barefoot, wearing bib overalls, and looking for all the world like Huck Finn tryouts on a movie set. I often felt like an outsider and was often treated like one. My outsider status was sometimes frustrating but not generally traumatic, in part because my inveterate reading gave me interesting and vivid companions who filled in the companionship gaps in my real life. Outsider kids need solace, and

I was certainly not the first child nor, I hope, the last, to find consoling sociability in stories that were richer in ideas and feelings than the forms of sociability generally available to me in my real life.

Stories in effect were my real home. In a short but intense book called *How Reading Changed My Life*, Anna Quindlen (another person who endured a miserable childhood) says that "it is like the rubbing of two sticks together to make a fire, the act of reading, an improbable pedestrian task that leads to heat and light. Perhaps this only becomes clear when one watches a child do it" (20). Reading as a "pedestrian task." An intriguing phrase. Quindlen does not say outright what she means by heat and light, but I suppose she means something like the heat of feeling and the light of knowing. Reared in my family's broken-glass nest of dark Faulknerian brooding, I certainly experienced the tremors of deep feeling, mostly underground, that my parents dealt with, or, more accurately, did *not* deal with, but no one ever offered me the light of learning. Things happened, but explanations were rarely forthcoming. I was ordered about, but not given reasons. Stories offered me a world of explanations and models. Reading may be pedestrian when it refers to such tasks as reading the newspaper or reading the washing label on a shirt, but when a child starts the literary pedestrianism of engaging with stories, her walk through one word after another can lead to a walk through one world after another, producing extraordinary results. So it was with me.

Mrs. Baumgartle and *Smoky the Crow*

I see with yesterday's vividness the image of me at age six starting my long literary, pedestrian trek in the living room of my family home in New Albany, Indiana, where I had just finished reading, all by myself, my first whole book, *Smoky the Crow*.[1] Had I been a six-year-old book reviewer, I would have gushed, "Best bird story of the year! A must-read avian adventure!" Because there were no children's books in my home, my self-conscious attempts at narrative identification prior to *Smoky the Crow* had been limited to my attempts in church to identify with the child Jesus. Despite squeezing my eyes and concentrating hard, however,

I never had enough data about Jesus to make him seem anything other than an odd little adult.

In reading *Smoky the Crow*, however, I enjoyed my first independent experience of full narrative engagement, and had that sense of going out of myself and living for the time *there* instead of *here*, that sense of simultaneous liberation and fulfillment that we all have when we go intensely *inside* a story. It makes no difference whether that story is on a movie screen or TV screen, in the pages of a book, or whether it comes from the speakers of a CD player or emanates from the mouth of a spinner of tales. I was hooked. I was as hooked as the ancient Greeks listening to the rhapsodists chanting about the Trojan War in the marketplace, as hooked as medieval warriors on mead benches listening to bards singing about King Arthur's round table, as hooked as my mother on the porch swing breathlessly reading fake stories about the scandalous capers of movie stars in the latest issue of *Silver Screen*. Until *Smoky the Crow*, reading had been a dull affair performed in the company of plodding peers, all of us under the supervision of the huge and formidable Mrs. Baumgartle (a name I am not making up), who was ready to pounce heavily on every predictable and irksome mistake made by a group of six-year-olds who had world-class talent for making predictable and irksome mistakes. *Smoky the Crow* was the story that first ignited what eventually became my professional and personal interest in all the different facets of language: the histories and meanings of individual words, words as images and metaphors, and words as story.

One of my earliest epiphanies about the quicksilver quirkiness of individual words occurred in Mrs. Baumgartle's class, as my reading group was struggling through what I considered the boring account of an airplane pilot using the magic of radio signals (magical in those long-ago days) to fly through bad weather by "staying on the beam." But while our poor pilot was trying *not* to crash his plane, I was definitely crashing the reading session by clowning around. Right in the middle of one of my most brilliant ripostes, however, Mrs. Baumgartle, like a recumbent grizzly grouchily awakened, grabbed me suddenly and smoothly by my shirt collar, lifted me in the air like a nine-ounce puppy, whacked me across the bottom with a nine-pound palm, and said with energetic exasperation, "Marshall Wayne, I wish *you* would 'stay on the beam'!"

Instantaneously and with great improbability, right in the middle of Midwestern Nowhere, the gods on Parnassus, probably needing new prescriptions for their glasses and probably thinking that they were zapping a genuine middle-class kid from a genuine city who would attend genuine schools, marked me (mocked me?) then and there as a future English professor. I know this because as I dangled at the end of Mrs. Baumgartle's arm, I found myself more interested by her pun on "beam" than I was upset by the whack on my bottom. The smack was a passing thing—I had been hit by smackers much more maliciously motivated than Mrs. Baumgartle—but I loved her play on "beam," a little word dance that opened a permanent window allowing me to see instantly, albeit only vaguely, that language could be fun.

Religious Fundamentalism and Linguistic Vividness

Being raised among Protestant fundamentalists offers lessons in linguistic vividness that last a lifetime. A woman in one of my father's churches with the unlikely name of Fern Turnipseed, for example, had, in a moment of either aesthetic amnesia or inspired comedy (I could never figure out which), named her son Forest Turnipseed. In addition to the comic delight I took in a mother/son duo named after plants, I found Fern to be linguistically fascinating even without Forest, for Fern had the gift—or the pathology, depending on your prejudice—of "speaking In tongues." At moments in church when Fern felt completely overcome with divine visitation, she would jump up in the middle of one of my father's sermons, swing herself around and around the nearest church pillar, and shout gibberish to the ceiling in an absolute frenzy of abandoned tears and religious inspiration. This performance sometimes stimulated two or three other people in the congregation to do the same thing, on which occasions our church service looked more like a mad house or a Friday night fraternity party than like anything considered religiously respectable by the Presbyterians (or even the Baptists) in their own churches on the other side of town, where people had landscaped yards. Fern was the queen of "shouters," a more or less technical term among us fundamentalists for folks with Fern's gifts, and her transformation from the woman she was all week long—a meek, repressed, tight-lipped, '50s housewife—into an oracular Delphic priestess mainlining a direct emotional jolt from the gods, or, as she believed, The One and Only God, was truly spectacular. It took me many years to learn that the linguistic part of Fern's startling phenomenon has a name, "glossolalia," but it certainly underscored for me that words, even incomprehensible words, could serve as the vehicle for an amazing range of human expressions.

I not only liked the meanings of individual words; I even liked their sounds and rhythms. As the son and grandson of ministers, I was raised in a word world shaped by the language of fiery evangelism and the Shakespearean locutions of the King James translation of the Bible. My grandfather literally raised the hair on the back of my neck as he preached in grave, sepulchral tones, "You sinners who don't repent at this altar tonight are like spiders that God is dangling over the yawning pit of hell by a brickle thread of life!" I immediately had a vision of thousands of people all squirming like spiders, about to be turned from frisky sinners into crispy sinners the moment God severed that "brickle" thread. Years later in college, I was amazed to find that my grandfather had somehow inherited this image from Jonathan Edwards's famous sermon called "Sinners in the Hands of an Angry God," which I am virtually certain that he never read. This image must have been passed down in an unbroken string of oral repetitions from one backwoods evangelist to another until it got to my grandfather—and to me—the language remaining vital and indelible across many generations.

Once reared in the word world of evangelistic fundamentalism, one cannot withdraw from it linguistically, no matter how far one withdraws from it theologically. Nor have I any desire to lose the sense I had then that salvation might hang on using or knowing just the right word in just the right way. There is much proof in the everyday world that one kind of salvation or other—the end of the war, the "guilty" or "not guilty" of a jury's decision, the final fracture or real reconciliation of a troubled marriage—does indeed hang on someone's knowing how to employ just the right word in just the right way at just the right time. We fundamentalists, however, generally construed "salvation" in a more literal way, and getting the language of contrition or scripture or doctrine *right* was vitally important. "Close enough" wordings were never close enough. Lack of precision was perilous. Not only the language of the King James Bible but the images from thousands of hellfire sermons and gospel hymns (both doleful and joyous) strengthen today the blood and bones of my own language. Many people may reject, as I did long ago, the theology of hellfire sermons, but theology aside, few discourses can equal these sermons for demonstrating to young people the power of vivid language.

At about age nine I attended a revival service in my grandfather's church and was captivated by a narrative description of Judgment Day proffered by the Reverend Kykendahl, an evangelist notorious even among us fundamentalists for his methods of building up a congregation's emotions over a week's time of nightly hellfire sermons. The heavenly story that Kykendahl painted on the night I am recalling was a conventional Christian portrayal of Judgment Day that depicted Jesus floating down from heaven surrounded by angels and smiling cherubs, all singing in triumph and joy. But while one narrative angle of this story focused on Jesus floating in the sky, the other narrative angle focused on earth and revealed a chilling picture of sinners weeping and wailing, gnashing their teeth, and praying for rocks and mountains to bury them from the sight of God's terrible judgment.

Just as Kykendahl was approaching meltdown intensity in the midst of telling this story, he acrobatically jumped into the front pew where I was sitting and accidentally kicked me in the head, suddenly raising the possibility that I might be catapulted to my own final judgment sooner than anyone expected (but I only turned out to be more startled than hurt). Later in the week, as Kykendahl orchestrated the rising emotional fever of the congregation attending these nightly services, he arranged for the church janitor to turn off the sanctuary lights at a prearranged cue in the sermon, at which point in the performance he ran up and down the dark aisles rattling a chain and imitating the frenzied shrieks of sinners in hell. It was a case of metaphor being turned into literal sound effects, a sort of primitive Dolby sound for anyone needing a religious jump start. We fundamentalists may have been over the top, but we did not take language for granted.

The language of the hymns in this religious tradition was often melodramatic and morose, filled with metaphors about the blood of Christ, slain lambs, lost sinners, sinking ships, heavenly gardens, the old rugged cross, the rock of ages, and final judgment. "There is a fountain filled with blood," intones one old hymn, "Drawn from Immanuel's veins; / And sinners plunged beneath that flood, / Lose all their guilty stains." The stouthearted fundamentalists among whom I spent my childhood never seemed daunted by the prospect of being washed in a fountain of blood, and they were serenely untroubled by any anxiety that violent religious imagery might damage the tender psyches of their young off- spring. I, on the other hand, as a child undoubtedly more earnest than God needed me to be, was positively riveted by metaphors of sinners drowning in an ocean of sin or bathing in fountains of blood.

The Embrace of Family Stories

When I wasn't at church being steeped in the metaphors of evangelistic fundamentalism or at school immersing myself in stories like *Smoky the Crow*, I was sharpening my sense of language and story in the embrace of oral family tales. Sitting in rocking chairs and porch swings on my grandfather's farm on summer evenings, eating popcorn and apples, I listened to the adults tell and retell the tale about Uncle Billy, who at six- teen lied about his age to join the Navy during World War II and was on a ship in the South Pacific hit by a kamikaze pilot; about Uncle Noral, who got locked in the outhouse by his two older brothers (one of them my father) and in his panic dug his way out through the filth at the bottom of the privy; about Uncle Wayne, who not only was the source of my middle name but was taken prisoner of war in Germany in 1944; about my great- grandfather Cox, who, when his family didn't want to leave the farm in the 1930s and move to town, allegedly burned down his house and barn; and about the logging and preaching my maternal grandfather did in the forests of southern Indiana in the early 1920s. And of course there was always a large number of suggestive and bloody Bible stories referred to so often in my world that they seemed like family tales themselves: King David secretly watching Bathsheba take a bath, Esther cutting off the head of Holofernes, Lot's daughters "lying" with their father (it took me years to understand the look on adults' faces when they solemnly but deliciously repeated this mysterious phrase about Lot "lying" with his daughters), Samson getting his hair cut by Delilah while he slept, and Saul being struck blind by God's light on the road to Damascus. All of these stories contain racy, stirring stuff for lads of thirteen or fourteen whose testosterone is just beginning to flow.

In the pre-television days of my childhood, one of my favorite family modes of taking in stories and acquiring sensitivity to language was listening to the radio. I had a particular love for the wooden Zenith tabletop model that my family owned. It had tubes that took about a week to warm up, it had an imposing gold needle that turned in a big circle to select the station, and it had a golden italic Z in the shape of a bolt of lightning that zapped diagonally across the entire front of the radio. This Z was a triple pun on the manufacturer's name, "Zenith," on the power of electricity, and on the mystery of radio signals. I listened not only to weekly radio narratives but also to "Walter Winchell," who always opened his program by speaking in a distinctively urgent, staccato voice—"Good evening, Mr. and Mrs. America and all the ships at sea"—while a clicking telegraph key could be heard in the background, ensuring that Winchell's narratives were, indeed, being heard all over the world simultaneously. I was too naive to ask myself why ships at sea might have any interest in Walter Winchell's gossipy little stories about politicians and movie stars, but that clicking telegraph key carried powerful proof to me of the universality of people's fascination for stories.

Stories: The Language of the Human Heart

Whenever human beings are most deeply moved by the great passions of life—grief, love, desire, anger, loss, outrage, profound happiness—they are likely to reach for special words or special forms of language—catechisms, eulogies, wedding vows, the affirmations that precede court testimony, baptisms, deathbed declarations—designed to capture the speakers' full depth of feeling. Without the words, it seems difficult for human beings to be fully present at our own deepest experiences. It is the job of words and stories, as Elder Olson says in his poem, "To see, to say / It was this way, this way" ("Prologue to His Book," 3). Metaphors and stories become in those moments and in those modes the language of the human heart as it works hard to know itself, not just as it is, but as it would like to be.

Nuala O'Faolain says of her own childhood reading, "I liked the words as much as the plot" (25). In O'Faolain's dreary childhood, stories introduced her to the idea that other lives were possible, and also to metaphors that were sources of beauty and excitement even in the midst of the mud and grime of Dublin's outskirts.

> In a scandalous book called *The Kansas City Milkman*—Mammy vaguely said I shouldn't read it—one character said about a woman, "What she needs is a roll in the hay." I didn't know what this meant—I saw a barn, in my head—but I loved its being a metaphor. A local boy was known as Buggy. "Don't call me that," he said, "I've a handle to me mug the same as you have." I murmured it over to myself: "A handle to me mug . . ." Halfway up the hill in Malahide there was a bench, with a little plaque on it that said PRO BONO PUBLICO. And on the side of the Chef sauce bottle—often on the table—there was a vertical column of words. "Piquant," I would say to myself as I dodged along beside the gurgling ditches on my way to school. "Piquant. Appetizing." (25–26)

Words shape the world. As an abstraction this idea is commonplace, but each time any of us bumps into specific instances of language's shaping power we experience anew its visceral effects. When King Lear says, "As flies to wanton school boys are we to th' gods; they kill us for their sport," the existential despair of a man who has come to believe that life is hopeless hits us like a heart attack (IV, i). When John Keats describes music as "yearning like a god in pain" ("The Eve of St. Agnes"), we feel at once the power of music to move the very foundations of our soul. When Mark Helprin tells us that a man tending a fire "rocked the logs with a poker, watching the red coals chip off into devil's candy" (354), he combines heat, hell, and Satan into an effortless, economical, and memorable linguistic expression. When Annie Proulx says that "Billy seemed stored in an envelope; the flap sometimes lifted, his flattened self sliding onto the table," we are given both a visual and tactile sense of Billy's constrained self, his flat demeanor (156). And when Charles Dickens describes "shaggy horses purged of all earthly passions . . . who, if required, would have stood stock still in a china shop, with a complete dinner-service at each hoof" (*Martin Chuzzlewit*, 70), he relishes right along with the reader his own comic absurdity. Such metaphors vivify language, and since human beings swim in language as fish swim in water, any systematic intensification of language cannot help but intensify the quality of life itself.

I gradually increased the breadth of my associations stirred by stories to the point where their pursuit, and my delight in them, has become one of the deepest habits of my heart. Literary language, literary people, and literary events occupy my mind in a way that I can only describe as "perpetual presences." I mean nothing metaphysical or mystical here. I simply mean that, for me, comparisons between, or associations with, real events and fictional events give me a constant set of references that allow me to toggle back and forth between fictional worlds and real life, deepening my understanding of both. I live in an echo chamber of literary and linguistic associations that begin with Homer and continue through the work of such contemporary authors as Cormack McCarthy, Toni Morrison, Ursula Hegi, J.M. Coetzee, and hundreds of others. On any given evening of my childhood you might have found me—after my duties of janitoring or paper delivering or lawn mowing or ironing or weeding or doing farmwork—lying on my bed lost in the world of *The Black Stallion*, or taking twenty minutes to remove my shoes and socks while concentrating on *Air Force Boys in the Big Battle*. On any given evening of my adulthood now, you might find me engaging in the same preoccupation, supported with generous pillows at my back as I read my latest novel of choice before going to sleep.

The constant literary echoes I live with amplify and deepen my experience. I enter a room, see a thin, intense stranger, and spontaneously recall Shakespeare's "Cassius has a lean and hungry look" (*Julius Caesar*, I, ii) I hear Pembleton on *Homicide* (a long-defunct TV police series) tell his partner Baylis that Baylis doesn't really own his goodness as a man until that goodness has been tested, and my mind immediately calls up that magnificent passage in *Areopagitica* where Milton expresses this same idea: "I cannot praise a fugitive and cloistered virtue, unexercised and unbreathed, that never sallies out and sees her adversary" (1006). I drive by a section of forest preserve in Chicago, and, unbidden,

I hear Robert Frost's voice saying, as I once heard it on a recording, "The woods are lovely, dark, and deep, / But I have miles to go before I sleep." I hear the muted melancholy in a friend's voice, and I suddenly think of Wordsworth's line in "Tintern Abbey" about "the still, sad music of humanity."

Stories: The Broadest Education Possible

Individual words are fascinating, and metaphors are powerful, but it is stories that most obviously give us information about other people's lives. We have practically no firsthand knowledge of most people's interior lives. Stories (whether fictional or not) are a common way of acquiring such knowledge. According to C. S. Lewis's troublesome student in the movie *Shadowlands,* "We read to know that we are not alone." The motive behind our constant demand for story lies, I think, in the involuntary and heartfelt shudder of repugnance we feel at the prospect of living a singular, isolated life. As Anna Quindlen says, "all of reading is really only finding ways to name ourselves, and, perhaps, to name the others around us so that they will no longer seem like strangers" (21).

Personal space and walled-off privacy are never final goals in life. They are only counterpoints to social life, friends, and community. In the absence of contact with others, our lives resemble nothing so much as single molecules trying to make up a universe. Another important value both of—and in—narrative is its ability to organize the data of chaotic experience, to refer beyond the data itself to larger meanings in the universe, and to *connect* that data to our own lives. As Bill Buford says in a *New Yorker* editorial, stories "protect us from chaos, and maybe that's what we, unblinkered at the end of the twentieth century, find ourselves craving. . . . Stories . . . are a fundamental unit of knowledge, the foundation of memory, essential to the way we make sense of our lives: the beginning, middle, and end of our personal and collective trajectories" (12). I do not take this to mean that all of stories' insights are *true*—I know, in fact, that they are not all true—but I know that stories' insights, whether true or not, comprise important *stuff* that constitute the means by which we negotiate our way toward the truth.

Obviously, my own most passionate love is for the stories that used to be called "great literature," but this is merely an effect of my training and education. I am under no illusion that great literature is narrative's only source of intense feelings and profound ideas. It is sheer snobbery to suppose that a science fiction movie or a TV show will always be less useful or less true, or even that it will be less artistic, necessarily, than a Shakespeare play or a Tudor history. This realization was driven home to me a few years ago when I was prowling through a used bookstore in a strange city during some of those odd, free hours that one stumbles on as a gift while attending a professional conference. Scanning volume titles in a happy trance, I ran across a copy of Zane Gray's *Riders of the Purple Sage,* one of the most beloved and often reread narratives of my childhood. My heart actually skipped a beat as I remembered the vivid pleasure this story had so often given me when I was eleven, and I thought, naturally, that I would buy it for sentimental reasons. As I leafed through it, however, I was astounded to find how badly written it was, how clunky the dialogue, how stagy the action, and how thin the characters. It made me realize that, for children at least, an *initial* definition of good reading may simply be whatever kind of reading most engages them, lifts their spirits up, and keeps their imagination alive. I put *Riders of the Purple Sage* back on the shelf unbought but not despised. I had no reason to take it home now, but I could still be grateful to it for the pleasure and education it had given me then.

Ideas from narratives do not lie passively in some arcane corner of the mind called "literary musings," but pass instead into the very warp and woof of everyday intellectual and emotional life. I think I hardly pass through one complete day, for example, without having some idea from *Hamlet* enter not just my mind but my relations to everyday life. I am persistently intrigued, for example, by Hamlet's idea expressed to Horatio just before his duel with Laertes that success in life is not always a matter of getting the right outcome. By Act 5, Hamlet has discovered that accidents, malice, and greed, at least in his world, are very likely to intervene such that desired outcomes or right outcomes are nearly impossible. In the face of this grim reality, success in life, says Hamlet, is *being ready* for whatever comes, not being able to control what comes. "The readiness is all," he says (V, ii).

But accidents, malice, and greed do not exist merely in Hamlet's world; they also exist in yours and mine, which makes "readiness is all" a useful perspective for anyone to contemplate. Would I have ever learned this idea without reading *Hamlet*? Almost certainly, yes. Failing to read *Hamlet* does not necessarily doom anyone to intellectual poverty. The redundancy of sources from which we can learn specific ideas means that we do not all have to know exactly the same sources in order to know generally the same things. However, stories' power to combine abstract ideas with concrete "speaking pictures"—as Aristotle and Philip Sidney so long ago observed—gives human beings the opportunity to learn how ideas actually work as the levers, pulleys, and weights of the world.

Most of all, I think narratives have taught me that people can often be larger than their circumstances. People whose lives start out as dramatically inauspicious as mine, O'Faolain's, or many other people's only illustrate by their extremity a general situation that applies to everyone. *All* of us are trying to figure out who to become, *given where we start and what we need to know.* The fact that some of us need to be "saved" and others merely need to "grow" does not mean that becoming a fully developed person is easy for anyone, nor does it mean that there is only one path of development. O'Faolain's path took her into journalism; mine took me into teaching. But educators do a lot of reporting, reporters do a lot of teaching, and all teachers and reporters deploy the power of stories even if some of them never pause to think critically about their reasons for doing so.

What stories educate us about the most is a question I will return to several times in the course of this book because no single answer from a single perspective will suffice. One good answer to start with, however, is given in J. M. Coetzee's *The Master of Petersburg.* Coetzee's central character in this novel happens to be the novelist Fyodor Dostoyevsky, who finds himself at a point of great anguish in his life because of the death of his son. "*What am I to do?* [he asks]. . . . If I were only in touch with my heart, might it be given to me to know?" (82). This startling and wonderful question—"if I were only in touch with my heart, might it be given to me to know?"—contains an insight that goes far toward explaining not only my love for literature but my sense of the important education that stories offer to us all. *Stories teach us how to maintain contact with our hearts.* Some stories lie to us about the human heart—have you watched a daytime soap opera lately?—but other stories teach us truths about ourselves and the human condition, and they accomplish this most humanizing of tasks because they take us both inside ourselves and outside to others, thus addressing the dual needs of our introspective and social natures all at once.

Despite the claim of C. S. Lewis's troublesome student that we read to learn we are not alone, we also read to *be* alone, to feel the pulse and the progress of our own interior imagination, to live in that special place within ourselves where our vicarious experience of others' lives is yet a solitary and reflective activity. As Katherine Paterson, the Newbery-winning children's author, says, "I have always felt that when it comes to exploring the geography of my inner life, great books are my most effective guide" (204). Because literature puts us in contact both with others' lives and with our own hearts, the study of narrative, at least to the dedicated, persistent learner, is nothing less than an attempt to come to some accurate assessment of life's value and purpose.

I dare say that Mrs. Baumgartle held no such lofty aim, at least not consciously, when she tried to keep me on the beam in reading class, yet all my life I have owed Mrs. Baumgartle a deep debt. As George Eliot says in *Middlemarch,* "the growing good of the world is partly dependent on unhistoric acts; and that things are not so ill with you and me as they might have been, is half owing to the number who lived faithfully a hidden life, and rest in unvisited tombs" (578). I have never visited Mrs. Baumgartle's tomb, but may she rest in peace. After what she had to put up with from me, she needs it. Mrs. Baumgartle was never famous, never honored, never pursued by reporters for her views or sound bites, but, insofar as I know, lived faithfully a hidden life working with first graders from a working-class neighborhood in a nondescript Midwestern town. It's as clear to me as a pane of crystal, however, that things are not so ill with me as they might be partly because of Mrs. Baumgartle's faithfulness. She did, after all, teach me to read, and reading led me to literature, and literature led me into *reading for life,* and reading for life has led me not only to a sense of existence most abundantly enlarged, but into worlds of feeling and thought whose scope can only be encompassed by the imagination, and whose depth can only be plumbed by the heart.

༺✦✕✦༻

CHAPTER TWO

What Is Ethical Agency, Why Should You Care, and What Do Stories Have to Do with *Your* Ethical Agency?

The Appetite for Stories

For human beings the pull of stories is primal. What oxygen is to our body, stories are to our emotions and imagination. We cannot flex our mental and imaginative muscles without drawing on the psychic energy and linguistic resources we have absorbed, in part, from our consumption of stories. In the words of Reynolds Price, "A need to tell and hear stories is essential to the species *Homo Sapiens*—second in necessity apparently after nourishment and before love and shelter. Millions survive without love or home, almost none in silence; the opposite of silence leads quickly to narrative, and the sound of story is the dominant sound of our lives, from the small accounts of our days' events to the vast incommunicable constructs of psychopaths" (4).

There are no non-storytelling cultures and no human beings who have been reared outside the field of influence generated by stories. We don't always understand or like particular stories, but we never lose our appetite for stories in general. Once past the issue of sheer physical survival, human lives are about feeling, believing, and judging, and stories profoundly map themselves onto this agenda of human concerns, because at the core of every story is a set of invitations to feel, to believe, and to judge as the story dictates. The cueing, prompting, and stimulating that we receive from stories to feel *this way,* to believe *this way,* and to judge *this way* bring our capacities for feeling, believing, and judging into active wakefulness. We pay a price for this cueing and stimulating because the emotions, beliefs, and judgments that stories ask us to make do not always convey accurate beliefs and judgments about the world, or emotions appropriate to the circumstances of our world, but we also get a lot in return for our complicity. We get pleasure, first of all—sometimes very deep pleasure—and, beyond that, we get an elemental stretching and strengthening of those basic capacities for feeling, believing, and judging that we cannot get through one hour of life without relying on. We also get configurations of data about *how* to feel in *this* way, *what* to believe on *this* front, *why* we should judge in *this* way, and these data sets possess important properties that call from us certain modes of personal development. First, literary data gives us information about the world that is much vaster and richer than we could ever encounter if we had to rely for data on our firsthand experience. Second, literary information is embedded in concrete details that help us imagine with vividness and particularity the realities of the world that the data represent.

Stories' invitations would hardly matter if stories were few and far between or if our encounters with them were superficial and infrequent, but we all know that everyday life is simply saturated with narratives. It turns out—if we stop to pay attention—that we are saying yes to stories' invitations many times a day and innumerable times over the course of a year. The question of how stories manage to affect us in the ways they do is the sand in my bed that won't let me rest. Skeptics sometimes claim that stories are *merely* verbal descriptions, and they refuse to believe that words describing *merely* made-up events can be important. Some skeptics like to point out the properties that stories *don't* possess. Stories don't have material mass, they might say, and stories are clearly not useful like opposable thumbs, recipes, or crescent wrenches. Stories don't vote and don't run governments, and many philosophers from Plato to John Locke to Jeremy Bentham to Michel Foucault to Jacques Derrida have argued strenuously that deep absorption of stories is not a good thing for either individual morality or social justice. Yet the truth is that Plato, Locke, Bentham, Foucault, and Derrida have been *spectacularly* unsuccessful in persuading anyone except a few jaded academics to stop liking stories. Stories enter our lives like yeast, bubbling into all corners of everyday life.

In part, the explanation for this can be attributed to the human appetite for experience. *Story is first of all a form of experience, not a form of intellectual discourse.* Storytelling and story listening arose as deeply affective, ethical, emotional, and social acts. These acts are profoundly companionable, the narrative threads stitching together the hearts of community members into a social web. Listen to the conversation among any group of friends or acquaintances for more than ten minutes, and chances are high that talk will turn to participants' accounts of the latest movie, play, or novel they have encountered. The remainder of the conversation will consist of the participants' own stories: how I did this, how Jane did that, how my parents said this, how I went here or went there, and on and on. The story of our lives is the stories we consume and the stories we tell. If these comments explain what I mean by the sand in my bed that won't let me rest, what remains is to explore the implications for human ethos of the fact that there is no appetite the world over, in either past or present time (including sex and food), that human beings feed as persistently and avidly as their appetite for stories.

Ethical Agency and Stories' Cumulative Effects

Stories' influence is conveyed not through any kind of mysterious or independent authority that stories generate but through the enticing *invitations* they extend, and what makes stories' invitations important to think about is that everyone says yes to narrative invitations almost all of the time. Once in a while we say no to a story—we refuse, that is, to respond emotionally, intellectually, or ethically in the way the story invites us to—but, overwhelmingly, even when we find the story less than gripping, we still say yes to its invitations with a fairly high degree of assent. That is, if we are looking to be entertained by a story, we will settle for a mediocre story or even one that we already know rather than do without. Can't make it to the starting time of the movie we really wanted to see? Never mind. We'll see the movie that was third on our list. When it comes to saying yes to stories' invitations, stories don't have to come and wrangle us. We are usually happy to step right up.

The influence that follows from these ready engagements with stories, mostly unthought about, stems from two forces: first, skilled storytellers know how to zero in on the hot buttons of human responsiveness (the basic passions and motives of life) with great artistic skill, and second, the rush of emotion we feel when assenting to stories liberates our minds and hearts from the everyday limitations of our own lives. Whenever we say yes to any story's invitations—especially invitations about how we should feel, what we should think, and how we should judge—we wind up investing a kind of authority in the invitation that it could never generate on its own. *It is the yielding that comes from within, not the authority imposed from without, that says most about who we are and who we shall become.* Dictators conquer, but stories infiltrate, with this important difference: few people invite dictators to conquer, but all people invite stories into their lives constantly—not only constantly, but with eagerness and persistence.

When the influence of these millions of yeses is multiplied by a lifetime, it follows that a life steeped in stories opens wide the door of our minds and hearts, mostly without our thinking much about it, to an infiltration of potential influence that moment by moment and story by story feels very slight, but that cumulatively and incrementally contributes powerfully to the formation of human souls. We cannot measure the effect on our health of each individual fork of food we eat or each individual dose of medicine we take, but we nevertheless know that, cumulatively and incrementally, those forks of food and those doses of medicine configure our bodies and condition our health in ways that, ultimately, can only be explained by tracing the effects back to the influence of those individual bites and those individual pills. So it is with the incremental influence exerted on our minds and hearts over time by the countless stories we tell and consume.

The reason *why* we mostly accept stories' invitations is simple to state: *refusing* to feel, believe, and judge as stories ask deprives us of the pleasure that stories are designed to give, not to mention the education that stories provide as a side benefit, and few of us are willing to give up a form of pleasure and education so congenial and fulfilling as yielding to the grip of a good story. Allow me to remind you, as I said previously, that most of us prefer even mediocre narratives to no narratives at all. The influence of narratives, however, despite our appetite for them, is always potential, never inevitable, and never absolutely predictable. In the end, stories work because we *want* them to work. The fact that stories *do* work—the fact that they cue our capacities for feeling, believing, and judging—inevitably raises questions about their potential influence on character, for what *is* character other than the particular configuration of our own ways of feeling, believing, and judging? *Every* influence that shapes character prompts us to evaluate whether that influence is good or bad for us. We are all agents in the world, and we all make choices about how to interact with other people that produce at least three consequences important for our ethical development.

First, the *ethical* choices we make about how to interact with others—lying rather than telling the truth, being generous rather than stingy, being compassionate rather than callous, being respectful rather than manipulative, being fair rather than unfair, and so on—are choices that not only have consequences for other people but, equally important, have profound consequences for us as well. These are the choices that create our own moral agency, or ethical character. Choices about how to interact with others do not merely *reflect* who we are but *create* who we are.

Second, our ethical choices cumulatively *reinforce* our sense of identity and thus over time inexorably configure a version of our self that forms the core of who we are. The interesting thing about our identity, however, is that it doesn't sit within us like a finished, solid object. Our ethical agency is not like a turned table leg or like any other once-and-for-all shaped thing. Selfhood is *not* a thing. It is a process. Character is always in motion: it is never fully static and never fully finished. The mechanism that drives the evolving development of our ethos, or character, is the choices we make, especially our choices about how to interact with others.

Third, our choices about how to interact with others influence the kind of agency that they have available to them. The classic example is the relationship between parents and children. Children whose parents are loving and supportive as opposed to children whose parents are unloving and neglectful wind up (as a result of their parents' choices) developing widely different senses of their own ethical agency.

The term "ethical agency" may sound unfamiliar to some of you, but it is a commonsense notion and can be defined in simple language. Ethical agency is not a theory; it is a set of actions. *Ethical agency is the concrete performance of moral and ethical choices within the everyday world of social relations.* Anyone's ethical agency is a general proclivity to treat other people in particular ways, and it produces signature ethical actions that we and others take to be "like" us, or "typical" of us. One person fudges on income taxes; another does not. One student cheats on a test; another does not. One scholar lies about his sources; another does not. One person squeezes out the time and energy to help a neighbor in trouble, while another neighbor doesn't even notice. One boss promotes the office suck-up, while another promotes the employee who has been outspokenly critical. One person habitually lashes out at friends and family members, while another person can be counted on to exert discipline and self-control. Expressing our general proclivities over and over as concrete forms of conduct deepens our sense of what actions—and what character—we think of as typically "us." Another term for anyone's "me" or everyone's "us" is "ethos."

All of us deal with ethical considerations persistently—they lie at the center of all human interactions—thus few of our thoughts about others are ethically neutral. They are deeply colored by speculations about the impression we are making, about the approval or the help we seek, about the disapproval we wish to avoid, and about the impression on us that other people make, beginning primarily with the impressions that we all give and receive as *ethical agents.* We may admire people for being strong, clever, brilliant, or talented, but we trust them and love them only when we think they are, at most, truly good or, at least, not malicious. In the words of moral philosopher Robert Louden,

> Moral considerations have ultimate importance not (as many philosophers have argued) because they form a tightly packaged set of

interests that can be shown to logically "override" all other competing sets of interests but rather because they concern values to which the pursuit of any and all interests, including scientific and technical ones, must answer. Morality is not just one narrow point of view competing against others.... [Its] ultimate importance is [a function of its] *pervasiveness*. Moral considerations literally appear able to pervade or permeate ... more areas and aspects of human life and action (and once they gain entry, to have, somehow, the final word) than do any other kinds of considerations.... *All* aspects of human life over which we exercise at least some degree of voluntary control have indirect moral relevance.... Morality's fundamental importance stems not from its "standing above" everything else but rather from the fact that it literally surrounds everything else, lies underneath everything else, and is continually embedded in everything else. (20, 59, 80)

We can escape, evade, or neutralize our ethical agency only by never interacting with other human beings. Only for hermits (not a major demographic) is this is an option. Except in instances of mental derangement, reflex actions, and involuntary physical processes such as digestion, there are no forms of human conduct that are ethically neutral. Choosing not to act is as much of an ethical choice as any other. Human interactions inevitably force us to make constant decisions about whether to be kind or unkind, generous or stingy, courageous or cowardly, honest or deceitful, compassionate or callous, self-controlled or self-indulgent, fair or unfair, faithful or unfaithful, respectful or manipulative, ashamed or shameless, open or closed, courteous or contemptuous, and so on. Ultimately, the choices that anyone makes over a lifetime configure his or her ethical identity, an identity that we call, in the deepest sense, "character" or "ethos."

Just as our bodies and minds develop healthily or unhealthily because of the formative influence of such variables as diet, exercise, hygiene, the presence or absence of pathogens in our environment, the presence or absence of problems in our DNA makeup, medical care, luck, and the various forms of mental practice in which we engage, our ethos is also subject to formative influences from at least three sources: (1) the *direct* prescriptions for good and bad conduct given to us by our parents and other caretakers, by our teachers and ministers, by our relatives and friends, and by the law; (2) the *indirect* ethical influence of our peers' attitudes and their conduct; and, finally, (3) the ethical *models* displayed by other people's conduct. Significantly, most of the ethical models in our lives come from stories rather than firsthand experience because all of us know a vastly larger set of fictional models than we will ever encounter in our limited, physical existence.

Thus we all *have* a moral (or immoral) character, and we all *do* ethical (or unethical) things. Everyday language shows this. Without embarrassment and without fear of serious challenge from others we often assert baldly ethical claims such as "cheating on tests is wrong," "short changing customers is dishonest," "murder of innocents is depraved," "infidelity is a betrayal," "stinginess among the rich is contemptible," "kindness is a virtue," "corrupt executives and politicians should be punished," "cruelty to animals is wicked," "rape is horrendous," and so on. Despite the aggressive assertions by some people that morality and ethics are bogus because all moral and ethical judgments are somehow "relative"—therefore not absolute and therefore not binding—we all make such judgments (*ceaselessly!*) about events in the world and about other people's agency, and we do so with confidence that our judgments have teeth that bite deeply into the meat of human affairs.

Do you need a few examples? We do not give rapists and thieves a mere tongue lashing; we send them to jail. We don't merely tell unfaithful spouses how disappointed we are; we divorce them. A friend lies to us? We stop returning his phone calls. We feel guilty for not dumping our pocket change in the jingling can of the legless guy on the corner, and we cover our conscience with the notion, almost the hope, that he's running a con. We write letters to the editor about the immorality of war. We flunk students who plagiarize. We expel students who violate the honor code. We feel justified in seeking legal redress (and sometimes legal punishment) when we have been treated unfairly. On and on, neither theoretical talk about the relativity of moral and ethical judgments nor some people's constant violation of ethical standards ever erases the relevancy of ethical judgments from the human agenda. It is worth repeating Louden's claim: ethical considerations saturate all social interactions.

Ethical Agency and the Developmental Imperative

But where does ethical agency, one's ethos, come from? Are we born with it, do we choose it, does someone program it into us, does it lie inside us like wisdom teeth just waiting to emerge, or what?

A full answer to this question requires many levels of response, but the first level of response demands our taking into account the fact that human beings are born ignorant and undeveloped, not knowledgeable and not fully formed. Thus human beings (unlike some other species) are fundamentally oriented toward *development*. Consider a contrary case. When a honeybee emerges from the pupae stage, it is *done* developing, and its active life has not even begun yet. A honeybee emerges both smart enough and developed enough to do what it needs to do without going to school or reading a honeybee manual. But when a human being emerges from the womb, almost all of its development still lies ahead of it. We do very few of the things that mark us as distinctively human with the kind of inborn knowledge that tells a honeybee how to pollinate flowers without ever having to take Pollination 101. Even those features for which human beings have inborn predispositions, such as reason, language, and imagination, still require development—*much* development—before we can use them robustly, diversely, vividly, and powerfully. As we pass through developmental stages we do not have to be greatly reflective or introspective to know that some kinds of "education" exert sledgehammer influences on our development: my parents' divorce, the death of my grandfather, the birth of my child, receiving the scholarship to go to Yale, adopting Jenelle, having a stroke, marrying Romeo instead of Paris, surviving hand-to-hand combat in Iraq, winning the Power Ball lottery, being swindled out of my money, winning the Pulitzer Prize, and so on. When we experience these kinds of events we are aware that "nothing will ever be the same," as we say, and we know this to be true from the first moment these events happen. Recognizing the developmental significance of what we are inclined to call "big" events requires little introspection. Even a fence post knows when it's been hit by a pile driver.

What we often fail to consider, however, is (1) that dramatic events comprise only a small percentage of the formative events in our lives and

(2) that dramatic events have the unfortunate tendency to rivet our attention and block our perception of incremental influences—the "small" influences that generate their power *cumulatively* but that we seldom wind up talking about in our memoirs or on therapists' couches. Comparatively small events may escape our notice altogether. It is of great formative significance in the long run, however, that life presents us nearly every moment with invitations to make one-after-another small decisions on the other side of which, potentially at least, nothing will ever be the same. The interesting thing about these kinds of decisions, however, is that we often fail to notice their importance. People who are forced to breathe polluted air every day do not think about the influence of the air's pollutants with every breath they take, but when they wind up with emphysema or lung cancer, it's not the labored breaths at the end that caused their problem. It was all the earlier breaths they did not think about.

Most of the formative choices that we make in life are not beyond our control, like avoiding some kinds of sickness by avoiding exposure to the germs that cause it, or avoiding car accidents by not driving. Many of our most formative choices would have made a great *alternative* difference if only we had *chosen* differently, but it isn't generally obvious to us when we make those millions of small choices that don't possess dramatic markers: choices about how to respond to someone's question when we're in a hurry or when we're annoyed, choices about how to respond to some person in a meeting whose egoism is driving us crazy, choices about how to respond to someone's deep anxiety over an issue that we think is small potatoes, choices about how to respond to a child's fears, choices about how to respond to just but stinging criticism, choices about how to respond to unfair criticism, choices about how to respond to our least liked person's need for reassurance and comfort, choices about how to respond to disappointment, loss, grief, and so on.

About these kinds of choices there are seldom any ethical billboards that flash us a message in huge letters, "THIS IS THE MOMENT YOU ARE BECOMING THE PERSON YOU WILL TURN OUT TO BE." Whether we have billboard clarity or not, however, such choices nevertheless form us, and when we consider that the main substance of life is comprised of just such moment-by-moment "small" choices—the choices that fill up the space between the big dramatic events that we all talk about—then it becomes apparent that *it is really the small but massively numerous small choices in our lives that are doing the work of formative development.* While we focus obsessively on the big traumas that drive us to drink or send us to therapy, our lack of awareness and thoughtfulness about the importance of life's innumerable "small" choices means that we often miss the most important data that tells the story of how we become the persons we turn out to be.

The character Dan, Roseanne's husband on the TV series *Roseanne,* a man who in his youth had been macho and rowdy, once said to his wife in a moment of amazed, if infrequent, self-insight, "You civilized me when I wasn't lookin'." Dan's point was that Roseanne's persistent but incremental influence over the years of their marriage had produced major changes in his character so gradually that he had never noticed the process and had only just at that moment become aware of the product. He had been led to make different kinds of choices about his life—and thus led to become a different kind of person—without realizing it. Like Dan, most of us are enduring changes all the time while we aren't even "lookin'." A typical failure of perception in most people's lives is the failure to see how stories play Roseanne's role in everyone's life, influencing and changing us while we aren't even looking.

The Incremental Influence of Assent

The extent to which the influence of stories on ethos escapes our attention is breathtaking. About other kinds of influence we are alert and yammering all the time. Books and articles flow like a river on such topics as whether teenagers should say yes or no to the attitudes and behavior of their peers, whether Americans are helping or harming themselves by taking so many mood-altering drugs, whether we should live close to interstate highways and in the midst of unrelenting noise pollution, whether aspiring professionals should say yes or no to the invitation to sacrifice time with children and spouse for more time on the job, whether someone who calls himself honest should say yes or no to the invitation to make an insider trading deal, whether someone who desires to think of herself as a concerned citizen should vote in every election, whether a spouse should say yes or no to the invitation for a one-night fling in a conference city far from home, and whether someone who thinks of himself as caring should say yes or no to the opportunity to help an ailing neighbor by cooking him a meal, shoveling his snowy sidewalk, or mowing his tall grass. But when it comes to the millions of yes-or-no choices we make in response to the stories that saturate our lives, we mostly fail to see the influence those choices exert on us. No one sees tectonic plates, but they have the power to move continents. No one notices my yeses and noes to the stories I take in, but in the deep underground of my moral imagination that pushes the visible part of my character upward into the world, the tectonic plates of that moral imagination are being formed by my countless decisions to say yes or no to various invitations, many of them presented to me—to all of us—by stories.

None of us is ever further away from the next narrative engagement that might affect us than our next conversation with a friend, the next click of the TV remote control, the next ballad wafting from our CD player, the next novel on our nightstand, or the next trip we make to the theater or the movies. As stories ask us to sympathize with heroes and heroines, feel antipathy for villains, rejoice with some characters' good fortune and feel sad at other characters' bad fortune, feel indignant when justice is trumped by evil, feel outraged when innocence is violated, and desire some outcomes while we dread other outcomes, and as we say yes and no to these invitations, as we always do, two things are happening: we grow to understand the story, and we grow to become the persons we are. What's at stake is nothing less than how a lifetime of yeses and noes turns us into the kinds of persons we become.

CHAPTER THREE

For Good or Ill

Stories as Ethical Education

Stories Swallow the World Whole

We find stories useful because they swallow the world whole, and in fact the domain of stories may be the only form of human learning other than religion that makes the attempt to encompass the entirety of human life and experience. Many people deny that they are getting an education when they engage with stories as "merely passing pleasures," but this denial is as unrealistic as the common claims of chain smokers and sun bathers that smoking and sunburns don't seriously increase their odds for developing lung cancer or melanomas. Passing pleasures can be many things besides passing; they may, in fact, become permanent habits of the body or mind. On the other hand, consuming narratives is not a negotiable practice for human beings because narrative education is indispensable to all of us almost all of the time.

Do not misunderstand the term "ethical education" in the subtitle of this chapter. Most people would probably understand this term to mean something like "teaching people to be good, as in not robbing liquor stores and not punching other people's noses." You know from reading chapter 2, however, that my definition of "ethical education" is not that narrow and is something more like "any kind of education that helps shape our ethos, whether that shaping power leads the learner to behave 'properly' or not." Not only is my definition of "ethical education" broad, but so is my understanding of the sources from which that education is derived: firsthand experience, the models we see in our companions and friends, the models we encounter in novels and biographies and histories, the lessons that we pick up from songs and jokes and family tales, the interpretations of life offered to us by movies and television, and so on.

As developmental agents trying to make our way in a complex, mysterious, and, at times, overwhelming world, we need all the help we can get, which is why we turn for assistance to science, history, philosophy, religion, and so on. But people who turn to science and religion for help in learning how to live usually don't mind admitting that they do so—in fact, they think that doing so demonstrates their sagacity—but when anyone suggests that this same educational motive explains their constant engagement with stories, many of these same people will vociferously deny the suggestion. This is when they offer the "stories are mere entertainment" rebuttal, as if entertainment and education never have anything to do with each other. People often forget that when they were children, the lessons they learned the fastest and deepest were the lessons that were the most entertaining. Our predilection for learning while being entertained does not diminish as we grow older, but it seems childish to us to admit this as adults, so we conveniently deny it.

Most forms of learning investigate the world by slicing it up into pieces. The three-hundred-year-long development of specialization in the academic disciplines offers the easiest example of this trend. Slicing-and-dicing has proved to be an immensely powerful strategy. From the idealizations of the natural sciences through the grammars of languages to the questionnaires of social scientists, the strategy of slicing the world up into discrete domains of inquiry that can be examined in great depth has proven itself to be spectacularly successful. However, when the knowledge that you and I most want is not specialized knowledge, but guidance about how to answer that ancient but always pressing question—"how should I live?"—then slicing-and-dicing becomes less useful.

Where in the world do you and I turn for information, guidance, models, and knowledge if the things we most want explained are how to live a whole life from beginning to end, including how to find happiness, how to spend money, how to love and what to love, how to have great sex, how to find rewarding work, how to deal with neighbors and relatives, how to think about the existence or nonexistence of a god or gods, how to deal with the perennial passions of life such as lust and anger and envy and pride and fear, how to balance the impulses for ambition and competition on the one hand with the need for companions and friends on the other hand, how to deal with grief and loss, how to deal with old age and weakness, and how to deal with the inevitability of death?

The only way you and I can pursue knowledge of life in this broadest sense is to swallow it whole, not partition it off into small sections, and the most powerful and comprehensive strategy that human beings possess for conducting holistic inquiries into life is narrative. Story swallows life whole and embeds its representations of human existence in all the concrete minutiae that determine the quality of everyday living. When we read *Middlemarch* or watch *The Wire* or *Rescue Me* or view *Citizen Kane*, we have the feeling that we are in concrete contact with the characters in these stories—as if it would take only the smallest twitch of the space-time continuum to allow us to move right into their worlds—which is never a feeling we have when engaging with mathematical proofs, maps, or scientific hypotheses.

In swallowing life whole, stories show us such features of existence as the operation of cause and effect, the surprises of coincidence, the motivations of passion and guilt and ambition and pride, the suspense attending outcomes, the conduct that creates or destroys the quality of our interactions with others, the tranquility or turbulence of our inner emotional lives, the configurations of success or failure, and so on. The contributions of other kinds of earthly learning are often profound and vastly valuable, but no form of earthly learning has an appetite for the world as broad as stories.

Why and When Do Stories Intersect with Ethos?

The "stories are mere entertainment" denial is curiously self-defeating. If, in fact, we probe the reasons *why* stories are so universally pursued, it is hard to avoid the inference that much of stories' compelling entertainment derives, in fact, from their educational power, and is generated precisely by stories' ability to educate us about people whose material circumstances, attitudes, ideas, motives, feelings, social/emotional entanglements, and destinies are different from (yet overlap with) our own. If whatever educates us also forms us, then it is not only fair but necessary—if we want to become thoughtful, self-determining persons—to evaluate ethically the influence of any kind of persistent education we engage in, particularly the kinds of persistent education that we voluntarily pursue, such as consuming one story after another in a never-ending sequence. (Not long ago at the end of the school year I asked one of my students how many movies she thought she might watch before next fall. "How many nights of the summer are there?" she responded.) Ethical criticism is all about the interrogation of these eagerly ingested forms of influence. *Not* doing ethical criticism leaves the discussion of stories' potential effects on character in the hands of doctrinaire moralists whose main mode of argument is a scorched-earth policy of holier-than-thou denunciation and intimidation.

Ethical discourse makes some people uncomfortable (perhaps because they mistake it for moralistic Sunday school talk?), and until very recently indeed, many academics—my professional colleagues—have emphatically rejected it because (I think) they consider it intellectually primitive. They are right. Ethical criticism *is* intellectually primitive. But "primitive" only underscores ethical criticism's importance: the primal issues in human beings' lives are always the most important and, in any event, are always unavoidable. We don't use the primitive medulla oblongata for doing calculus, but if the medulla oblongata isn't doing its job, we have no breath or pulse to do calculus with. Ethical considerations have this kind of primal importance. The fact that oppressive ideologies have often been foisted off as positive ethical programs ("the white man's burden" and "a woman's place is in the home," for example) does not mean that ethics either can or should be gotten rid of. Whether we would be better off without ethics is a moot point. Ethical considerations infiltrate every human interaction not because we don't try hard enough to filter them out but because there *is* no filtering them out.

Does this sound like an exaggeration? Perhaps you think big issues that on their face have no obvious ethical significance—accidents, for example, or disease, talents, and luck—have as much or even more to do with the texture and quality of everyday life as human interactions with their inevitable ethical baggage. There is a sense in which you are right, but there are two things that must be kept in mind. First, accidents, luck, talents, and disease may set the circumstances of people's lives, but people's *reactions* to these circumstances are more determinative of the quality of life than the circumstances themselves, as evinced by the fact that some people who suffer catastrophic debilitation from accident or disease maintain a high quality of life and others do not (Stephen Hawking comes to mind). If the circumstances were everything, these differences could not exist.

Second, human existence is so deeply rooted in ethical considerations that people cultivate ethical interpretations even about ethically neutral events. It's hard to believe that catching a cold or winning the lottery possesses any ethical significance, but people's typical response to catching a cold is to assign agency and blame. "Damn. I'll bet I caught this cold from that person who sneezed in my direction at the faculty lunch table last Wednesday" (ethical significance: that person is treating me unfairly by being careless with his cold germs). Most people who win the lottery cannot help feeling that their success requires a deeper explanation than blind odds. Lottery winners habitually claim that some agent—God, Lady Luck (as opposed to blind luck), dead Grandma's spirit, Providence, life itself, or whatever—is rewarding them (ethical significance: someone or something cares about my needs; someone wants to see me well-off).

Ethical judgments are so natural to us that many people are unaware of the extent to which they are engaging in such activity. When an acquaintance unexpectedly humiliates you, you may offer a typical kind of pop psychology explanation—"Mark's loveless childhood set him up for lashing out at people"—but what you are outraged about is ethics, not psychology: "Mark's hostile ridicule of me was so *unfair*, so *mean-spirited*, so *unkind*, so *ungenerous*, so *uncharitable*!" When your spouse leaves your artist garret home to run off with a rich heart surgeon, you may offer a typical kind of pop economic explanation—"Mercenary women favor rich men, not starving artists"—but what you are outraged about is ethics, not economics: "Susan's dumping me for that fat rat's-ass doctor was so *dishonest*, so *self-indulgent*, so *selfish*, so *callous*, so *cruel*! *Vows* had been made! I have been *betrayed, hurt, dishonored*!"

There are many interesting and important issues about narratives not explained by this line of argument, but what it does explain is the *use* we make of narratives. Narratives give us educational information about how to deal with life's conundrums, perplexities, ambitions, motives, attitudes, actions, explanations, feelings, values, ideas, and human types. And all of us *need* narratives because we know, if we stop to think about it, that firsthand life cannot offer us all the education we need in order to grapple with the world's complexities. Firsthand life for human beings everywhere[1] is comparatively narrow, dominated by routine, and, most important of all, *short*. Life is not well structured to give any of us a truly broad education about its typical predicaments, permutations, and puzzles. All of us are limited to occupying a single spot of space and time *at* a time, and all too briefly.

Every culture fills in the educational gaps left by firsthand experience by means of stories. As Philip Sidney said so long ago (in 1583), "poetry hath [ever] been the first light-giver to ignorance" (83). Stories' ethical visions enlighten our ignorance by giving us information that goes deeper than mere description. The real problem of life for human beings is not deciding on the one "right" description of the world, because the truth is that we can live quite comfortably as the fervent believers of many (and sometimes vast) descriptive errors. You can live as complete and happy a life thinking that the world is flat as you can knowing that it's round, but if you cannot read other people's ethical dispositions—if you cannot tell whether other people are prone to help you or harm you, deceive you or tell you the truth, hate you or love you, be kind or unkind to you, be generous or stingy with you, and so on—then it won't matter if you think your world is flat or round because it will just be a mess. The real problem in life is knowing how to *judge* things, and this is a problem that, over and over, narratives' ethical visions help us think about in richer ways than if we had to rely solely on our own firsthand experience.

What *Is* a Story's "Ethical Vision"?

If my phrase "a story's ethical vision" does not seem sufficiently clear, I simply mean that no story can get told in any medium without an ethical vision of some kind that supports and informs it. *A story's ethical vision is a particular configuration of rights and wrongs that any story puts in motion within a represented human context.* Every author has ways of letting us know which characters deserve our sympathy and which do not, whose ambitions we should support and whose ambitions we should fear, and so on. Whether we are talking about "The Three Little Pigs" or *A Farewell to Arms* (a novel that has been inaccurately said to contain no moral judgments), each story requires us to approve and disapprove—not just vaguely, but intensely and vividly—of its characters and their actions. Furthermore, readers *must* make these ethical judgments. They are not discretionary, for they form the most important part of our understanding of the story to begin with.

The ethical vision of *A Farewell to Arms*, for example, asks us to admire and like Frederick Henry, to abhor the actions of the army officers who try to execute him, and to believe that Henry's love for Catherine is good—not just pleasant, and not just good relative to time and place, but good absolutely, ethically good—good in a way that lifts Henry's character above the sordidness and horror of war, and improves it by healing his depression, making him gentle, giving him hope, and bringing him joy. To understand the ethical vision of Hemingway's story, or any other, is imaginatively to ingest the possibility that the narrative actions—and the narrative values—we have just encountered may occur in the real world. In one obvious and important way they *do* exist in the real world. Ingested possibilities that form a part of our potential repertoire of real actions also form a part of our real ethical character. Surely the content of ethical character is precisely equivalent to the number and kind of choices that one perceives possible in the world of action. Consumers of story who imaginatively ingest the worlds of human actions laid out for them in stories are potentially made over in the shape of the ethical vision of the stories that they both love and hate.

It follows that consumers of story conduct aesthetic and moral responses to stories at the same time, not at separate times. How would one separate, for example, the ethical blunders from the aesthetic blunders of the reader who thought that the wolf was the protagonist in *Little Red Riding Hood* or who thought that the ending of *King Lear* was truly funny? *Not to understand the ethical vision of a story is also not to understand its aesthetic shape.* To understand an ethical vision is to see it as a possibility, and to see things as possibilities generates the choices out of which we make our lives. In the words of Matthew Kieran, "Art as such typically stimulates and engages the imagination in order to promote a sound appreciation of what the imaginings concern and thus serves to promote imaginative understanding. . . . It is through the imaginative understanding that art is tightly linked to our moral aspect. Our moral perception and sensibilities are themselves dependent upon our imaginative understanding of the world, people, and forms of life" (342).

To return to my definition, a story's ethical vision is a particular configuration of rights and wrongs that any story puts in motion within a represented human context. If stories are about human interactions (or about creatures who, like human beings, possess ethical agency, even if they happen to be animals, sentient robots, or space aliens), and if human interactions are saturated with ethical considerations, then every representation of human actions in a story has to order those ethical considerations in some way that allows readers to make sense out of what happens. The ethical vision of both persons and stories includes all of those actions, thoughts, motives, and attitudes we feel that we and others *ought* to do or *ought not* to do, and it includes the *ethical criteria* by which we judge ourselves and others to be *good* or *not good.* The core of everyone's everyday existence is a set of ethical considerations.

The ethical vision of a story operates in the same way that it does in our lives: it is foundational to our sense that we can live a flourishing life, or that we must live with danger, deprivation, discomfort, or injustice. The ethical vision of a story is its attempt to capture the valences of all those rights and wrongs that operate at the core of its characters' everyday existence. If we ask whether all this talk about ethics raises any significant questions about the ways in which people react to the content of stories—and to the criticism or praise they may heap on that content—the answer is, of course, yes. A vast amount of practical ethical criticism about stories is going on all the time. It seldom announces itself *as* ethical—today's ethical critics often pretend to making political, social, or religious points—yet the ethical criticism or praise that we heap on stories is not hard to find. Scratch the surface of the political, social, or religious criticism of soap operas or grand operas or violent

TV programs or sexually graphic movies or smarmy song lyrics, and you will find an ethical premise lurking underneath. The interests of ethical criticism may be confused or obscured by being proffered as any kind of discourse *but* ethical, but they are not thereby diminished.

Asserting that stories exert ethical influence on those who consume them does *not* entail a belief that stories exert their influence on us *coercively,* the way political actions or law enforcement policies or physical forces do. But stating that stories work noncoercively also does not mean that the influence is superficial. Tony Kushner, the playwright of *Angels in America*, makes this point "just right" (to quote Goldilocks) in a *New York Times* interview, and the clarity and keenness of his insight make it worth quoting at length.

> It's never the case that a work of art is directly responsible for changing the world. Only activism, direct political action, does that. But art can help change people, who then decide to change their own lives, change their neighborhood, their community, their society, their world. *I don't think art alone changes people, but consciousness, the life of the mind, is a critical force for change and art helps the shaping of consciousness.* For instance, I have always felt, and I get this in part from my experience making plays and productions, and also from William Shakespeare and Bertolt Brecht, that watching theater teaches people a way of looking at the world with a doubleness of vision that's immensely influential—transformative, even. . . . On stage and off, in the theater and in the real world, "things," as W. S. Gilbert put it, "are seldom what they seem." . . .
>
> Again, no one learns to see the world anew entirely because of plays or books or paintings or dance concerts. Art has a power, but it's an indirect power. Art suggests. When people are ready to receive such suggestion, it can and does translate into action, but the readiness is all. *People make the world; art is one of many ways we do that.* (June 4, 2004; emphasis added)

People in general as well as literary professionals are not only deeply passionate but also clearly concerned about ethics when they argue about a large and diverse range of issues related to story. These issues and arguments, in motion all the time, include but are not limited to the following:

- *character formation:* how poems, TV programs, movies, novels, song lyrics, and so on influence readers' beliefs, imagination, and feelings
- *learning about life:* how narratives, including fictions, teach lessons about everyday life, about the age-old question of how to live
- *imitation of values:* how readers and viewers imitate the attitudes and values and conduct of characters from literature, TV, movies, and other narratives
- *social attitudes:* how narratives influence people's understanding or misunderstanding of, sympathy with, or detachment from such social constituencies as ethnic groups, racial minorities, non-Europeans, non-Americans, women, and people with disabilities
- *civics and civility:* how television, movies, novels, and rap lyrics influence young people's views about public civility, honesty, violence, authority, social and political institutions, women, race relations, the environment, and the law
- *history and class:* how narratives influence readers' views about history, class, democracy, commercialism, and so on

Direct Imitation of Stories

I receive especially obdurate resistance to ethical criticism from my most well-educated and well-read colleagues. I once had a professional colleague attempt to trivialize my interest in the ethics of narratives by saying, "So as an ethical critic you would object to a novel that gave me a vivid and sympathetic portrayal of an ax murderer on the grounds that reading it might turn me into an ax murderer, right?" Well—no. I'm not worried in her case that any fiction she reads could ever turn her into an ax murderer. But, *in principle*, she has a point.

Direct imitations of stories do occur and clearly produce ethical consequences. I venture to assert, moreover, that we all engage in direct imitation of narrative models much more frequently than we think.

The reason we think that *we* are the ones "above" such influence is that we largely think of direct imitation only in its most sensationalistic and gross forms. We think of the hoodlums in New York who, immediately after the release of the movie *Money Train* (1995), killed a man by imitating the movie's horrific scene in which a subway ticket seller is squirted with gasoline and burned to death in his toll booth. Or we remember the two boys who accidentally killed themselves in New Jersey when, right after the release of the movie *The Program* (also in 1995), they tried lying down in the middle of the freeway, intending like the movie heroes to let the cars straddle them harmlessly. Or we remember the large number of young people who, after reading *On the Road* in the 1960s, bought Volkswagen buses and struck out for the highways and byways of America in direct imitation of Jack Kerouac. In all of these cases we undoubtedly think, "How gullible, how immature, how uncritical, how unlike me. I could never be like that."

But it all depends on what "like that" means, doesn't it? Like the droll response that Mark Twain once made to an announcement about his death, our confidence in the immovability of our character may be not only factually premature but intellectually complacent and uncritical. We all do the same thing as the people in the sensational examples from the previous paragraph—academics and intellectuals as much as anyone else—*not* by committing immoral or grossly imitative *actions*, at least not often, but we do imitate less obviously tangible features of story such as *values* and *attitudes* and *ideas* and *beliefs*. In the end, of course, our actions grow out of our values, attitudes, ideas, and beliefs, so the line of influence from stories to actions may not be as indirect as many of us would like to think, but as long as we persist in thinking that this line of influence is only remote or nonexistent, the ways that stories do indeed influence us will remain hidden from our own perception.

Firsthand Experience versus Secondhand Experience

Another often repeated objection to ethical criticism is based on the assumption that stories' effects cannot penetrate to our ethical core because they are only secondhand experiences. This is a mistaken notion.

We cannot separate the things we love from who we become when we love them, and it does not matter whether the things we love are beer and Skittles, chess, rock 'n' roll, people in real life, or people in stories. Experience is hardly ever firsthand *or* secondhand. It's usually both. Moreover the line between them is usually unclear. Stories have a peculiar power to blur firsthand and secondhand experience because, as Jerome Bruner says of autobiography (which I think may be said of all the narratives we deeply experience), "eventually the culturally shaped cognitive and linguistic processes that guide the self-telling of life narratives achieve the power to structure perceptual experience, to organize memory, to segment and purpose-build the very 'events' of a life" (15).

Significantly, stories provide more powerful accounts for most of us than abstract philosophical, psychological, or even theological accounts, for only stories can offer us the comprehensive view of a whole life. To quote James Q. Wilson, "Novelists may do a better job of explaining character formation than social scientists" (145). Those who wish to dismiss the formative power of stories because of their secondhand status fail to consider that in the secondhand realm of story we experience an immediacy of feeling, a rush of emotion, and a flow of sensations that frequently surpass the intensity and flow of firsthand experience. (One can see why Plato so deeply distrusted literature's effects. He saw more clearly than most thinkers how literature's empiricism teaches its auditors to *care,* and care deeply about, precisely those features of life that he was most interested in teaching people *not* to care about, namely, how life's physical and emotional aspects *feel.*)

Stories lift us out of the here-and-now and take us to the there-and-then. Reading a narrative, or seeing one (in a movie or drama), is itself a firsthand experience, even if the events and characters being depicted are fictional. One does not *imagine* reading *Great Expectations* or watching *Lost* or listening to a narrative ballad, even though one imagines the events that these narratives depict. Moreover, just because we imagine the events and characters in *Great Expectations* does *not* mean that we also imagine the emotional, intellectual, and ethical responses triggered by the narrative representations.

Why is this important? Because if our emotional, intellectual, and ethical responses to stories are the same emotional, intellectual, and ethical responses we have to life, then the thesis I am developing in this book becomes both clearer and more compelling. If I am right, we toggle back and forth between life and stories, and each of these domains assists us in understanding the other. We do not have to pretend that the secondhand experiences of story are real in a firsthand sense. On the other hand, the difference between firsthand and secondhand experiences does not necessarily force us to conclude that story is less of an influence on us than real life merely because it is secondhand. In the words of Peter Lamarque, "we can know something is fictional but still take it seriously without having to believe or even half-believe it. We can reflect on, and be moved by, a thought independently of accepting it as true" (302). Or as Samuel Johnson puts the issue (with his usual cogency and economy) in his "Preface to Shakespeare," "the reflection that strikes the heart is not that the evils before us are real evils, but that they are evils to which we ourselves may be exposed. . . . Imitations produce pain or pleasure not because they are mistaken for realities, but *because they bring realities to mind*" (224; emphasis added). And when realities are brought to mind by the "as if" of story, the "as if" characters and events can lead us to ideas, values, views, and feelings that mold us as readily as firsthand experience.

So much of human experience is of the kind we have when we are reading or viewing narratives that the obvious differences between reading stories and living life may blind us to deep similarities. It is true that when I read about Huck's desire to escape the widow Douglas or read about Sethe's choice to murder her infant daughter, or when I watch President Bartlett on *West Wing* agonize over his advisers' recommendation to authorize a covert assassination or watch Luke Skywalker come to the shattering realization that Darth Vader is his father, I am not with these characters physically. It is also true that I am not doing any of the things the narrative characters are doing, but these differences should not blind us to the deep truth that *much of life's firsthand experiences are also lived in the mind's eye and not only when we are consuming stories.*

Every time I daydream about traveling abroad or winning the lottery, every time I visualize myself teaching my class, every time I plan ahead for my children's education or a vacation, every time my heart beats faster in anticipation of a sexual encounter, I am living in my mind's eye. I am not "really" doing the things I picture, if (and only if) "really" is reserved exclusively for physical action. But I am undeniably having some kind of "experience" of these events, an experience that is sometimes more intense, full, and vivid than these same events might be if I experienced them in the body instead of in the mind's eye. I live as fully in those moments of imagination, dream, and story—sometimes more fully—as in any other moment.

The line between what counts as firsthand and what is secondhand experience is not clear precisely because our imagination lets us live at more than one level both simultaneously and sequentially. Shakespeare's Julius Caesar refers to this power of the imagination when he says, "Cowards die many times before their deaths; / The valiant never taste of death but once" (II, ii). When we take stories to heart, we *live* in them, and they live in us; we are not holding them away from us at fingertips' distance. Insisting that they are only secondhand experience misses this blurring and blending of story living and real-life living. A lot of real, everyday living just *is* story living.

The double consciousness we adopt as consumers of stories—the consciousness that allows us to be "with" Huck on the Mississippi or "with" Indiana Jones in *Raiders of the Lost Ark* or "with" Henry James in Leon Edel's great biography, and to be simultaneously in our living rooms with our feet up, offers the potential for us to come at experience from different directions simultaneously. That is, stories allow us, *at the same time we are intimately involved,* to back off from them more consistently and at a further distance than we can from real-life experiences, thus allowing stories, in many cases, to be more educational than real life. In stories we can have intimacy and distance at the same time. In Martha Nussbaum's words,

How can literature show us or train us in anything, when, as we have said, the very moral abilities that make for good reading are the ones that are allegedly in need of development? James's artistic analogy has already, I think, shown us an answer to this question. When we examine our own lives, we have so many obstacles to correct vision, so many motives to blindness and stupidity. The "vulgar heat" of jealousy and personal interest comes between us and the loving perception of each particular. A novel, just because it is not our life, places us in a moral position that is favorable for perception and it shows us what it would be like to take up that position in life. We find here love without possessiveness, attention without bias, involvement without panic. (162)

The double consciousness that makes it possible to back off from narrative more consistently than from real life is a difference that yields a vast educational power. As Iris Murdoch writes, "art, especially literature, is a great hall of reflection where we can all meet and where everything under the sun can be examined and considered. . . . Art is far and away the most educational thing we have" (86).

Stories as a Primal Need

The reason why the intellectual's protest against ethical criticism on the grounds that "I could never be that naive" misses the point is that our ceaseless consumption of stories is not driven by naiveté but by need. Storytelling techniques may sometimes be sophisticated, but, fundamentally, stories as a response to and an extension of human nature are not sophisticated intellectual enterprises. They endlessly recycle enduring human preoccupations, and, overwhelmingly, human preoccupations are not issues of intellect. They are issues of emotion, imagination, perception, drives, needs, and social relations. Even the most sophisticated and intellectual of storytellers, such as Henry James and James Joyce, recognize in their bones what academic and professional critics sometimes fail to recognize in their heads, namely, that human beings tell and consume stories because they *need* to.

Stories display the universality of such *emotions*, for example, as fear, grief, hatred, envy, remorse, compassion, lust, anger, confusion, shame, despair, and joy. We can tell that these emotions are common to humankind because they crop up again and again in stories across many cultural divides. Second, stories from all cultures also display such common human *motives* as ambition, pride, greed, sex, dominance, honor, revenge, self-defense, familial protection, and the impulse to compensate for perceived weakness, failures, or deprivations. Third, stories from all cultures display such common human *actions* as cruelty, tenderness, work, honesty, dishonesty, laziness, treachery, infidelity, loyalty, making war, making peace, making love, telling stories, listening to stories, learning from experience, refusing to learn from experience, expressing hatred, conquering nature, being conquered by nature, and so on. Fourth, stories from all cultures display the commonness of such *existential conditions* as happiness, despair, loneliness, self-confidence, insecurity, self-love, self-loathing, fear of death, hopefulness about the future, hopelessness about the future, regret, nostalgia, and so on. If these emotions were not transcultural, translations of literature and other forms of story would not and could not work, for translation can only work if the concepts referred to and expressed by the original language *exist* in both the culture and the language into which the original is translated.

I do not mean to be making an argument against difference or making a covert claim that difference does not count. Of course difference counts. Of course people from different cultures, languages, and ethnic traditions deal differently, sometimes extravagantly differently, with emotions, actions, motives, and existential conditions. But these coping differences should not blind us to the fact that what is being coped with are universal facts of human nature and experience. We remain distinctively human in all of our different contexts. The fact that the finches of the Galapagos Islands might nest differently from the finches in my backyard does not mean that they are not both finches. Human nature is no more ad hoc than finch nature, although human conduct is immensely more varied because its contexts are immensely more varied and because the means of mediation, especially speech and writing, permit different mediations not only to be preserved but to be built on—and thus made more and more different in appearance—from generation to generation.

But whether I am watching a movie about Japanese warriors in the fourteenth century, or reading an epic poem of war from an ancient Greek culture, or reading a novel of modern African life, or listening to a ballad expressing the lament of Asian yak herders, I *know*—that is, I recognize as human—the emotions, motives, actions, and existential states being represented. I can recognize, understand, and sympathize with what is represented because the referents are universal to my species. Multicultural claims about the moral obligation to "respect" the integrity of all cultures and ethnic perspectives carry force only because there exists, underlying those claims, a commonality of human nature that is silently being taken for granted as the only grounds on which the imperative of "respect" can possess intellectual or moral coherence. Storytelling is perhaps the most universal of all human activities that shows our commonness.

The moment we begin socializing with others, and this would include all those times when we are socializing with others in our heads and hearts, not just at physical sites, storytelling forms the primary matrix of our interactions. As long as we are with other people, we may be playing golf, painting the den, or taking a power walk, but all the time we are bonding to our companions by telling and consuming stories. Can you recall *any* conversation longer than fifteen minutes in which either you or your interlocutors didn't say something like, "Let me tell you what happened to me the other day," or "This reminds me of something that happened when I was a kid," or "You'll never guess what Jamison said to me at lunch yesterday," and then someone launches into the story of what happened, what is remembered, or what was said? Such stuff, such telling and consuming of stories, is one of our most important forms of individual expression and social cohesion. And this doesn't even count the stories as art—either their significance or their number—that we read in books; watch in movie houses, in theaters, or on TV; or listen to in songs, sermons, commercials, jokes, books on tape, and so on. In subsequent chapters I continue to examine in detail both why and how this perpetual traffic in all kinds of stories helps us become the persons we turn out to be.

CHAPTER FOUR

Stories and the Ethics of Experience

The Difference between Experiencing and Knowing

Mere experience is not as educational as people usually think. We are fond of adages like "the school of hard knocks" and "experience is the best teacher," but the truth is that raw experience unmediated by reflection, theories, and thought can teach us little. Commonplace wisdom frequently asserts that the objects, people, and activities we experience most intimately are the things we know best, but if this is so, then why do spouses, family members, and colleagues whom we see every day in intimate circumstances frequently misunderstand, misinterpret, and mislead each other in completely confabulating but oh-so-common ways?

The most obvious feature of commonplace wisdom—the usual source of these honorific claims about the educational power of experience—is its failure to see that the world is stranger, more complex, and more subtle than commonplace observation can detect. Unless a second activity occurs that goes beyond experience—*conceptualization*—the meaning of experience can remain forever opaque. Does burning my hand on a hot stove teach me not to touch the next hot stove I encounter? Only if I am able to construct a concept that goes beyond my experience, only if I am able to make the inductive generalization "a hot stove will *always* burn my hand if

I touch it—including the hot surfaces of stoves that I have not yet seen or experienced." But notice something crucial here: *the knowledge about hot stoves lies in the concept, in the inductive generalization, not in the experience itself.* Getting burned happens to my hand, but the knowledge of what this experience means gets constructed in my brain, not in my hand.

Plato seems to be the first thinker to have argued that knowledge is always knowledge of concepts, not of experience, but interestingly, Plato's elevation of concepts over experience has received powerful reformulation and reinforcement from modern philosophers of science, some of whom have been arguing for at least the last forty years that many facts, as in "the facts of nature," are created by theories, not by experience. This is because no one knows what *counts* as a fact until she or he has some theory that yields the criteria for ignoring some aspects of reality as non-facts and taking other aspects into account *as* facts. In the history of science, facts that existed at one point in time, like the existence of phlogiston or ether, can become non-facts at another point in time. The facts of phlogiston and ether were created by theories, not by nature.

Human beings possess the ability to have knowledge of some things they have never experienced at all. Educated adults in the West all have some notion, for example, of such concepts or places as perfect justice, traveling at the speed of light, absolute zero, and Tokyo, even though none of us has experience of the first three, and only some of us have had experience of the fourth. Human beings can also have firsthand experience that doesn't necessarily yield knowledge. I can experience a burning sensation on my back, for example, but have no knowledge of whether this experience is being created by a hot piece of metal or a cold piece of dry ice. I can experience the taste of spices and herbs in a salad dressing but have no knowledge of which spices and herbs are producing the distinctive taste. Experience does not always lead to knowledge. Think about the number of people you know who commit the same self-destructive, foolish, or illogical mistakes over and over. If experience is such a great teacher, why don't alcoholics and drug addicts, who experience firsthand the losses and pain that their conduct leads to, learn how to quit drinking or shooting up? The catalog of their experiences grows larger and larger, but they learn nothing except, perhaps, that experience itself does not yield the knowledge they need for self-control. It's not that their experience isn't intense enough or that it's illusory. The problem is that they don't successfully conceptualize any alternative to it.

The Kind of Knowledge We Get from Stories

So what does all of this talk about experience and knowledge have to do with consuming and telling stories? A great deal. Stories give us experience but not just raw experience. Stories give us *conceptualized* experience. A story offers us the same chance to apply its representations to the world the way we might apply any concept or idea, such as justice or gravity to the world, in order to improve our understanding of it. This does not mean that writers necessarily have an educational aim in mind when they write—such as "help my readers arrive at a better understanding of the world"—it merely means that this is the way stories work. This also explains one important reason why we never tire of engaging with stories: the world of experience is so complicated, and the potential meanings of experience are so elusive, that we can never have enough rich sources of ideas and concepts to help us achieve the conceptualized understanding of the world that we need.

The concepts that are stories have a metaphorical relationship to the real world, which means that the vision of a novel—or the vision of a stage drama, movie, TV sitcom, ballad, or epic poem—metaphorically "stands for" the world of real-life experience and events. *Middlemarch* is a visionary metaphor of provincial nineteenth-century English life no less than Burns's "red, red rose" is a metaphor for his "love," no less than *Roseanne* is a metaphorical vision of a late-twentieth-century American working-class family, and no less than *All My Children* is a metaphorical vision of the early-twenty-first-century American leisure class pursuing the fulfillments of "true love" while wearing the latest fashions and talking the latest small talk. The stories "stand for" the world of experience. Nelson Goodman, a philosopher of aesthetics, put it this way: "Fiction, then . . . applies truly neither to nothing nor to diaphanous possible worlds but, albeit metaphorically, to actual worlds. . . . The so-called possible worlds of fiction lie within actual worlds. Fiction operates in actual worlds in much the same way as nonfiction" (104). Goodman's comment helps explain why the vivid and powerful embrace of stories turns them into thoroughly conceptualized, deeply embedded *facts* of our experience, as easily available for recollection or reference as all of our firsthand, biographical facts. The sheer mental act of *understanding* a story entails that we bend our minds around the arc of the story's metaphor. Once we do this, the "bend" we make will never allow our minds to assume precisely their former shape. The metaphor, once I have made it mine—an ownership that I cannot avoid, at least temporarily, because ownership is contained within the act of understanding itself—has now become a fact of my life in at least three important senses.

First, it has become a fact of my experience. The act of reading, viewing, or listening—figuring out the metaphor of the story and having been figured by it—is now part of my personal history, a fact of my biography. The understanding that I have won is now woven into my intellectual fabric. Not only can I subsequently *not* refuse to know what the story has taught me to know; I cannot make what I know mean something else without reimagining the whole metaphor.

Second, the metaphor of the story is not just a fact of my *personal* history or perception but is probably a fact of *communal* history and perception as well. Once certain stories become widely shared (and now that movies and TV series are easily available as DVDs, they begin to share the material longevity that used to belong only to books), they become the potential basis for collective discourse. Whether we are talking about the story of George Washington chopping down the cherry tree, Abe Lincoln walking miles to return a penny, Rosa Parks refusing to sit in the back of the bus, Lou Gehrig playing baseball with broken bones in both hands, the novel and the movie of *Gone With the Wind*, the story and the movies of *A Christmas Carol* and *Jane Eyre,* or the apparently endless reruns of *I Love Lucy,* these stories seize the imagination and invite the assent not just of individuals but of whole groups.

The facts of history—or of current society, for that matter—may be more powerfully interpreted for society as a whole by stories than by history or statistics. To millions of TV viewers in the sixties, for example, the fictional Archie Bunker of *All in the Family* did more to convey the truth of certain white, middle-class attitudes about race relations, family values, the importance of neighborhoods, and the industrial work ethic than all of the statistically laden government reports of the day all put together (who actually reads government reports?). It is often the case that facts' relevance for living is not easily seen until they are cast into narrative form. This does not mean, of course, that stolidly factual accounts are valueless, but it is to say that their value often remains potential, like the nutritional value of food, until it is digested, and *reality seems much more thoroughly digestible as story than as disembodied fact.* In the words of Benedict Carey,

> Researchers have found that the human brain has a natural affinity for narrative construction. People tend to remember facts more accurately if they encounter them in a story rather than in a list, studies find; and they rate legal arguments as more convincing when built into narrative tales rather than on legal precedent. . . . Taken together, these findings suggest a kind of give and take between life stories and individual memories, between the larger screenplay and the individual scenes. The way people replay and recast memories, day by day, deepens and reshapes their larger life story. And as it evolves, that larger story in turn colors the interpretation of the scenes.

The value of historical facts is not that they are facts but that they are historically conceptualized. Their value as facts does not become accessible to most people until they see them in a narrative that makes them meaningful.

Third, a story is a fact in and of itself. Its independent material existence makes it a fact in and of the world. It has an existence apart from any single reader, listener, or viewer. As consumers of narrative we *re*construct others' metaphors of the world when we read novels, watch movies and TV, or attend plays, but the original construction remains a definable property of the narratives themselves. Stories have their own status in the world. No matter how much I may *want* certain outcomes in stories, my desires do not determine the arc of the story. Hamlet always dies at the end of *Hamlet*. Marianne Dashwood always marries Colonel Brandon, not Willoughby, at the end of *Sense and Sensibility*. Sirius Black always dies at the end of *Harry Potter and the Order of the Phoenix*.

Indeed, the power of narratives to teach us anything about the world *depends* on their autonomy. If we make stories say whatever *we* want them to say, we rob ourselves of stories' ability to introduce us to new ideas, concepts, or points of view. Since story consumers are first of all human beings who know at some deep level that they *need* to learn about the world, they are not likely ever to sacrifice totally the education that narratives offer for the mere egotistical pleasure of making every story come out the way they want it to. There is simply not enough in it for them. The *pleasure* of stories as well as their educational power lies in their enabling readers to *escape* the ego, not to imprison all of the world's wonderful diversity *within* the ego.

Understanding fictional characters' experiences in stories requires that we leave the home base of ego and stretch ourselves vicariously to live in the world of feeling and ideas beyond our own ballpark. This is how *all* education works. In the words of James Redfield, "The aims of education are the aims of life; education is simply the general term we use for the process by which we become wiser than we were" (171). Narrative experience is simply education in its most comprehensive form. From the epics of Homer to the novels of Helprin, the ethical implications of ingesting stories remain relevant for us all. If we are ever to succeed at cultivating compassion for the sufferings of others, or empathic appreciation of their joys—if we are ever to succeed in treating other people on the basis of moral principle rather than self-interest, or, as Kant puts it, if we are ever to succeed at treating other people as ends rather than as means—then we absolutely *must* learn how to leave the home base of ego. Contemporary social scientists are becoming more and more interested in the way narratives help us develop empathy. "[Current] researchers argue that to experience true empathy is an act of great sophistication, *requiring that one be able to run a narrative through one's mind* about what happened to the sufferer to bring the individual to his or her current state, and what might be done to help. To empathize is to understand beginnings, middles and possible ends" (Angier 7; emphasis added).

In *The Last Happy Occasion*, Alan Shapiro tells a story about how a neighbor's hostile dog knocked down his pregnant wife and then nearly killed the Shapiros' own dog. Shapiro reports being so deeply angry that for years he was unable "to think about [the dog's owner] without wanting to perform a host of tortures on the most sensitive parts of his anatomy" (161–62). And yet as he reflects on the experience and constructs a narrated version of it for the book he is writing, he notices that turning the event into a story invites him to enter what he calls a "contemplative field," where both he and the reader are invited to back off from the rawness of the experience and to consider conceptualized alternatives to firsthand feelings of revenge and anger:

> Freed from the tyranny of sheer event . . . the contemplative field I enter when I write about this man now, and that you enter when you read about him, affords us both a latitude of response and attention not available in the experience itself. This contemplative field enables us to cultivate what Wayne Booth calls an upward hypocrisy, pretending to more sympathetic understanding than we ordinarily have. It enables us to enter into the inner world of people we might shun or dismiss in the normal course of our nonreading lives. This is the value of imaginative contemplation. . . . I'd like to think that the imaginative work of writing this, of telling and retelling this story over the years, will bring me sooner to a more inclusive, more flexible grasp of the experience. (160–61)

Stephen Pinker of Harvard, psychologist and philosopher of science, and Rebecca Goldstein of Princeton, professor of philosophy and novelist, have conducted a fascinating conversation in *The Seed Salon* pursuing just this line of thought, Pinker from the perspective of evolutionary psychology and Goldstein from the perspective of a working artist.

> **SP:** And that brings us back to fiction. One problem for anyone like me who believes in a fixed human nature, including a fixed moral sense, is to explain how human behavior could have changed so radically over a few centuries or millennia. Much of the world has seen an end to slavery, to genocide for convenience, to torture as a routine form of criminal punishment, to capital punishment for property crimes, to human sacrifice, to rape as the spoils of war, to the ownership of women. We seem to be turning into a nicer species. . . . We have a much lower rate of death in warfare than in prestate, hunter-gatherer societies.

RG: So we're getting less cruel.

SP: We are getting less cruel, and the question is . . . why did it happen? *What stretched our innate capacity for empathy? And one answer is mediums that force us to take other people's perspectives, such as journalism, history, and realistic fiction.*

RG: *Storytelling does it.*

SP: By allowing you to project yourself into the lives of people of different times and places and races, in a way that wouldn't spontaneously occur to you, fiction can force you into the perspective of a person unlike yourself, who might otherwise seem subhuman.

RG: There's a fundamental role that storytelling is always playing in the moral life. To try to see somebody on their own terms, which is part of what it is to be moral, is to try to make sense of their world, to try to tell the story of their life as they would tell it. . . . I think storytelling, in general, has a moral use. . . . We train children by telling them stories. We try to get them to feel their way into other lives, and that itself is something. If we had no capacity for that there would be no hope. . . .

SP: *Fiction can be a kind of moral technology.*

RG: *Storytelling is something that can awaken attentiveness, engagement, and empathy to a life that isn't one's own. And to be attentive, engaged, empathetic: that is moral. . . .*

SP: When it comes to fictional narratives, I suspect there is an adaptive benefit as well. One problem we all face is how to act in a world that presents a vast combinatorial space of possibilities, especially when it comes to other people. I can do any of ten things, and you can do any of ten things in response to each of those ten things, and I can do ten things in response to your response, and so on. There is an explosion of possibilities that no mortal mind can deduce in advance. What fiction might do is allow people to play out, in their minds' eyes, hypothetical courses of action in hypothetical circumstances, which would then allow them to anticipate what would happen if they ever faced those situations in reality. (47–49; emphasis added)

While we today use psychological terms such as "bonding" or "empathy" for such flights beyond the ego, the Romantic poet Percy Shelley simply calls it love: "The great secret of morals is love; or a going out of our nature, and an identification of ourselves with . . . [that] which exists in thought, action, or person, not our own" (40). To attend to narrative as one of the facts in a world larger than our own interests helps us resist a disfiguring self-obsession. As Nelson Goodman asserts, "the arts must be taken no less seriously than the sciences as modes of discovery, creation, and enlargement of knowledge in the broad sense of advancement of understanding" (102). Until we ceaseless consumers of stories understand that our responses occur on a continuum with our responses to real life— until we understand that these responses to story constitute an important kind of *practice* at forming responses to real life—we are likely to vastly underrate the potential ethical significance of our relationships with narratives. Fiction, says Brian Hall, "is always moral, regardless of the morality, immorality or amorality of the lives the fiction portrays. To help you see through another's eyes, to undermine parochial certainty—how could this not bear on morality? . . . Enlightened transformation goes to the heart of the artistic goal of literature. *(Naturally, this means that fiction can be bad for you, too).* . . . Fiction can teach you again and again what you think you already know" (23; emphasis added).

Stories Represent Life But Have the Unity of Art: Why Does This Matter?

It is precisely because stories look like life and yet differ from life and yet *relate* to life that we find them endlessly fascinating. The act of taking in stories is like looking into a magical mirror that hints it will tell us the secrets of life not just on the other side of the mirror but on our own side as well. There are many implications to stories' analogical relationship to real life, but I will limit my attention to two of these implications here. The first implication I have already touched on, so I will mention it only briefly, and that is that stories always stimulate ethical responses as much as they stimulate emotional and intellectual responses. This is because ethical categories comprise the most important part of our "reading" of new acquaintances. Not using ethical categories to understand other people would make them appear to us mostly as blanks devoid of interest. None of us can imagine living this way. I don't mean that none of us can imagine living *happily* this way; I mean that none of us can imagine living this way at all. But if this is so, then it follows that we will bring our ethical standards into play in all of our social relations, including those we conduct with narrative characters.

The second implication of stories' status as analogous-to-but-different-from-real-life is their greater unity and organization. Achieving greater unity and organization in our own lives—what we often call "getting our act together" or "achieving focus"—is a goal that most of us pursue. Some people do so purposefully, some wistfully; some do so with fair success, some never seem to have success at all. For all of us, however, achieving a life that feels unified for any long stretch of time is difficult. None of us ever achieves it permanently. The reason is that the unity of life is primarily a product of consciousness—a function of memory—not a unity of parts. But works of art do not have consciousness or memory; they have aesthetic strategies. Thus, while we know "it is I" doing all the different things in our day, that sense of continuity, or unity, is not the same thing as the parts of life all fitting together. I remember that it was I mowing the grass in the morning and writing this book in the afternoon. That sense of continuity certainly provides one kind of unity in my life, but I'm flummoxed if you ask me whether the two parts fit together the way any two images in a poem or any two themes in a musical composition fit together. They don't. The only connection between grass mowing and writing this book is that I am the same person doing both parts. Too much of my life—and yours—gives us the sense that the parts *don't* fit together. In contrast, the analogies of fictions and other narratives provide us with points of comparison that let us see what greater focus, organization, and unity our lives *might* possess.

Stories provide this comparative function because the unity of art is based on just the kind of unity that our lives lack: a unity of parts. Each shade of color in a painting, each chord in a piece of music, each word in a sonnet (even the punctuation), each scene in a well-made TV drama or sitcom *fits*. An artwork is not conscious of itself as we are, but its parts resonate with each other in a way that the parts of our lives seldom do.

The parts that make up individual works of art have precisely the kind of internal resonance with each other that keeps us peering at them for the secret of achieving such harmonious resonance in *our* lives. Many of us have the nagging sense that our suitcase of life is always revealing to others the straggling ends of underwear and neckties that we never succeed in getting tidily packed. But good art seems never to straggle its underwear and neckties unless, indeed, the straggling clothes are a deliberate aesthetic strategy, in which case the representation of straggling is not really an inherent incoherence. Thus we look at art—and especially, perhaps, at narrative art—with all the fascination of creatures who on our side of the mirror feel desperate to incorporate in our own lives some of the unity manifested by the art on the other side of the mirror.[1]

Poor Ophelia says in her famous mad scene, "Lord, we know what we are, but not what we may be" (*Hamlet* IV, v). Ophelia is right, but for the purposes of my argument here she might have gone on to complete her thought. "We know not what we may be[come]," *but we are intensely interested.* The story of our own lives engrosses us for the same reason that all other stories engross us: we want to see how things turn out. We can't wait to see how *we* turn out. But what is the process by which human beings "turn out" to become anything at all other than what accident and impulse shape us to be?

We have already seen in the honeybee comparison that human beings don't automatically "turn out" according to internal programming. (As Aristotle would say, human beings' destinies do not have internal efficient causes.) Human beings have to get an education, or, rather, many different kinds of education—the most important kind being an education in how to interact with other human beings—in order to have anything that resembles a full human life. However, life simply does not allow us sufficiently rich forms of firsthand socialization to guarantee that we'll learn all we need to know. As I have already noted, we don't live long enough. We can't change our sex, our era, our skin color, our parents. We can't learn enough languages or live a full span of life in different cultures. And so on. Stories fill the gap between the education we get and the education we need.

In the words of Scott Sanders, "every work of literature is the drawing of a charmed circle, since we can write about only a piece of the world. Within that circle, language shines meaning onto gestures, whispers, images, and objects" (206). Not all stories are works of literature, of course, which means that the "language" of some stories is not primarily language at all but images; nevertheless, the same truth holds. Kathryn Morton understands the deep connection between the stories we encounter and the lives we lead.

> Fiction gives us the names and symbols in a grammar of experience. . . . The truth about people can best be known as people know it. It is a package deal, and the package best adapted to convey a sense of the human condition is the novel. . . .
>
> Novelists give us demonstration classes in what is the ultimate work of us all, for by days and years we must create the narrative of our own lives. A pawky, artless mess we easily make of it. . . . It is lonely work; we are all amateurs. To glance up and see a great novelist offering a story of rare, sweet wit and grace is to feel that our heart has found its home. . . .
>
> These books are showing me ways of being I could never have managed alone. *I am not killing time, I'm trying to make a life.* (2; emphasis added)

Our impulse for intimacy with stories stems from the heart's core, where we hunger for knowledge about the practices and arts of being human. Story is neither a dispensable nor a discretionary item in the human enterprise. Nancy Willard, poet, novelist, and children's book author, puts it this way:

> The teller tells the story he has made out of bits he has seen and pieces he has heard. His telling brings these fragments together, and in that healing synthesis, he gives the wasted hours of our lives an order they don't have and a radiance that only God and the artist can perceive. We get up, we go to work, we come home dead tired, and sometimes we wonder what we are doing on this planet. And we know that in the great schemelessness of things, our own importance is a lie. Is the object of the game to tell that lie? Yes, to tell the lie. But in telling, to make it true. (112)

Stories and Patterns, the Basis of Meaning

Life doesn't come with any wash-and-care labels. Data and stimuli ceaselessly stream at us from all sides, and from inside, but we are left to make a life, plus a meaning, on our own. In the meantime, our bodies, minds, and the universe give us more information than we can process, more data than we can interpret, more experience than we can digest. Signals come to us raw, undifferentiated, uninterpreted, and unself-announcing. On our end, the receiving end, we are mere mortals and cannot swallow everything, much less digest it. We *must* engage in ceaseless editing, interpretation, labeling, and patterning. We receive information, but what we need, and thus try to construct, is meaning. Creating the patterns that order the chaos is the main project of human beings everywhere.

Although we have no certain way of knowing whether pattern is any more an inevitable feature of the universe than chaos, we cannot do without at least an operational faith that it is, for without it we cannot construct any meaning at all. We shrink from thinking that all the repetitions in the world that look like patterns are really just coincidence. According to a conversation between the Daimon and the Lesser Zadkiel, who oversee the life and development of the central character, Francis Cornish, in Robertson Davies's *What's Bred in the Bone*, coincidence is merely "a useful, dismissive word for people who cannot bear the idea of pattern shaping their own lives. Coincidence is what they call pattern in which they cannot discern something they are prepared to accept as meaning" (207). Regardless of the ontological status of coincidence *or* pattern, functionally we can only make meaning out of patterns, not coincidence, and our most consistent strategy for turning information into news is to shape our experience into stories.

In the words of Alasdair MacIntyre, "Every society enacts its own history as a more or less coherent dramatic narrative, a story in which each of us has to find his or her own place as a character, in order to know how to participate in it and how to continue it further. . . . It is through narrative that [children] learn to hope and to fear, to love and to hate, to dream and to want, to understand and to identify" (11). To switch metaphors, we swim in narrative as the native element most congenial to our human sensibilities, an element in which we learn to recognize both the other members and types of our own kind and the possible relations that we as individuals may establish with them. What pattern gives us is a way of separating things into coherent categories as a primary strategy for getting to know about them. But we are built such that we can erect a meaning for our own lives only if we have knowledge about other people's lives.

The features of story that make it so much more compelling than any other form of learning seem to be the following: its capacity for holistic representations of human life; its capacity to embed represented lives into a fully realized context of concrete details; and its capacity to vivify and identify those issues about which human beings tend to be in a perpetual froth of concern such as personal development, love and marriage, money and power, sex and other pleasures, religion and ideas, justice and injustice, good and evil, honor and dishonor, shame and redemption, comfort and deprivation, love and hate, and the causes of happiness and misery. In the end, human beings rely on narrative's capacity to pattern the chaotic "stuff" of raw experience into intelligible and meaningful shapes.

Simply knowing that issues of human belief, happiness, and misery are important does not tell us how to deal with them. Forms of human happiness are inescapably plural and maddeningly incommensurate. While we always know that we want to be happy, we are often completely in the dark about what will *make* us happy, and even when we think we know that *this* or *that* will make us happy, we are not sure how to rank *this* or *that* among the other self-excluding activities that might also make us happy. Stories assist the human dilemma of making choices by allowing us to negotiate *vicariously* among different lines of action and thought—and to take a good long look at possible concrete consequences—across a wider scope of possibilities than would ever be possible on the basis of firsthand experience alone.

In the words of Nuala O'Faolain, speaking of her youth, "novels were what I cared about. They asked the questions I wanted answered. How do lives get lived? How is love found?" (30). Unless all of our time and energy are being spent on sheer physical survival, O'Faolain's questions identify life's most important and highly messy layer of "primitive" issues. Only story can swallow this messiness whole and make sense of it.

CHAPTER FIVE

Judgment that Bites, Assent that Risks

"Dr. Gregory, Surely You Don't Advocate (gasp) *Censorship*?"

My college students get their hackles up at any suggestion from me or other critics that their interactions with narratives in print, film, or television might offer grounds for ethical concern. "Dr. Gregory, do you support *censorship*?" they ask, the word dripping with italics, as if "censorship" uttered in a tone of scandalized indignation would, like a magical incantation, simply make ethical discourse evaporate. "No, I'm opposed to censorship," I say, but when I ask them whether they think someone ought to exercise some kind of judgment or control over the stories that their younger siblings, nephews, cousins, and nieces are allowed to consume, they immediately support the idea.

My students readily agree that the principle of potential influence—the same principle that they had a moment ago strongly repudiated—is in fact valid when applied to "younger kids." When I ask them to identify the threshold age for being influenced by stories—and when I ask them to justify their confidence that they themselves have crossed that threshold—the conversation gets muddled, but they do not back away from the idea that "young kids" should have their consumption of certain kinds of stories monitored and controlled by responsible adults.

63

"Those *Halloween* movies are just not appropriate for eight-year-olds" is a typical kind of judgment. When I suggest that it is perhaps unfair to deny their younger relatives the same freedom to consume different kinds of stories that they demand for themselves, they resist. In other words, my students exhibit two strong ethical intuitions here: first, that they themselves are not vulnerable to ethical influence from stories, and second, that younger children are vulnerable. That these two intuitions are often contradictory and always ill-defined does not shake my students' belief in their reliability. In the personal story that follows, in which my wife and I face the issue of stories' potential influence as both parents and professional teachers, I unpack in detail just how much bite this issue of our ethical intuitions possesses—and how little it has to do with censorship. Finally, I will show reasons why the superficial belief that only "young kids" are susceptible to the ethical influence of stories is unreflective and naïve.

"Good Will to Men"—You Can Open Your Stereotype Now

It was Christmas eve, 1973. Among the gifts my wife and I were wrapping for our three-year-old daughter, Mellie, was a large, one-volume collection of "fifty favorite children's stories." As we sat leafing through the collection preparatory to wrapping it, smiling at stories we recalled from our own childhoods, we lost our smiles as we found ourselves increasingly shocked at the stereotypes that blatantly appeared in some of the stories. One story about "what mommies and daddies do" showed Daddy coming home from the office in a suit as Mommy, dressed in an apron and high heels and wearing a pearl necklace, was baking cookies. Another story was about an African-American maid—yes, a maid!—represented by the racist "Aunt Jemima" image, who took good care of her white family, while yet another story sagely offered our young daughter the sexist view that "little girls are sugar and spice and everything nice," but that "little boys are rats and snails and puppy dog tails."

Did these images and words present us with an ethical problem? My wife and I certainly thought so. We were not keen on saturating Mellie's impressionable young mind with such stereotypical falsehoods about her social world, but what should we do? We were not naïve enough to believe that we could protect Mellie from the stereotyped images that would surround her every day of her life—graphic, verbal, or embodied—but this didn't erase our queasiness at being among the first agents to introduce such images to her and to suggest our approval of them by making them *gifts*. Stories, we knew, would always form part of Mellie's education about life. The question was, and always is, what knowledge or views does an education from narratives offer? J. Hillis Miller proposes the following answer: "What do we learn from fictions? We learn the nature of things as they are. We need fictions in order to experiment with possible selves and to learn to take our places in the real world, to play our parts there. . . . With fictions we investigate, perhaps invent, the meaning of human life" (69).

Even as my wife and I pondered such issues, which for us were, and are, the stuff of daily thinking and work, we also had to laugh at ourselves. Here we were treating an innocent looking collection of children's stories as if it were a vial of poison. On the other hand, the book was telling us that "little girls are sugar and spice and everything nice!" *Please!* Our homey little Christmas eve with sweet Christmas lights and honey smooth carols was being fretted by ethical and political conundrums definitely *not* in harmony with the strains of "peace on earth, good will toward men" wafting serenely from our stereo. We veered back and forth between commending ourselves as thoughtful parents and laughing at ourselves as goofy intellectuals.[1]

Perhaps, we said to ourselves, we're like those doctor parents who, because they know too much about germs, infection, and death rates, worry themselves into a case of the hives every time their children get the flu. On the other hand, it didn't work to dismiss the whole issue as the heated product of our oh-so-literary imaginations and overeducated minds. Our expertise in analyzing textual nuances convinced us that these stories conveyed highly persuasive lessons in social stereotypes, all reinforced by such aesthetic strategies as engaging rhymes, coherent little plots, vivid characters, colorful illustrations, and accessible language. To attempt to deny what we knew about stories' educational power put us in the position of a professional tire changer trying to deny that he knows a lug nut when he sees one.

Nonetheless, even in such a private, domestic context, and even in the case of our own three-year-old daughter, it still made my wife and me uneasy to contemplate direct control over other people's art. We were adept at taking our students through all the arguments traditionally mustered against institutionalized censorship. On the other hand still again, our daughter was not the general public, we were not a government agency, and our actions as parents would not decide public policy for others. We were just trying to be good parents, and no matter how silly we felt, we were still stuck with the question of what to do with the objectionable stories in this collection. As the narrator says in Robert Browning's "Porphyria's Lover," we "found a thing to do" (74). Browning's mad narrator strangles his mistress. My wife and I brought out the razor blades instead. We found that by pushing the two halves of the fat anthology down flat at the opening of the stories we objected to, we could neatly cut them out of the book one page at a time.

Like my students, some of you may be tempted to gasp *"censorship"* in italics, but censorship consists of institutionalized, legalized forms of control over the books, movies, and TV programs that citizens are allowed to peruse or that publishers are allowed to sell. Censorship is not parents holding standards about what kinds of influence are appropriate (or inappropriate) for their children's development. What parent has not felt this responsibility? All of us are shocked when we see parents *failing* at it. "Did you know that Mark took his four-year-old son with him when he went to see *Nightmare on Elm Street*? What was he thinking?" In the West for at least the last 150 years, society has generally become more and more confused about where to find the criteria—or even the analytical vocabulary—for discussing such issues. At the same time that some people argue that the First Amendment protects all words and most images, other people try to rip *Huckleberry Finn* and *Catcher in the Rye* from school library shelves. Still other parents worry about the effects of "Aunt Jemima" images in their children's picture books.

One thing my Christmas eve story suggests is that being opposed to censorship—or supporting it, for that matter—does nothing to answer the question of how all of us, not just children, are influenced by the words and images of the fictions we encounter. That censorship issues are always a flash point for passion bears witness to people's intuitions that fictions possess the power not just to entertain and divert but to influence. If the ethical influence of stories was really the nonissue that many people, including most of my students, wish to claim that it is, why would censorship ever arise as a controversial topic? If just being opposed to censorship, or just being for it, settled the issue, we could all take sides and agree to disagree. But people of good will, good conscience, and good arguments don't just disagree about censorship. They disagree in hundreds of different ways about not only what the ethical influence of stories might be, but even how to *talk about* ethical influence. In the remainder of this chapter I will clarify at least one of the major issues that bedevil ethical discourse by analyzing the nature and content of narrative assent.

What Happens When We Give Assent?

When we assent to a story's demands—when we feel as it asks us to feel, when we believe as it asks us to believe, and when we judge as it asks us to judge—what happens to us is that we take another step in becoming the persons that we turn out to be. This claim receives an especially clear restatement by the philosopher Richard Eldridge in *On Moral Personhood*.

> It is in and through narrative itself that we lead our lives as persons. . . . Persons are not, it seems, "just" real material entities. . . . They lead lives out of ongoing narratives, make choices out of them. These narratives and the lives and choices that they shape are in turn structured by assumptions about narrative unity, coherence, and closure that are tested in narrative writing in general, and in particular in fiction, where the influence of contingencies can yield to the imperative to achieve coherence. . . . It seems that literary narratives and personhood are, one might say, internal to one another. (11–12)
>
> We can attain moral consciousness only as we see our personhood and its demands reflected to us in the lives of others that are recounted to us in narrative art, while our collective responses themselves determine narrative art's relevant and proper exemplars. (60)

Leroy Searle employs particularly felicitous phrasing when he asserts that "*the imaginative text . . . is the essential experiment upon ourselves,* to see, through reading intently and exactly, what practices, what stances relative to the world, what attitudes and values actually can and do command our assent—and above all, with what concrete practical effect" (1255; emphasis added).

I do not have a formula for telling anyone which stories she or he should assent to and which to dissent from. Even if I did, what would be the point? For the most part, people do not shape their responses to stories because of what critics say, but based on the stories themselves. Or do they? In our society the usual way of talking about consuming anything, including stories, emphasizes the mastery of the consumer. The consumer, we say, is king. Right? Maybe not. The language of the market ceaselessly flatters the autonomy of consumers—"freedom of choice" is repeated ad nauseum—but, for the most part, marketers, not customers, do the ruling. The language of consumer autonomy is just market spin. Consumers do indeed have many choices, but these are not choices that they have selected. They are choices that marketers limit consumers to, and besides, marketers know how to stimulate, motivate, and herd consumers into directions desired by the manufacturers, corporations, and businesses that hire them. Surely, making choices that marketers have selected for us in advance is not making choices.

What does this have to do with stories? Much. Just as people need to become sufficiently sophisticated to understand their bogus sovereignty as consumers when they buy cars and toasters, they also need to become more sophisticated in the way they understand their diminished sovereignty as consumers who go to movies, watch TV, and read novels. At a superficial level of analysis it is clear that TVs and books do not turn themselves on or open themselves up at their own volition. Nobody marches patrons into movie or stage theaters at gunpoint. But to infer from this absence of crude coercion that the consumer is king is certainly not the whole story about story any more than it is the whole story about shopping. It is *especially* not the whole story about story because the most common motive that takes us to story in the first place has nothing to do with the desire for mastery. *Our impulse for stories is, in fact, the desire to give up mastery and to let the story direct and shape our attention, feelings, judgments, and ideas*, at least for the time that we and the story are inter-acting. For the most part we go to story because we *desire* to assent.

The yielding that we give to stories may look like giving ourselves away, or voluntarily diminishing ourselves, but the truth is that such yielding bolsters our sense of self by giving us the data for seeing our real selves in relation to other selves. This data is crucial to our ability to create an authentic self. In the words of Kenneth Asher, whose comments about literature apply to stories in general, "Most of us see our lives—to use E. M. Forster's distinction—as a plot rather than a sequence of happen-ings. We try to make our past—even our past mistakes—a coherent part of the complete narrative of our lives. When we familiarize ourselves with the literary tradition we enter a storehouse of alternative selves. These narratives help us to shape the selves that we would become" (4). We traf-fic in stories, in other words, in order to be lifted up and out of our or-dinary selves. Sometimes after the escape from ordinary life afforded by stories, we get better traction on everyday life when we return to it, the way traveling abroad can give us a fresher look at everyday life when we return home. C. S. Lewis is positively eloquent in his description of the psychology of assent. Like Asher, he is speaking of literary experience, but what he says is generally true of our responses to stories in any medium.

> You *submit* to the text, *you relinquish yourself,* because you need to be transported. You know with complete certitude that, when you are yourself, you are only, at best, half alive [emphasis added]. . . . When it's the real thing, literature enlarges us; strips the film of familiarity from the world; creates bonds of sympathy with all kinds, even with evil characters, who we learn are all in the family. . . . I confess to never having been able to get enough of the real thing. . . . All the great, veil-piercing books . . . [are] great *because* veil-piercing. Books propel me out of the narrow life that I lead in my own little world, offering me revelations of strangers, who turn out not to be totally strange; a variety of real worlds, unveiled for me, for the first time. . . . It's the literary experience of liberation. (63)

"Like an importunate lover," says Alan Shapiro, "*poetry solicits our assent;* it invites . . . a willing submission to its own belief that this rather than that is better, worthier, more interesting. It woos our pliable attention to the things it trusts, and draws it away from the things it doesn't. Each poem pleads, whatever else its words are saying, Come be with me and be my love" (88; emphasis added). Sven Birkerts calls such yielding "the time of the self" or "deep time": those moments of our lives when the power of story liberates us from the anxieties and constraints of daily living and introduces us to the generous education of living other people's lives. He writes, "The time of the self is deep time, duration time, time that is essentially characterized by our obliviousness to it. To the degree that we immerse ourselves in a book, listen to music, sink into the visual realm of a painting—to that degree we surrender our awareness of the present as a coordinate on a grid. We relinquish the governing construct of the now, exchanging it for content, feeling, and absorption" (193).

Can Narrative Assent Be Dangerous? Why?

But what do we do with the claims made by some people that certain stories are bad for us? We can all think of stories that issue invitations, for example, to feel contempt for women and minorities (think of all the racist and sexist movies from *Birth of a Nation* to *Pretty Woman*), as well as invitations that lead us to feel gratuitous lust, invitations that incite a hunger for violence, invitations to rationalize self-indulgence, and so on.

On the other hand, none of us is going to deprive ourselves of affiliations either in life or in stories *because* of such danger. Life offers many dangerous invitations—falling in love, running for office, finding friends, sometimes just breathing the air and drinking the water—but if we try to protect ourselves from life's dangers by withdrawing from life, we give up more than we gain. We may reject narrative affiliations just as we sometimes reject real-life affiliations, and for the same reasons—because of someone's bad character, because of someone's inane shallowness, or just because we can't stand the way somebody talks—but both in life and in stories we generally begin by giving people the benefit of the doubt because the danger of being misled or mistreated is not as harmful or scary to us as the deprivations of loneliness. No matter how disappointing the results of assent may turn out to be, there is no adventure or growth without it. No one has to become a credulous nincompoop in order to grow, but cast-iron *dissent* stultifies growth altogether.

Dissent is of course important and sometimes leads to critically important or even to heroically important acts of social, political, and ethical resistance. My claim is not that dissent is valueless, but that learning requires the risks of assent before we can even know what positions require dissent. In the words of Wayne Booth, who is the only contemporary critic to invest any prolonged analysis of this issue, "we discover the powers of narrative only in an act of surrender. . . . To *begin* with doubt, as we are told that scientists do, employing some criterion of 'falsifiability,' some test in which suspicion is primary, is simply to destroy the datum" (*Company*, 32). Or as Booth put it many years earlier in *Modern Dogma and the Rhetoric of Assent*, where he is speaking about the grounds of belief in general, not just belief in narratives, "there is a sense in which assent and affirmation are more fundamental than negation, in both logic and experience. . . . From birth our primary movement is toward the world, to grasp it, assenting to and taking in other selves, new truths, the whole world. . . . Each of us makes himself or herself by assenting to and incorporating whoever and whatever represents life at its most immediate and persuasive. *Our negatives are learned as we discover violations of our affirmings*" (194; emphasis added). Our fundamental assent to stories' requirements about what we should pay attention to lies so close to the heart of my topic, story's potential power for ethical influence, that it deserves a more detailed analysis.

Does Assent to Stories Have a Content of Its Own?

Because "assent" is not a technical term, it is tempting to assume that we all share some transparent notion of its meaning, but, as a matter of fact, this is unlikely. So far, I have argued that assent is a kind of yielding, but what exactly does this mean? What does one *do* when one yields? Is it as simple as it sounds? If assent is just mindlessly going blank, then maybe it's not something anyone should recommend. If assent is the complete squashing of all critical intelligence, then perhaps again it's not such a good thing. We can begin to sort the nuanced meanings of assent, however, if we cease thinking of it as an emotional disposition or an intellectual stance and begin thinking of it as a kind of *practice*, a kind of specific *behavior*. Allow me to suggest, then, that assent is a *practice* and is comprised of at least four moves.

Willing Suspension of Disbelief

The first move is to take the attitude that Coleridge identifies in *Biographia Literaria* as a "willing suspension of disbelief for the moment, which constitutes poetic faith" (326). This is an agreement on the auditor's part not to reject the data of any story out of hand and not to start out truculent or combative.[2] To initiate the narrative transaction by temporarily placing one's own beliefs in neutral is not to completely squash them. In yielding to a story, the reader or viewer softens the membrane of ego in order to respond *not* as we might respond in real life, but as the *story* seems to require. Nuala O'Faolain's wonderful phrase "becoming surefooted on the high-wire of the author's intention" (27) calls attention to this nonegotistical collaboration with story. Assent takes the story's data as the *given* of the narrative experience and forestalls the possibility of deep criticism or rejection until we see what the story contains and what possible value it holds. Most of us reserve the right to reject a story later if we feel we must, but only narrow-minded readers choose to cheat themselves out of a story's possible value before they've even had a chance to experience it.

Vicarious Experimentation

One huge advantage offered by narrative experience over real-life experience as a guide for navigating everyday living is that narrative modes of living are *vicarious*. Testing things out in the mind's eye—reviewing the world we do *not* want to live in as well as the world we *do* want to live in—offers immense savings in real-life energy and allows us to avoid paying the real-life cost of bad choices. Mark Johnson, a philosopher of moral theory, develops this point in his book on the implications of cognitive science for ethics.

(1) Narrative supplies and reveals the themes by which we seek to unify the temporal, historical dimension of our existence, and with-

out which our lives would be a meaningless jumble of disconnected events. (2) Narrative can illuminate purposes, plans, and goals, which are the forms by which our lives have some direction, motivation, and significance for us. There is no other cognitive-experiential structure that blends these two basic dimensions of human existence. . . . Only narrative encompasses both the temporality and the purposive organization at the general level at which we pursue overarching unity and meaning for our lives." (*Moral Imagination*, 170–71)

Receptivity to Narrative Energy

The third move involved in assent includes a receptivity for what Northrop Frye has aptly identified as "the transfer of imaginative energy from [story] to the [auditor]" (129). Without our willingness to become a medium for the energy of powerful stories, their final transport into the world never gets completed. The story never lands. Assent is Ingredient X, the secret or at least mysterious compound that has to be added to a narrative before *any* of its potentialities can be liberated. In the words of Paula Fox, "imagination is a bridge between the provincialism of the self and the great world" (553) .

Taking Pleasure in Narratives

The fourth move involved in assent includes a willingness to take *pleasure* in the representations that literary art places before us. Even resistant responses to story must be based on the pleasure of recognizing false views and taking pleasure in possessing superior views. "We have no sympathy but what is propagated by pleasure," says Wordsworth, "no knowledge, that is, no general principles drawn from the contemplation of particular facts, but what has been built up by pleasure. . . . Knowledge is pleasure; and where [a man] has no pleasure he has no knowledge" (Preface, 292). Most of us generally have no problem assenting to pleasure, of course—we don't need Wordsworth to teach us that we like being pleased—but there has long been a persistent thread of thought in Western culture that has always been suspicious of pleasure in itself, and especially suspicious of the pleasure that people take in stories.

Plato was the first voice in the West to articulate such suspicion, but he was certainly not the last. Monastic orders in the Middle Ages were designed to remove monks from the temptations of pleasure, and Puritans in the seventeenth century closed the English theaters because they were suspicious of "worldly" pleasures. Modern literary critics like Roland Barthes, Michel Foucault, and Judith Fetterley have asserted that taking pleasure in stories makes us naively and dangerously vulnerable to colonization by corrupt political values. All three critics I just mentioned represent the views of many others as well, all of whom see the pleasure offered by story as a device of political entrapment, like the angler fish's "bait" that it projects from its snout as a way of luring smaller fish into its maw. This view raises a question about the status of pleasure itself in human experience, an issue to which I now turn.

Is Pleasure a Primary or Secondary State of Being?

At first glance it might seem that pleasure is an elemental thing-in-itself, but a second glance suggests that all pleasure ultimately depends on something else. Even the pleasures of the body that might seem to require nothing but *having* a body—the pleasures, for example, of sweetness, softness, rest, sex, and so on—*don't* depend on *merely* having a body, but on having a body that is in good working order, that is in decent health, and that is in harmony with our minds. Sex, for example, is not pleasure of an undifferentiated or absolute kind. Sex is *not* pleasure, for example, in cases of rape and prostitution or when performed by bodies that are sick and minds that are distracted or sorrowful.

So what is the most elemental pleasure offered by stories? It is mostly the deep pleasure of learning. In the words of Nobel laureate Joseph Brodsky, "we read not for reading's sake but to *learn*. Hence the need for . . . works that bring the human predicament, in all its diversity, into its sharpest possible focus" (97; emphasis added). Learning about the human predicament in all of its diversity is a pleasure, as *all* real learning is pleasure. Socrates claimed in the *Philebus* that thought leading to wisdom is more valuable than pleasure and has no roots in anything outside itself, but we all know that thought and pleasure are sometimes genuinely mingled. As philosopher Karen Hanson says, "Plato would do better to remember . . . that the pleasures of learning may depend on some antecedent pain—the disturbing awareness of one's own ignorance" ("Pleasures of Thought," 5). Alleviating ignorance is among the greatest pleasures that motivate human beings to keep intimate company with narrative art.

Assent to Print Stories versus Assent to Media Stories

My argument in favor of assent not only is about stories that come to us by means of media—print, movies, TV, audio recordings, songs, and so on—but extends to stories whose only technologies are the voice and ear. Narratives and poems in an oral culture impose the same request for assent upon listeners that printed narratives and poems impose upon readers in literate cultures. In fact, the appeal for assent demanded by oral stories is the *same* insistent demand for assent claimed of us by media stories. Stories delivered orally or on television and in movies demand *immediate* assent. Only print stories give us the luxury of *reflective* assent that allows us to take our eyes from the page, think about what we have just read, and then resume reading on our own schedule. Only print stories allow readers to go back and reread, to look up a word in the dictionary, or take a break and come back to the story later, and so on. (Even though the emerging practice of watching movies and TV programs on DVDs does offer a flexibility for pausing and reflecting not available to us when watching TV the "old fashioned" way and still not available to us when watching movies in the theater, it seems obvious that people's habits of TV watching do not include taking advantage of this opportunity for *reflective* assent, although research on this issue is lacking.) An orally delivered story allows no time for quibbling, pondering, or otherwise negotiating with it. (For more on the differences among print stories, media stories, and oral stories, see Neil Postman and Eric Havelock.)

Activating the Imagination: Narrative's Concrete Particulars

Once assent to a story has been given, the potential force it possesses for inviting ethical change in the consumer rests on the workings of the vicarious imagination. I have now made several references to the vicarious imagination, but what exactly *is* it? Let me begin to answer by turning to the testimony of the Russian writer Aleksey Peshkov, who wrote under the pen name of Maxim Gorky (1868–1936). While working as a young man in conditions that were physically and morally degrading, Gorky discovered that imaginative assent to stories provided him not with mere escape—and certainly not escap*ism*—but with a better and more fulfilling mode of existence. What we shall be interested in analyzing is how stories helped him accomplish this benefit. The passage is brilliantly evocative and worth quoting at length.

> There was much in my environment that was wicked and savage, and gave birth to a feeling of acute loathing. . . . It was in such accursed conditions that I first began to read. . . .
>
> The more I read, the closer books bound me to the world and the more vivid and significant life became for me. I saw that there were people whose life was worse and harder than mine. Though I derived some comfort from this, I did not grow reconciled to the outrageous facts of the life about me. I saw too that there were such who were able to live a life of interest and happiness in a way none about me knew how to. From the pages of almost every book sounded a subdued but insistent message that perturbed me, called me into the unknown, and plucked at my heart. All men were suffering in one way or another; all were dissatisfied with life and sought something that was better, and this made them closer and more understandable to me. Books enshrouded the whole world in a mournful aspiration towards better things, and each one of them seemed a soul tacked down to paper by characters and words which came to life the moment my eyes and my mind came into contact with them.
>
> I often wept as I read—so moving were the stories about people, so dear and close did they become to me. Lad as I was, pestered with senseless toil and berated with senseless vituperation, I promised myself in the most solemn of terms that I would help people and render them honest service when I grew up.
>
> Like some wondrous birds out of fairy tales, books sang their songs to me and spoke to me as though communing with one languishing in

prison; they sang of the variety and richness of life, of man's audacity in his strivings towards goodness and beauty. The more I read, the more a wholesome and kindly spirit filled my heart, and I grew calmer, my self-confidence developed, my work improved, and I paid ever less heed to the innumerable spurns life was dealing me.

Each book was a rung in my ascent from the brutish to the human, towards an understanding of a better life and a thirst after that life. (11, 16–17)

Because Gorky's testimony about narrative itself takes the form of narrative, it both encapsulates and exemplifies the chief elements of my argument about the connection between assent and ethical influence.

Story Is Concrete, Not Abstract

Stories deal not in abstractions but in details that have the capacity to hit the gut and the head all at once. We experience the concrete details of a story one by one and in a deliberate and aesthetically controlled sequence. ("Each one of them seemed a soul tacked down to paper by characters and words which came to life the moment my eyes and my mind came into contact with them.") "Man has been given the tool of art," says Viktor Shklovsky, the Russian formalist, "in order to return sensation to our limbs, in order to make us feel objects, *to make a stone feel stony*" (6; emphasis added). Elder Olson, in trying to define the nature of "a work of art," emphasizes that a work of art can only be experienced as a particular unique object, not as a set of universals or propositions or precepts.

A work of art is a particular, and a special kind of particular. It cannot be known through a universal. . . . I cannot know any particulars about *Hamlet* because I know about tragedy. Euripides' *Tyro* is a lost work; it was a tragedy; what do you know of it? Further, the work of art is a particular that cannot be known through the account of someone else. . . . I may learn accidental bits and pieces from accounts; the form I must experience directly, through the workings of my own mind upon the data of my own sensations. A work of art is not merely a particular; it is a unique particular. It has its qualities to be, not an individual representing a class, but what it is uniquely. (*On Value Judgments*, 311)

No work of narrative, no story in any medium, can make the stone feel stony without vivid particularity, without concreteness.

Story Triggers the Vicarious Imagination

It is story's concreteness that activates the vicarious imagination, our ability to experience the thoughts, actions, and emotions of others as if they were our own. ("I often wept as I read—so moving were the stories about people, so dear and close did they become to me.") This kind of vicarious experience appeals to us because such experience helps satisfy our desire for learning, companionship, and intimacy. We remain hungry to learn about others' lives because such learning helps us understand our own. ("I saw that there were people . . . who were able to live a life of interest and happiness in a way none about me knew how to.") We desire companionship and intimacy because, as Aristotle said long ago and as many social scientists have repeated many times since, human beings are social animals. ("Like some wondrous birds out of fairy tales, books sang their songs to me and spoke to me as though communing with one languishing in prison.")

Vicarious Experiences Create the Potential for "Ethotic" Effects

In addressing our desires for intimacy and companionship, the vicarious experiences of story allow us to stock our memories with snapshots or, perhaps more accurately, mental movies of many of life's typical situations. Stories offer us at least the knowledge of recognition, and to recognize things for what they are is not a mean or superficial form of learning. Such learning also enables us to see ourselves and our own circumstances more clearly. ("From the pages of almost every book sounded a subdued but insistent message that perturbed me, called me into the unknown and plucked at my heart. All men were suffering in one way or another; all were dissatisfied with life and sought something that was better, and this made them closer and more understandable to me.") Second, these vicarious experiences influence the formation of selves. The wider and more varied our experience with narrative is, the larger repertory we acquire of imaginative scenarios for how we might live and who we might be. ("The more I read, the more a wholesome and kindly spirit filled my heart, and I grew calmer, my self-confidence developed, my work improved, and I paid ever less heed to the innumerable spurns life was dealing me.")

In other words, narratives constitute not only a concrete *record* of fictional characters' lives but a concrete *experience* in the lives of readers. In his essay "Of Diversion" Montaigne captures the difference between mental abstractions and gutsy concreteness: "I look upon death carelessly when I look upon it universally [that is, abstractly], as the end of life. I insult over it in gross, but in detail it domineers over me: the tears of a footman, the disposing of my clothes, the touch of a friendly hand, a common consolation, discourages and softens me" (67). Cynthia Ozick takes Olson's and Montaigne's point about particularity and elaborates its consequences for consumers of story with great insight. Her brilliant analysis is about literature but applies equally well to story in general.

> In [the] steady interpretive light [of story] we can make distinctions; we can see that one thing is not interchangeable with another thing; that not everything is the same; that the Holocaust is different, God knows, from a corncob. So we arrive, at last, at the pulse and purpose of literature: to reject the blur of the "universal"; to distinguish one life from another, to illumine diversity; to light up the least grain of being, to show how it is concretely individual, particularized from any other, to tell, in all the marvel of its singularity, the separate holiness of the least grain. *Literature is the recognition of the particular.* (248; emphasis in the original)

The imagination cannot feed on abstractions and generalizations. It needs images, textures, sensations, smells, sounds, tastes: the look and feel of particular things in particular contexts.

Narrative's Particulars versus Organized Lists

So why do not *all* concretely rendered arrangements of events move us the way stories move us? Laundry lists, bills of sale, menus, telephone books, and college schedules all give us solid, concrete details. They also have a kind of thematic unity to them, so why do they never strike us as narrative art or as literature? Because these arrangements of particulars, while they may inform us, do not *move* us; because even though they all contain verbal representations of one concrete detail after another, *like* stories, these details are not arranged *as* stories: "4 long-sleeved white shirts, no starch"; "250 gross of number two, cedar-cased, eraser-tipped, yellow Ticonderoga lead pencils"; "EN 382 Studies in Major Authors: Jane Austen. MWF 10:00–10:50. Jordan Hall 342. M. Gregory. Open to juniors and seniors only." These items include concrete, particularized information, but nothing that moves us ethically or emotionally. There is no human interaction, no drama, no conflict, no character. The concrete details of stories are not moving just because they are concrete, but because they concretely *represent the dynamics of human life*, and it is always *life* that interests us. It is learning to see life's patterns that moves us and, in moving us, educates us and, in educating us, shapes us.

CHAPTER SIX

 formatting-ornament

Story as Companionship

Companions of the Mind, Companions of the Flesh

So—you have given your assent to the story. You're hooked. You're not going to walk out on the movie or the play, you've taken your finger off the remote control, you've marked your place in the novel for tonight's pillow-propped reading, and you're going to accompany this story to the end. I have already suggested two things that this assent will get for you: pleasure and education. But just as we saw in the previous chapter that "assent" can be a vague term until it is unpacked, so the term "pleasure" can also be vague until unpacked. Depending on our motives and aims, we can take pleasure in eating or not eating, pleasure in being with others or being alone. It will help us understand the potential influence of stories if we become more precise about the highly varied kinds of pleasure that people find in story.

One primary pleasure that stories give us is enduring and significant companionships. As creatures social to the core, all human beings know that the quality of human life is largely synonymous with the quality of our companionships. We all require companions as part of a complete life, but one of the most important and easily overlooked features of companionship is the extent to which we enjoy our companionships not just in the flesh but in the mind. We enjoy our real-life companions when we think about them in our imagination, in our memories, and in our mind's eye, not just when we are with them physically. Firsthand separation in the flesh—depending on how absolute it is and how long it lasts—undoubtedly puts a strain on companionship, but everyone knows about human beings' ability to remain profoundly bonded to companions that they see only infrequently. There are doubtless epistolary friends (all prior to 1990, no doubt) or email friends or chat-room friends who have never met in the flesh at all.

The commonness of mind's-eye companionship may blind us to its importance both as a cognitive feature of human brains and as a highly significant dimension of sociability. As an important feature of our psychic life, mind's-eye friendship helps explain not only the richness of human experience but also the significance of narrative companionships. *Having real-life companions whom we do not always see in the flesh is not very different from having narrative companions whom we also do not see in the flesh.* Making companionship work among those who cannot see each other is easy for human beings, and it follows that real-life companionships conducted mainly in the mind's eye can be an immense influence on us. How many choices in life have you pondered in light of the question "What would my father do in this case (or my spouse or my mentor or my best friend)?" Few people seem to think about the way narrative companionships can play the same monitoring role in our lives as real-life friends whose "presence" may only be a mind's eye presence rather than a physical presence.

My wife, for example, is a persistent companion of my life even when we are separated. So is Elizabeth Bennett, but just because Elizabeth Bennett is *always* separated from me in the flesh and my wife is only sometimes separated from me in the flesh does not prevent Elizabeth from also being a persistent companion. How would you know where to draw the line between "real life" and "imagined life" anyway? If I am imagining, is not the act of imagining a real event in my real life? I am not imagining doing my imagining. And if I tell you *what* I am imagining—especially if I tell you about it in the form of a compelling story—do not my imagined scenarios become real events in your life as well, insofar as whatever you imagine is as much a real part of your life as what you feel with your senses? There is less of a gulf between real experiences and imagined experiences than we think.

We *use* narrative companions in many of the same ways and for many of the same reasons that we use companions in the flesh: for company, for imagined conversations, for sources of ideas, for models of conduct, and so on. We also use them to corroborate our own desires and impulses and values, to show us ways of acting and feeling, and to correct us when we misjudge or go wrong. For example, whenever I am tempted in academic meetings to tell off obnoxious colleagues, I am always reproved by the mental image of Atticus Finch's magisterial courtesy even to his enemies in *To Kill a Mockingbird*. Through the many stages of writing and rewriting that have produced this book, I have enjoyed the persistent presence of Wayne Booth, my decades long mentor, coauthor, and friend as a sometimes physical critic and counselor, but more often as a mind's eye critic and counselor, and his presence whether we were both in his study in Chicago drinking tea and joking or whether he was only a voice in my head in Indianapolis has helped me write this book more successfully than I would ever have been able to write it without him (see Booth and Gregory, "The Unbroken Continuum"). In everyday life, such comments to ourselves as "I should put money in that Salvation Army Christmas can; it's not the season to be a Scrooge" also show us making use of mind's eye fictional companions as monitors of our real-life conduct.

Affiliation versus Individualism

Ever since the European Romantic movement in the early nineteenth century, Western society has been developing (and deepening) a vast flotilla of views about the importance of individualism. But after every single advantage of individual self-development, individual self-expression, individual self-actualization, and so on has been toted, touted, and calculated right down to the last decimal place, the larger and more important truth about life is that no fulfilled or satisfied version of it can be achieved on the basis of solitary individuality. It is paradoxical but true that individualism only counts for us if we can use it *socially*, in our interactions with others.

Our society's contemporary emphasis on the importance of the private, solitary individual, an emphasis strongly influenced by market ideology about the individual consumer, leads many people to believe that self-fulfillment as a kind of one-person achievement is life's primary goal.[1] The myth of the isolated, self-sufficient hero has been with us in Anglo-American society at least since Byron wrote *Manfred* in 1817, and we keep revisiting the *Manfred* archetype in thousands of novels, movies, TV programs, and songs that tell us over and over the bogus narrative of the isolated hero who achieves a higher plane of existence *because* of his isolation. But no matter how many times this story gets retold, the truth remains that solitary self-fulfillment is not possible. Doing things "my way" (the title of a vastly popular song in the 1960s recorded by Frank Sinatra) can be cripplingly lonely to creatures whose evolutionary history has programmed them to be irreversibly social.

The primary goal of life is not personal fulfillment but interpersonal fulfillment, not solitary fixation but social affiliation. "Affiliation" comes from the Latin word *affiliare,* meaning "to adopt as a son," and affiliating with others thus suggests joining with them not casually or from mere self-interest, but with a kind of mutual regard, the strongest model of which is family relations. James Q. Wilson has surveyed moral codes examined in anthropological studies conducted in a wide array of different cultures and makes a general point derived from these studies suggesting how our social selves are linked to our ethical selves:

> Man is by nature a social animal. Our moral nature grows directly out of our social nature. We express sympathy for the plight of others both because we value their company (and so wish to convince them of our companionable qualities) and because we can feel the pain of others even when not in their company. (121)
>
> This innate sensitivity to the feelings of others . . . is so powerful that it makes us grasp not only the feelings of friends and family members but also those of some strangers, many fictional characters, and even animals. . . . Scarcely a waking hour passes when we do not wonder how we appear in the eyes of others. . . . Our sociability generates our moral sense. (140)

Social existence is the default mode of existence for all human beings. In the words of Wayne Booth, "I am not bounded by my skin. . . . I am a kind of focal point in a field of forces . . . and hence essentially *affiliated*. . . . To be *joined,* in other words, is my primary, natural condition" (*Company,* 230–40). The loneliness we feel in the absence of others is not just an annoyance or a discomfort. If it goes on long enough, it depresses us and can sometimes make us psychotic or suicidal. Even in prisons, where, it seems safe to assume, the inmates could be collectively described as among the least charming companions on the planet, still the worst punishment for anyone is to be placed in "the hole"—solitary confinement. One deep intuition tells us that our need for companions is nonnegotiable. A second deep intuition tells us that narrated companionships can be deeply satisfying and rich in their own right, not as a poor substitute for real-life companionships but as highly significant adjuncts and supplements.

Two Examples of Affiliation as Self-Completion: Sanders and Dickens

Scott Russell Sanders

Affiliation is not the same thing as aggregation. We aggregate with people on hurried streets and in busy hallways, but affiliation is more like a product of what Northrop Frye calls "moods of identification." In *The Educated Imagination*, Frye asks his readers to imagine that they have been stranded on a desert island. Much of the time in such circumstances, Frye says, most of us would find ourselves disassociated from our locale, which would strike us much more as an environment than as a home. However, he says, from time to time "in this Robinson Crusoe life I've assigned you, you may have *moods of complete peacefulness and joy, moods when you accept your island and everything around you.* You wouldn't have such moods very often, and when you had them, they'd be *moods of identification, when you felt that the island was a part of you and you a part of it*" (18; emphasis added).

There are many fictional accounts of such moods of identification not just with nature, as in the Frye quote, but with other people. These would be times when we feel other people to be a part of us and we a part of them. This is often the language of lovers, as in "you complete me" or

"I feel like only half a person when you are gone." To feel this connection is affiliation of the richest kind, and insofar as we wish to live the richest kind of life, we cannot do without it. There are many people who *do* do without it, of course, but only at the loss of a richness usually imposed by circumstances, not sought by choice. And firsthand experience never offers us enough of it. All of us supplement life's parsimonious distribution of the best companionships by turning to the supplementary companionships in stories. One of America's best essay writers, Scott Russell Sanders, tells a story of companionship that illustrates its happy fulfillment among affiliated, not just aggregated, individuals. His story also illustrates Frye's notion of "moods of identification":

> One delicious afternoon while my daughter Eva was home from college for spring vacation, she invited two neighbor girls to help her make bread. The girls are sisters, five-year-old Alexandra and ten-year-old Rachel, both frolicky, with eager dark eyes and shining faces. They live just down the street from us . . . and whenever they see me pass by . . . they ask about Eva, whom they adore.
>
> I was in the yard that afternoon mulching flower beds . . . but how could I stay outside, when so much beauty and laughter and spunk were gathered in the kitchen?
>
> I kept looking in on the cooks, until Eva finally asked, "Daddy, you wouldn't like to knead some dough, would you?"
>
> "I'd love to," I said. "You sure there's room for me?" . . .
>
> Eva and the girls and I jostled like birds too numerous for a nest. We spattered flour everywhere. We told stories. We joked. All the while I bobbed on a current of bliss, delighting in the feel of live dough beneath my fingers, the smell of yeast, the piping of child-voices so much like the birdsong cascading through our open window, the prospect of whole-wheat loaves hot from the oven. . . . *[These are the] times when I have felt a deep and complex joy, a sense of being exactly where I should be and doing exactly what I should do. . . .*
>
> It is as though I spend my days wandering about, chasing false scents, lost, and then occasionally, for a few ticks of the heart, I stumble onto the path. While making bread with my daughter and her two young friends, I was on the path. So I recall that time now as a way of

keeping company with Eva, who has gone back to college, but also as a way of discovering in our common life a reservoir of power and hope. (65–67; emphasis added)

Such a moment provides not just a *sense* of possessing an enlarged and more complete existence. It is the very thing itself. At this level of affiliation, common life and individual life reinforce each other in an elemental, recursive loop. Stories often provide our best education for learning what these occasions look and feel like.

Charles Dickens

Quite differently from Sanders, Charles Dickens also provides a portrait of true human companionship, and his portrait makes clear that what Sanders felicitously calls "common life [as] a reservoir of power and hope" is not limited to persons of cultivated sensibilities like Sanders and his family, but really is *common,* available not just to those who are educated and "sensitive" but to us all simply because we are human. In his account of the Cratchit family's Christmas feast to which Scrooge is taken by the Ghost of Christmas Present, Dickens captures with vividness and poignancy the exuberant participation of all the Cratchits in the family celebration. The scene of Christmas dinner represents a brilliant vision of how connectedness can mask or at least diminish the sting of every other deprivation. The plum pudding emerges from the wash house.

> Oh, a wonderful pudding! Bob Cratchit said, and calmly too, that he regarded it as the greatest success achieved by Mrs. Cratchit since their marriage. Mrs. Cratchit said that now the weight was off her mind, she would confess she had had her doubts about the quantity of flour. *Everybody had something to say about it,* but nobody said or thought it was at all a small pudding for a large family. It would have been flat heresy to do so. . . .
> There was nothing of high mark in this. They were not a handsome family; they were not well dressed; their shoes were far from being water-proof; their clothes were scanty; and Pewter might have known, and very likely did, the inside of a pawn-broker's. *But they*

were happy, grateful, pleased with one another, and contented with the time. ("Christmas Carol," 46, 49; emphasis added)

What riches of companionship Dickens gives these poor Cratchits. How often do any of us feel in *any* company that we are "happy, grateful, pleased with one another, and contented with the time"? Most of us might think ourselves fortunate to possess even one of these graces, especially if we could possess it with any consistency. There could hardly be a more striking contrast to the prison house of the isolated, subjective ego than the spectacle of the Cratchits' family feast, a communion in which each family member has something to say and simultaneously feels his own importance to the group, feels the importance of every other member of the family, and feels bonded to the group and the occasion. What more could affiliation do for us?

Full Knowledge of Fictional Characters versus
Partial Knowledge of Real-Life Companions

The potential influence of narrative companions is generated in large part by their aura of concrete reality. Here is something close to a paradox. Why is it that a coworker whom I see every day in three-dimensional, fleshly reality will sometimes remain more of an abstraction or a mystery to me than characters from stories who exist only in my imagination?

The explanation seems to be that in real life we only see people from the outside if that is all they choose to reveal. Life forces us mostly to *infer* what people's interior states might be—their motives, their feelings, their self-talk, and so on—and, moreover, our inferences are not always right. My inability to see the interior of real people's lives, combined with people's general reluctance to expose that interior, often forces me to see only a type or a stereotype or a cliché when I would like to see the distinctiveness of the individual. I would like in many instances to be the companion of other people's hearts—all of us would at least like to feel that we know better the people whom we see frequently—but convention, self-protection, decorum, propriety, and routine (routine, perhaps, most of all) keep us separated. The inferences I am forced to make about others can actually work as a kind of screen between me and them, and that screen can even diminish my sense of their concrete reality.

In the case of most narrated characters, however, I have a rich sense of their complete depths. I see them all the way down and all the way through. The data about them is complete, and it is all contained within the story. This doesn't mean that all fictional characters' lives are simple. Commentary about Hamlet and Captain Ahab will apparently go on forever, but everyone doing such commentary knows that all the data is in the text. No one will ever discover Hamlet's or Ahab's secret diaries or the records of their therapy sessions. In contrast with my paucity of knowledge about the interior lives of most of my real-life companions, fictional characters show me *their* interior lives abundantly and vividly. What you see is what you get in a way that is never true of real-life companions. As George Santayana says,

> The great characters of poetry—a Hamlet, a Don Quixote, an Achilles—are no averages, they are not even a collection of salient traits common to certain classes of men. They seem to be persons; that is, their actions and words seem to spring from the inward nature of an individual soul. Goethe is reported to have said that he conceived the character of his Gretchen entirely without observation of originals. And, indeed, he would probably not have found any. His creation rather is the original to which we may occasionally think we see some likeness in real maidens. *It is the fiction here that is the standard of naturalness.* And on this, as on so many occasions, we may repeat the saying that poetry is truer than history. (110; emphasis added)

Aristotle long ago claimed that stories were truer than history because stories show principles while history shows sequence. The novelist William Gass pushes this notion even further and claims that fictional characters are the only objects in whom we can see an *essence* of human character in a way that we never can in real life. Stories constitute the domain, Gass says, "where characters, unlike ourselves, freed from existence, can shine like essence, and purely Be" (54). Gass believes so deeply in the ontological status of narrated characters, in fact, that he argues against the ages-old understanding of them as imitations. To him, they have a deeper and more real status than mere imitations. In Gass's view, *we* are the imitations. Narrated characters capture the real essences of which real life offers only pale shadows.

> Gatsby is not an imitation, for there is nothing he imitates. Actually, if he were a copy, an illusion, [a] sort of shade or shadow, he would not be called a character at all. He must be unique, entirely himself, as if he had a self to be. He is required, in fact, to act *in character,* like a cat in a sack. No, theories of character are not absurd in the way representational theories are; they are absurd in a grander way, for the belief in Hamlet (which audiences often seem to have) is like the belief in God—incomprehensible to reason—and one is inclined to seek a motive. . . . [Our motive in reading literature isn't to pursue life] but the point and purpose of life—its facility, its use. . . . Here you have half the history of our criticism in the novel. Entire books have been written about the characters in Dickens, Trollope, Tolstoi, Faulkner. But why not? Entire books have been written about God, his cohorts, and the fallen angels. (37–39)

Narrative Intensity: We Consume Stories, But They Also Consume Us

It is useful to remind ourselves that, in narrative interactions, when we embrace stories because we love them, we need to remember that loving is an activity that always changes us, regardless of whom or what we love: money, God, liquor, chess, classical music, rock music, a person, *Hamlet*, or Hamlet. When it's a story we are consumed by, our intimacy with it seems incapable of being exhausted by multiple exposures. We can't get enough of the things we love. Some of us will go see a new production of *Hamlet* every theater season if we can find one. Millions of children just keep rereading the Harry Potter novels. I had a mother in a bookstore tell me not long ago that she was worried because of her ten-year-old daughter's profound expectation that when she turned eleven she would receive an owl message informing her of her admission to Hogwarts. Juanita Havill recalls as a child reading a story about a young boy working in the Welsh mines who is killed in an accident. "I identified totally with this boy from another time and . . . when I finished the book, my mother asked me why I was crying and I couldn't explain it. So closely had I identified with the miner's son that when I wiped the tears off my cheek, I looked at my fingers to see if they had been blackened by coal dust" (96). Narrated reality sometimes seems realer than real life, but the ways in which this intensity carries over to real life are complicated to understand and talk about.

It is not the case, for example, that learning to love characters in stories always or automatically leads to loving people in real life. If it did, we could rely on stories as a kind of foolproof education in compassion. But stories can only extend invitations. They cannot coerce. Certainly there are some people who love narrative characters the way they love dogs—passionately—but who cannot muster up sympathy for their relatives or their neighbors. Surely it is safe to say, however, that persons whose ethical imaginations *do* take in the sufferings and joys of their real-life neighbors have acquired at least part of this sensitivity by practicing its deployment in response to the lives of narrative companions. Havill's description of her mother reading a novel seems a perfect description of someone caught up in the repetition of a primordial act of identification with others: "My mother read as if her life depended upon it. . . . She would open a book and disappear. She didn't fidget or nibble snacks or look up. While reading, she had an expression of calm, transported by the story to another place" (94). The specific consequences of constantly consuming stories are not predictable, but to deny the likelihood of consequences altogether is not plausible. In the words of William Monroe,

> When we expose our functional repertoire of scripts and patterns to the inclusion of a powerfully wrought symbolic strategy, we make ourselves vulnerable to displacement and transformation. Will this new program or "application" work like a computer virus or "Trojan horse" retarding our processes and disabling other functions? Or will it increase our capacities, allowing us to know and to do marvelous things formerly closed off from us? We can never know in advance exactly what will happen when we open ourselves to encounter even a familiar work. (23)

A particularly vivid account attesting to the depth of identification we can attain with narrative companions is provided by Robert Pinsky. "I know a woman who as a child," he says, "used to be afraid to begin a new book. In the inert little object, in the squared-off ranks of black sentences, lay a terrible power she had not elected: within a few pages she would become subject to that power. She might start to care about the fate of a character the author could thwart, humiliate, or even kill, the character a hostage not even to fortune but to the authorial need to create just that caring my friend dreaded while also craving it" (205–6). I once had a student, one of my department's brightest English majors, say practically the same thing to me after literary criticism class one day. "I never finish a novel," she reported. "I get so invested in the characters that I can't stand the possibility of something happening to them that I don't want to happen."

We are so sensitive to the pull of narrative appeals that a story can make me care about characters even when I am not privy to all of the details of what is happening to them or even when I enter the story in the middle of things. I have noticed, for example, that if I am flipping channels on TV and come across a thriller or a suspense program in which children are in danger, I immediately experience an anxiety that leads me to hustle on past the scene to avoid seeing that danger, usually some form of violence, descend on innocent heads. I can bear such scenes (usually) if I have been following a story from the beginning and have thus invested my time and energy in seeing it through, but to see violence or ill fortune descend on innocent people in random visitations—the clicks of my remote control *are* random—is more distress than I voluntarily desire. What's interesting is that my understanding of what's likely to come down the narrative path of the story is practically instantaneous—I need only a bare minimum of the story's data, an instantaneous exposure to the expression on characters' faces, the background music, the tonality of the color palette—in order to understand what is going on. The instantaneousness of my response suggests that human brains have an almost preternatural ability—it would actually be a protocol of our evolved cognition—to pick up story cues without having to "interpret" them in any clumsy, self-conscious way in whatever media we are habituated to encountering stories in the first place.

If what I have just said is true, this suggests that our responsiveness to the cues that indicate people's conditions in both real life and in stories is *natural* not just in the weak sense of common but in the strong sense of inborn. It makes sense to suppose that in human beings' long evolutionary history, those persons who could most quickly and accurately perceive in other people the signs of danger (or the opportunities for mating or sharing resources) had the highest survival rates, and thus sent their genes forward into future generations more often than those who were dim-witted or confused about signs of danger, distress, or sexual invitation.

As long as the narrative companions whose lives we are following look like recognizable human beings in recognizable human situations, we immediately take it for granted that their situations apply at least potentially to us. Almost any kind of situation can, no matter how removed from the reality of everyday life, be made to *appear* temporarily plausible. The genres of science fiction, fantasy, and horror films prove this claim dramatically. In a good science fiction film or novel, we can be made to care about the existence of aliens traveling on space ships going faster than light speed more than we care about the real-life suburban schmucks stuck in traffic every day on their way to the office.

Mark Rudman reports of his youthful reading that "when things were turning out too badly in stories, I wanted to intervene, as Buster Keaton's projectionist in *Sherlock Jr.* [1923] does when he dreams himself into the film he's showing" (213–14). While there are many such testaments to what this kind of caring feels like, perhaps no one has created a more vivid description of it than Jane Hamilton in her first novel, *The Book of Ruth*. The young, first-person narrator, Ruth, maintains throughout the whole novel a thread of commentary about the effects on her mind and heart of the novels that she listens to on tape with a blind woman, Mrs. Finch, for whom Ruth serves as a companion, tape changer, and story kibitzer. Ruth is deeply familiar with that terrible sense of caring that Pinsky describes, the kind of caring-accompanied-by-dread that Ruth captures in these breathless words:

Once, we were listening to a book called *The Mill on the Floss,* and we were finally, after twenty reels, right near the end. I had a terrible feeling about Maggie, that her days were numbered, and that water was going to be responsible. I couldn't bear it. I thought about her constantly at school, hoping the best, although my heart told me she didn't have a chance in the world. I bumped into people in the halls and they pushed me away with their elbows. They didn't know Maggie was the only person on my mind. I was desperate to hear the end. (56)

Ruth lives so intensely with story companions that she even imagines having interactions with them. As Ruth gets to know Daisy, for example, the beautiful but slutty bad girl of her school, Ruth uses *Pride and Prejudice* as her reference point for understanding a young woman so unlike herself. "To me [Daisy] looked like Mr. Darcy's twin sister. In the book Miss Finch and I read, *Pride and Prejudice,* Mr. Darcy didn't have a twin sister, but you never know, he could have had one they were ashamed of" (86). Ruth develops such a sense of intimacy with her narrative companions that even the authors begin to take on real-life solidity. When Ruth is frustrated by her inability to find the words to describe a distant aunt whose social class and education are so much higher than Ruth's own that she seems like a visitor from another planet, Ruth spontaneously thinks, "I wish I could hire Charles Dickens to describe Aunt Sid. I don't have a chance in the world to do her justice" (249).

Like Ruth in Hamilton's story, the monster in Mary Shelley's famous novel provides another picture of a character with extremely limited experience and no education who finds in narratives the clue to making sense out of human conduct. After his escape from Dr. Frankenstein's laboratory, the monster secretly spies on the residents of an isolated cottage to learn about human life, but Shelley knew that her monster could not learn to understand the human condition on the basis of distanced, noninteracting observations. Thus she arranges for the monster to steal a portmanteau that contains stories: *Paradise Lost,* a volume of *Plutarch's Lives,* and Goethe's *Sorrows of Young Werther.* Like anyone new or inexperienced in the world—Jane Hamilton's Ruth, or you and I in our youth—Shelley's monster becomes aware of just how limited his long range information about human beings is the moment he begins reading his purloined stories. In viewing people but not interacting with them, the monster was unable to learn about those matters of the heart that stories so effortlessly give him knowledge of.

I can hardly describe to you the effect of these books. They produced in me an infinity of new images and feelings. . . . The cottage of my protectors had been the only school in which I had studied human nature; but [*Plutarch's Lives*] developed new and mightier scenes of action. I read of men concerned in public affairs, governing or massacring their species. I felt the greatest ardor for virtue arise within me, and abhorrence for vice, as far as I understood the signification of those terms. . . . But *Paradise Lost* excited different and far deeper emotions. . . . It moved every feeling of wonder and awe that the picture of an omnipotent God warring with his creatures was capable of exciting. (134–35)

Does Adulthood Inoculate Us Against Stories' Ethical Influences?

As you saw at the beginning of chapter 5, my students resist the notion that they might be influenced by the stories they ingest, primarily on the grounds of their self-imputed maturity. Youngsters are susceptible to influence, they admit, but not adults. My students seem typical of adults in general on this front, most of whom easily assume that only children consume stories with the kind of intensity that renders them vulnerable to influence, but this assumption is both implausible and unrealistic. The compulsive gambler or drinker who claims he isn't governed by his habit is about as plausible as the adult who says that she's never influenced by story. As I watch people view their favorite TV programs or sit with me in movies, as I listen to conversations among my students and others about what's happening on their favorite soap operas, and as I listen to the collective, rapt responses of theater and movie audiences, it seems a more accurate description of the power of story to say that instead of outgrowing it—instead of adulthood taking us beyond our tendency for childish absorption—engaging with stories is precisely the one activity that can pull us back into imaginative absorption more readily and more pleasurably than any other. As we age, we outgrow many kinds of pleasure that delighted us in childhood, but we never outgrow the pleasure of stories.

Adults often get as deeply attached to companions both in real life and in stories as do children, not because they are childishly flawed, but because stories work for human beings at all developmental levels. I know some professional women—attorneys and executives—for example, who have seen *Pretty Woman* more than twenty times, and I know some men who have seen *The Magnificent Seven* or *Rocky* the same number of times. Since the principle that what moves us also forms us seems incontrovertible—especially if we voluntarily seek to be moved by an experience over and over—why would it be the case that adults are invulnerable to ethical influence from the companions they love or hate in stories?

CHAPTER SEVEN

ໜຈⰂⰂⰂⰂⰂⰂ

Ethics of Narrative in a Practical Vein

Ethical Invitations in

Katherine Anne Porter's "The Grave"

What Keeps Us Hooked—or Not?

A full account of narrative transactions raises the question of why we so seldom avail ourselves of our absolute freedom to walk out on any voluntary narrative interaction at any time. I have suggested some of the reasons that lie within us—our general desires for learning, pleasure, companionship, and so on—but now I want to analyze some of the reasons that are located in narrative themselves rather than in general human motives. It takes more than *initial* assent to keep us bonded over time. What stratagems do stories employ that create the kinds of deep bonding with readers that previous quotations describe?

Another way to ask this question is, what are stories' delivery systems? What kinds of hooks allow the story *out there* to become a gripping sequence of mental events *in here,* inside my head and heart? This analysis must show how a reader's or viewer's initial assent may begin in human need, as I have previously suggested, but also gets worked up by the story such that it becomes *a patterned set of responses,* shaped and directed from word one to word last (or from scene one to scene last, and so on, depending on the story's medium) by such means as building suspense, creating sympathy, developing belief, structuring desire, and generating such emotions as indignation and satisfaction, likes and dislikes, hopes and anxieties, gratification and frustration, and so on.

Responses to Narratives Are *Directed*, Not Random or Purely Idiosyncratic

We do not decide willy-nilly which characters in stories we want to see rewarded and punished. If we were all making independent and random responses, it would be hard to explain why everyone in a movie laughs at the same time, feels suspense at the same time, and feels gratified or scared at the same time. If human beings' default responses to stories were random or idiosyncratic, there would be no way to explain why no one ever sides with the wolf over the three little pigs or with Claudius over Hamlet or with Jack Palance over Alan Ladd in *Shane* or with Darth Vader over Luke Skywalker in *Star Wars*. No one ever thinks that *Anna Karenina* is slapstick or weeps for Elmer Fudd. But if we are not reacting to stories randomly, then it follows that some kind of deliberately deployed stimuli are effectively *patterning* our responses, not just *poking* them.

What are the strategies that accomplish this patterning? The rakish smile of the hero in an action film is not just a product of Jude Law's or Jackie Chan's or Samuel Jackson's good looks. That rakish smile is an aesthetic strategy (a technical achievement on the actor's part), and it is designed, first, to project an ethos for the character and, second, to make story consumers *like* (or dislike) that ethos. In real life, a rakish smile may be a habitual smirk, or it may be an accident, or it may be a sign of gas pain. In a narrative, however, that smile, and all other such details, are deliberately developed cues that prompt readers and viewers to assent to—or to make—the judgments, beliefs, or feelings that they *must* make if the story is to succeed.

That the central character of Mary McCarthy's short story "Artists in Uniform" is wearing Ferragamo shoes is not a random detail. It is an aesthetic strategy that positions the character's social class relative to the unsophisticated Midwesterners in the club car of the train she is traveling on, and also makes readers see her as an East Coast sophisticate and an intellectual snob. In short, the reference to Mary McCarthy's shoes (the shoes were indeed hers; she later wrote about the autobiographical dimensions of the story, and even uses her own name in the story itself) leads us to experience certain emotions, to refer to certain concepts, and to make certain ethical judgments (on the presumption that we find the reverse snobbery of Midwestern hicks, as well as Eastern intellectuals and their straightforward snobbery, both blameworthy).

Plot as Ethical Trajectory

Most people think of plot as an account of mere sequences: "First this happens and then that happens and then something else happens and then the story ends." But if plot were really just a sequence of events, there would be no way to distinguish stories from real life, because "a sequence of events" defines equally well both plots and life. Yet everyone knows that the events in stories are in fact more connected and unified than the events of everyday life. Even stories designed to show life as fragmented and people as disconnected are not themselves fragmented and disconnected. If they were, we would never be able to know that they were *about* fragmented lives and disconnected people. As Aristotle long ago pointed out in his *Poetics,* plot is a single, overarching action—it's the idea of the story—that lies behind the representation of its events.

The story's elemental idea, moreover, describes not just an aesthetic shape as it unfolds, but an ethical shape as well. In other words, *the arc of a particular plot is also the arc of a particular ethical trajectory.* The plot shows how people in stories become the persons they turn out to be, and our participation in their movement from Point A to Point B and beyond involves us in assuming beliefs, having feelings, and making judgments that, once we have made them, exert pressure on the ethical trajectory of our own lives. The philosopher Mary Midgley provides an insight about the origin of morals that also offers an insight into the origin of plots. "If we ask what is the source of the authority of morals," she says, "we are not looking outward for a sanction from the rulers, or for a contract. We are looking inward for a *need*, for some psychological fact about us that makes it deeply distressing to us to live shapelessly, incoherently, discontinuously, meaninglessly—to live without standards" (153).

To live without standards, to live completely shapelessly, is incompatible with living socially, and social living is the only mode of life available to us. Thus society requires ethical standards and life requires something like plot. The forward movement of our lives is never sufficiently intelligible to us, so we create visions of the intelligibility we seek in the plots of our stories and, subsequently, try to make our lives resemble our stories. Psychological researchers at Northwestern University have found that the life stories told by troubled patients are useful both as diagnostic tools and as therapy. On the therapy front, researchers have discovered "a kind of give and take between life stories and individual memories, between the larger screenplay and the individual scenes. The way people replay and recast memories, day by day, deepens and reshapes their larger life story. And as it evolves, that larger story in turn colors the interpretation of the scenes" (Carey, 3). Stephen Wayne, a political scientist at Georgetown University who has studied John McCain, said of Mr. McCain's approach to his 2008 presidential campaign, "politics was imitating art. It is almost as if McCain had described himself as a literary character, and then he tried to be that person in real life" (Kirkpatrick). With his usual precocity, Oscar Wilde anticipated these lines of thought about the relations between story and life in the nineteenth century, as, indeed, his famous quip shows: "life imitates art far more than art imitates life. . . . A great artist invents a type, and life tries to copy it" (680–81). Artists invent not only types of persons, however, but also kinds of plots, and it takes only a moment's reflection to see how strongly a given plot, in addition to being an aesthetic design, is also *a design that extends an invitation for deep ethical responses.*

A plot shows us the actions and sequences of human life: how experience begins, how it develops, how the developments can be confusing but can also come into swift and sudden focus, and how complications may be resolved, which often entails (but not always) the participants coming to *see* and *understand* the design of which they are a part and, by means of that seeing and understanding, growing and developing as human beings or, if they fail to see and understand, coming to stultification or degeneration. The ersatz plots of our real lives and the real plots of our stories both anticipate inevitable endings: death for the real-life person, *finis* for the story. Neither lives nor stories can go on forever. Our knowledge of this fact gives plot a dimension of significance that resonates with our knowledge of the certainty of *endings*. Peter Brooks, who has thought carefully about this dimension of plot and its deep appeal to our longing for a life of form rather than chaos, says that

> the narrative must tend toward its end, seek illumination in its own death. Yet this must be the right death, the correct end. . . . The improper end indeed lurks throughout narrative, frequently as the wrong choice: choice of the wrong casket, misapprehension of the magical agent, false erotic object choice. . . . The desire of the text (the desire of reading) is hence desire for the end, but desire for the end reached only through the at least minimally complicated detour, the intentional deviance, in tension, which is the plot of narrative. (103–4)

Katherine Anne Porter's "The Grave"

In what follows I am going to do two things. While engaging in the practical analysis of a story, I will argue in a more general way about the ethical dimension of storytellers' aesthetic strategies and choices. In the history of ethical criticism, the typical humanist approach to ethical criticism is illustrated by Matthew Arnold's comment near the end of his "Preface to *Poems, 1853*" that "*I know not how it is,* but their commerce with the ancients appears to me to produce, in those who constantly practice it, a steadying and composing effect upon their judgment, not of literary works only, but of men and events in general" (493; emphasis added). Arnold is right, of course, because his caveat—"in those who constantly practice it"—captures the point I have been making that any activity we do persistently and voluntarily is likely to configure not just what we do but who we are. The credit that Arnold deserves for this insight, however, is undercut when he deliberately evades detailed analysis by saying, "*I know not how it is.*" Ethical criticism can no longer get away with these evasions. In my practical analysis of the story that follows, I am going to *say* "how it is."

Ideally, it would be most useful to do a three-way comparative analysis of a print story, a movie, and a TV program. I must override this ideal, however, in order to make available to you all of the data I will be analyzing. Thus I have chosen to analyze a work of literature that I can include here in its entirety. This will allow you to check all the data of the story at the same time I am working with it. In this story, Katherine Anne Porter's "The Grave," the occasional ellipses are the author's, who employs them as a matter of style. I have numbered the paragraphs for ease of reference in the analysis that follows.

THE GRAVE

by Katherine Anne Porter

1. The grandfather, dead for more than thirty years, had been twice disturbed in his long repose by the constancy and possessiveness of his widow. She removed his bones first to Louisiana and then to Texas as if she had set out to find her own burial place, knowing well she would never return to the places she had left. In Texas she set up a small cemetery in a corner of her first farm, and as the family connection grew, and oddments of relations came over from Kentucky to settle, it contained at last about twenty graves. After the grandmother's death, part of her land was to be sold for the benefit of certain of her children, and the cemetery happened to lie in the part set aside for sale. It was necessary to take up the bodies and bury them again in the family plot in the big new public cemetery, where the grandmother had been buried. At last her husband was to lie beside her for eternity, as she had planned.

2. The family cemetery had been a pleasant small neglected garden of tangled rose bushes and ragged cedar trees and cypress, the simple flat stones rising out of uncropped sweet-smelling wild grass. The graves were lying open and empty one burning day when Miranda and her brother Paul, who often went together to hunt rabbits and doves, propped their twenty-two Winchester rifles carefully against the rail fence, climbed over and explored among the graves. She was nine years old and he was twelve.

3. They peered into the pits all shaped alike with such purposeful accuracy, and looking at each other with pleased adventurous eyes, they said in solemn tones: "These were graves!" trying by words to shape a special, suitable emotion in their minds, but they felt nothing except an agreeable thrill of wonder: they were seeing a new sight, doing something they had not done before. In them both there was also a small disappointment at the entire commonplaceness of the actual spectacle. Even if it had once contained a coffin for years upon years, when the coffin was gone a grave was just a hole in the ground. Miranda leaped into the pit that had held her grandfather's bones. Scratching around aimlessly and pleasurably as any young animal, she scooped up a lump of earth and weighed it in her palm. It had a pleasantly sweet, corrupt smell, being mixed with cedar needles and small leaves, and as the crumbs fell apart, she saw a silver dove no larger than a hazel nut, with spread wings and a neat fan-shaped tail. The breast had a deep round hollow in it. Turning it up to the fierce sunlight, she saw that the inside of the hollow was cut in little whorls. She scrambled out, over the pile of loose earth that had fallen back into one end of the grave, calling to Paul that she had found something, he must guess what . . . His head appeared smiling over the rim of another grave. He waved a closed hand at her. "I've got something too!" They ran to compare treasures, making a game of it, so many guesses each, all wrong, and a final show-down with opened palms. Paul had found a thin wide gold ring carved with intricate flowers and leaves. Miranda was smitten at sight of the ring and wished to have it. Paul seemed more impressed by the dove. They made a trade, with some little bickering. After he had got the dove in his hand, Paul said, "Don't you know what this is? This is a screw head for a *coffin!* . . . I'll bet nobody else in the world has one like this!"

4. Miranda glanced at it without covetousness. She had the gold ring on her thumb; it fitted perfectly. "Maybe we ought to go now," she said. "Maybe one of the niggers 'll see us and tell somebody." They knew the land had been sold, the cemetery was no longer theirs, and they felt like trespassers. They climbed back over the fence, slung their rifles loosely under their arms—they had been shooting at targets with various kinds of firearms since they were seven years old—and set out to look for the rabbits and doves or whatever small game might happen along. On

these expeditions Miranda always followed at Paul's heels along the path, obeying instructions about handling her gun when going through fences; learning how to stand it up properly so it would not slip and fire unexpectedly; how to wait her time for a shot and not just bang away in the air without looking, spoiling shots for Paul, who really could hit things if given a chance. Now and then, in her excitement at seeing birds whiz up suddenly before her face, or a rabbit leap across her very toes, she lost her head, and almost without sighting she flung her rifle up and pulled the trigger. She hardly ever hit any sort of mark. She had no proper sense of hunting at all. Her brother would be often completely disgusted with her. "You don't care whether you get your bird or not," he said. "That's no way to hunt." Miranda could not understand his indignation. She had seen him smash his hat and yell with fury when he had missed his aim. "What I like about shooting," said Miranda, with exasperating inconsequence, "is pulling the trigger and hearing the noise."

5. "Then, by golly," said Paul, "whyn't you go back to the range and shoot at bulls-eyes?"

6. "I'd just as soon," said Miranda, "only like this, we walk around more."

7. "Well, you just stay behind and stop spoiling my shots," said Paul, who, when he made a kill, wanted to be certain he had made it. Miranda, who alone brought down a bird once in twenty rounds, always claimed as her own any game they got when they fired at the same moment. It was tiresome and unfair and her brother was sick of it.

8. "Now, the first dove we see, or the first rabbit, it's mine," he told her. "And the next will be yours. Remember that and don't get smarty."

9. "What about snakes?" asked Miranda idly. "Can I have the first snake?"

10. Waving her thumb gently and watching her gold ring glitter, Miranda lost interest in shooting. She was wearing her summer roughing outfit: dark blue overalls, a light blue shirt, a hired-man's straw hat, and thick brown sandals. Her brother had the same outfit except his was a sober hickory-nut color. Ordinarily Miranda preferred her overalls to any other dress, though it was making rather a scandal in the countryside, for the year was 1903, and in the back country the law of female decorum had teeth in it. Her father had been criticized for letting his

girls dress like boys and go careering around astride barebacked horses. Big sister Maria, the really independent and fearless one, in spite of her rather affected ways, rode at a dead run with only a rope knotted around her horse's nose. It was said the motherless family was running down, with the grandmother no longer there to hold it together. It was known that she had discriminated against her son Harry in her will, and that he was in straits about money. Some of his old neighbors reflected with vicious satisfaction that now he would probably not be so stiff-necked, nor have any more high-stepping horses either. Miranda knew this, though she could not say how. She had met along the road old women of the kind who smoked corn-cob pipes, who had treated her grandmother with most sincere respect. They slanted their gummy old eyes side-ways at the granddaughter and said, "Ain't you ashamed of yoself, Missy? It's aginst the Scriptures to dress like that. Whut yo Pappy thinkin' about?" Miranda, with her powerful social sense, which was like a fine set of antennae radiating from every pore of her skin, would feel ashamed because she knew well it was rude and ill-bred to shock anybody, even bad-tempered old crones, though she had faith in her father's judgment and was perfectly comfortable in the clothes. Her father had said, "They're just what you need, and they'll save your dresses for school . . ." This sounded quite simple and natural to her. She had been brought up in rigorous economy. Wastefulness was vulgar. It was also a sin. These were truths; she had heard them repeated many times and never once disputed.

11. Now the ring, shining with the serene purity of fine gold on her rather grubby thumb, turned her feelings against her overalls and sockless feet, toes sticking through the thick brown leather straps. She wanted to go back to the farmhouse, take a good cold bath, dust herself with plenty of Maria's violet talcum powder—provided Maria was not present to object, of course—put on the thinnest, most becoming dress she owned, with a big sash, and sit in a wicker chair under the trees . . . These things were not all she wanted, of course; she had vague stirrings of desire for luxury and a grand way of living which could not take precise form in her imagination but were founded on family legend of past wealth and leisure. These immediate comforts were what she could have, and she wanted them at once. She lagged rather far behind Paul, and once she thought of just turning back without a word and going home.

She stopped, thinking that Paul would never do that to her, and so she would have to tell him. When a rabbit leaped, she let Paul have it without dispute. He killed it with one shot.

12. When she came up with him, he was already kneeling, examining the wound, the rabbit trailing from his hands. "Right through the head," he said complacently, as if he had aimed for it. He took out his sharp, competent bowie knife and started to skin the body. He did it very cleanly and quickly. Uncle Jimbilly knew how to prepare the skins so that Miranda always had fur coats for her dolls, for though she never cared much for her dolls she liked seeing them in fur coats. The children knelt facing each other over the dead animal. Miranda watched admiringly while her brother stripped the skin away as if he were taking off a glove. The flayed flesh emerged dark scarlet, sleek, firm; Miranda with thumb and finger felt the long fine muscles with the silvery flat strips binding them to the joints. Brother lifted the oddly bloated belly. "Look," he said, in a low amazed voice. "It was going to have young ones."

13. Very carefully he slit the thin flesh from the center ribs to the flanks, and a scarlet bag appeared. He slit again and pulled the bag open, and there lay a bundle of tiny rabbits, each wrapped in a thin scarlet veil. The brother pulled these off and there they were, dark gray, their sleek wet down lying in minute even ripples, like a baby's head just washed, their unbelievably small delicate ears folded close, their little blind faces almost featureless.

14. Miranda said, "Oh, I want to *see*," under her breath. She looked and looked—excited but not frightened, for she was accustomed to the sight of animals killed in hunting—filled with pity and astonishment and a kind of shocked delight in the wonderful little creatures for their own sakes, they were so pretty. She touched one of them ever so carefully, "Ah, there's blood running over them," she said and began to tremble without knowing why. Yet she wanted most deeply to see and to know. Having seen, she felt at once as if she had known all along. The very memory of her former ignorance faded, she had always known just this. No one had ever told her anything outright, she had been rather unobservant of the animal life around her because she was so accustomed to animals. They seemed simply disorderly and unaccountably rude in their habits, but altogether natural and not very interesting. Her brother had spoken as if he

had known about everything all along. He may have seen all this before. He had never said a word to her, but she knew now a part at least of what he knew. She understood a little of the secret, formless intuitions in her own mind and body, which had been clearing up, taking form, so gradually and so steadily she had not realized that she was learning what she had to know. Paul said cautiously, as if he were talking about something forbidden: "They were just about ready to be born." His voice dropped on the last word. "I know," said Miranda, "like kittens. I know, like babies." She was quietly and terribly agitated, standing again with her rifle under her arm, looking down at the bloody heap. "I don't want the skin," she said, "I won't have it." Paul buried the young rabbits again in their mother's body, wrapped the skin around her, carried her to a clump of sage bushes, and hid her away. He came out again at once and said to Miranda, with an eager friendliness, a confidential tone quite unusual in him, as if he were taking her into an important secret on equal terms: "Listen now. Now you listen to me, and don't ever forget. Don't you ever tell a living soul that you saw this. Don't tell a soul. Don't tell Dad because I'll get into trouble. He'll say I'm leading you into things you ought not to do. He's always saying that. So now don't you go and forget and blab out sometime the way you're always doing . . . Now, that's a secret. Don't you tell."

15. Miranda never told, she did not even wish to tell anybody. She thought about the whole worrisome affair with confused unhappiness for a few days. Then it sank quietly into her mind and was heaped over by accumulated thousands of impressions, for nearly twenty years. One day she was picking her path among the puddles and crushed refuse of a market street in a strange city of a strange country, when without warning, plain and clear in its true colors as if she looked through a frame upon a scene that had not stirred nor changed since the moment it happened, the episode of that far-off day leaped from its burial place before her mind's eye. She was so reasonlessly horrified she halted suddenly staring, the scene before her eyes dimmed by the vision back of them. An Indian vendor had held up before her a tray of dyed sugar sweets, in the shapes of all kinds of small creatures: birds, baby chicks, baby rabbits, lambs, baby pigs. They were in gay colors and smelled of vanilla, maybe. . . . It was a very hot day and the smell in the market, with its piles of raw flesh and wilting flowers, was like the mingled sweetness and corruption she had

smelled that other day in the empty cemetery at home: the day she had remembered always until now vaguely as the time she and her brother had found treasure in the opened graves. Instantly upon this thought the dreadful vision faded, and she saw clearly her brother, whose childhood face she had forgotten, standing again in the blazing sunshine, again twelve years old, a pleased sober smile in his eyes, turning the silver dove over and over in his hands.

The Ethics of Plot

To turn, then, to an analysis of this plot, we can see that the story's single overarching action begins with an *initial instability* that shows us nine-year-old Miranda—when she is just beginning to feel the first stirrings of female identity—encountering highly charged data from everyday life about her role as a female and her destiny as a human being. The data concerning what it means to be a human being is conveyed by the graves of Miranda's forebears, in which she and her brother Paul each find a treasure, and the data about what it means for Miranda to be female is conveyed by the dead pregnant rabbit whom Paul has shot and whose body becomes a grave for the babies the mother rabbit was about to bring into life.

The *complications* of the plot spin out of the facts—first, that Miranda is too young to understand fully her own relation to mortality as a human being, and, second, that she is also too young to understand her potential relation to procreation as a female. Since she does not really understand the data she is looking at but finds it troubling—troubling *because* she does not understand it and also troubling because even the part she *dimly* understands, that all things are born to die, is too frightening to confront seriously at such a young age—she buries it in the grave of her memory, "heaped over by accumulated thousands of impressions" (¶15), where it appears to vanish.

The *crisis* of the plot is Miranda's experience of a moment of true panic—terror, really—that unexpectedly descends on her twenty years later, when, now twenty-nine and either visiting or living in India, Miranda suddenly comes into the presence of smells and sights that bring back to her with overwhelming clarity the sights and smells she experienced on that long-ago afternoon when she was in her forebears' graveyard with her brother and he shot the pregnant rabbit.

The *resolution* of the plot is Miranda's overcoming of blind fear as she finally completes the action begun twenty years before, namely, as she finally comes to a full realization and acceptance of three things: the mortality of human existence, the personal participation in that mortality that is her destiny as a member of the human race, and the contribution to ongoing life that is potentially hers as a woman, whose ability to bear life at once opposes mortality while ultimately yielding to it.

The plot of "The Grave" has an intellectual content—the idea that life and death move into and against each other in an existential dance of profound tension—and it invites us as readers to feel this idea as a deep truth that, once seen and accepted, aligns us with fundamental forces driving the universe: not only are human beings born to die but so are stars, planets, mountain ranges, oceans, and every other thing. Porter's plot invites us to believe that seeing life's simultaneous resistance and yielding to death gives us real knowledge about life, knowledge as solid as right angles or Newton's second law of motion.

The final movement of this plot, Miranda's acceptance of her own mortality, invites us to replace our own fear of death as a terrifying annihilation with an acceptance: death as the systole to life's diastole. As the vehicle of such an invitation, this plot offers its readers comfort—not the sort of easy or sentimental comfort that says "believe this doctrine and you will be saved," but the comfort of inviting us to believe that by living *and* dying we are participating in a cosmic rhythm that, insofar as we are willing to acknowledge it, brings us close to feeling, even if we cannot fully fathom, the beating heart of the universe itself.

Of course, different readers of "The Grave" may think such ideas are humbug and claptrap, but I am not arguing that every reader must believe what "The Grave" (or any other story) asks us to believe. My argument is rather that *for the time we spend reading this story*, some responses such as these I have just described are impossible to avoid as long as we engage with the story assentively enough in order for it to *work*. If we do try to avoid these responses, then we are going to be stopping at every point in the story to quarrel, or we are going to be stopping at every point in confusion, and this is not the way we read stories, view movies, watch TV, or listen to song lyrics. We may *think* we don't believe the lyrics of a song or the plot of a story, but the only way we could really vote our disbelief is by throwing the book in the corner or turning off the radio or walking out of the movie, and while this is something we always *can* do, it is something we seldom *actually* do.

So once again we confront a kind of paradox about stories' potential ethical effects. Nothing *forces* me to agree with the assumptions about life that underlie "The Grave," but the very practice of attentive reading, of genuine engagement, entails such agreement whether we realize it or whether we would, outside of the story, welcome it. Telling ourselves or others that we don't believe what the TV program or the movie or the novel asks us to believe is a kind of technical denial with little existential and intellectual credibility. Such denials ignore the fact that while consumers are enjoying the program, the song, the movie, or the novel, and *at least* for as long as they persist in this enjoyment, they *are* believing what the story asks them to believe. Belief, at least in an operational sense, is necessary corridor to the pleasure that the story delivers.

The Ethics of Style

By "style" I mean all those techniques of *linguistic heightening* that elicit precision of perception, depth of emotional response, clarity of ideas, and direction of judgment. Porter's word choice in "The Grave," her diction, unrolls before us a verbal scroll of references to death, life-in-death, death-in-life, birth, youth, old age, and graves. The barrage of such references in a story of such brevity gives us the emotional effect of being steeped in a certain range of emotional connotations generated by the story's characteristic words and images. The first image in the story is that of Paul and Miranda, near the beginning of their lives, "scratching around aimlessly and pleasurably as any young animal" (¶3) in the empty graves that had once held the bones of their forebears. The metaphorical collapsing of human and animal boundaries—Paul and Miranda viewed narratively as young animals—foreshadows both the violent animal death that occurs later in the story and, more subtly, the eventual death of the human children who are now so completely unaware of mortality even as they scratch around in the very pit of it. As readers we cannot help seeing that as these forebears are now all dead, so shall these children become. We also see that as these children are now, so these forebears once were.

In E. Annie Proulx's *The Shipping News* a character is described this way: "If life was an arc of light that began in darkness, ended in darkness, the first part of his life had happened in ordinary glare. Here it was as though he had found a polarized lens that deepened and intensified all seen through it" (241). Porter's literary style in "The Grave" is like a polarizing lens that allows us to see through the ordinary glare of everyday life more deeply and intensely than we usually do. The invitation she extends to see things "her" way is difficult to deny, and once the invitation is accepted, the consequence is that "The Grave" will lead engaged readers to think more keenly and deeply about how to achieve clarity in their own lives against the backdrop of a deeply felt, not just an intellectually acknowledged, mortality.

As "The Grave" continues, one grave after another appears: the graves of Miranda's and Paul's family, the mother rabbit's body, the living sage bush that becomes a new cemetery, and Miranda's memory, which becomes a twenty-year grave for her recollection of this afternoon's events, "heaped over by accumulated thousands of impressions." The final grave image in the story is less explicit but symbolically powerful and occurs in the single most emphatic spot in the story, the final sentence, where readers see young Paul, a timeless representation of vigorous youth, turning over and over in his hand a coffin screw, the perfect symbol of universal and inevitable death, his own as well as Miranda's, yours, and mine. The dove presents death to us as a fact that can be accepted with peace—death as an integral part of life—rather than resisted with bitterness and resentment.

The children's deliberately "solemn tones: These were graves!" (¶3) economically evokes their shallow understanding of mortality at the story's beginning. They are trying to generate an emotion using an affected tone of voice to simulate an understanding of what they cannot really grasp, and this sets up for us as readers a kind of baseline recognition of what Paul and Miranda do and do not know, thus allowing us to accept as plausible and to feel as poignant the later tones of their *real* emotion when they examine the body of the dead pregnant rabbit. Paul's "low amazed voice" when he realizes that "it was going to have young ones" (¶12) and Miranda's "pity and astonishment and a kind of shocked delight in the wonderful little creatures for their own sakes" (¶14) that thrills through her words "Oh, I want to *see*" stand in marked contrast to the children's trumped-up earlier emotion in "These were graves!"

The story also invites readers to dread the possibility that the children will encounter the truth about life-in-death and death-in-life in some frightful way. A tragic encounter is not beyond possibility. Porter exploits both our general knowledge of the world and the kinds of possibilities that typically surround children in life as well as in other narratives to heighten our anxiety about what these two children might face, or learn, next. Paul and Miranda are both carrying guns, they are children, and accidents happen. Or they could run into dangerous forms of wildlife, especially in the backwoods of Texas in 1903—wolves or bears, perhaps—that could teach them horribly about life and death. Or one of them could get bitten by a rattlesnake, or fall into a hole or off a ledge—the possibilities of danger are numerous, and a story that opens with children rooting around in graves makes us wonder if danger will indeed materialize. Such suspense is a time-honored hook by which storytellers of all kinds keep their readers, viewers, and listeners engaged.

There is a logic of suspense that helps explain why suspense is always such a surefire narrative device for hooking readers. The hook is the vulnerability we all feel about our own existence. None of us can read the future, but we all know we are vulnerable to a huge variety of ever-present dangers, and to some degree this uncertainty—and an instinctive resistance to it—helps shape every human ethos. Thus, in suggesting by the art of her story that Paul and Miranda might be in danger, Porter immediately hooks us. We want to see if danger appears or not and, if it does, whether the children will escape, because we, like them, are always in the presence of dangers we cannot foresee and don't know if we will escape from, dangers as close as the next drive to the grocery store or as unseen as a loose blood clot chugging along in an artery. Moreover, adults seem programmed to respond with greater anxiety when children are in danger than when their peers or older people are in the same danger. Thus Porter—whether she thinks about these issues at a conscious level is irrelevant—exploits built-in generic sympathies as a foundation for the story's more specific aesthetic sympathies.

Another important stylistic device in "The Grave" is a running thread of olfactory images that mingles the odor of sweet-smelling life and the corrupt smell of death, reinforcing the story's invitation for us to feel concretely the importance of the story's leading idea about life-in-death and death-in-life. The mention of repeated exhumations of family corpses buried, presumably, in plain wooden boxes (Texas backwoods, 1903) suggests implicitly the odors of decay, and contrasts strongly with an explicit reference to the cemetery as "a pleasant small neglected garden of tangled rose bushes and . . . sweet-smelling wild grass" (¶2). Next occurs the highly charged but seemingly casual description of the odor in the open graves as a "pleasantly sweet, corrupt smell" (¶3). The way this particular odor combines the sweet smell of growing grass and the odor of rot expresses the heart of the story's ethical vision with not only physical and emotional redolence, but also great intellectual and verbal economy.

Twenty years later, when Miranda is in the Indian marketplace, it is this particular odor, "the mingled sweetness and corruption she had smelled that other day in the empty cemetery at home" (¶15), that unexpectedly triggers her memory of this childhood day, the day when she and Paul had looked on the images of life-in-death and death-in-life. One thinks instantly of the most famous example in literature of a recollection stirred up by taste and odor, Proust's claim that "when from a long-distant past nothing subsists, after the people are dead, after the things are broken and scattered, still, alone, more fragile, but with more vitality, more unsubstantial, more persistent, more faithful, the smell and taste of things remain" (36). The mingled odor of sweetness and rot instantly takes Miranda back to a recollection of the disturbing sights and feelings of that long-ago day and makes us readers feel that we are present at a great moment, not a great moment in the history of world politics or public affairs, but a great moment in the development of any human being. It is that moment when, according to whatever constraints and conditioning of culture they have absorbed, young persons peer through the door of mortality and see for the first time that the shadows lurking there are their own.

The role we should play as adults in helping children lose their innocence about mortality is a touchy issue for many people, who resist educating children about life's dark truths—loss, grief, failure, suffering. (Does this reluctance help explain our society's tendency to go to the other extreme and support one Disney narrative after another?) Adults' uncertainty about how much "reality" to force on children, and when to do it, is the topic of Thomas Gray's famous poem, "Ode on a Distant Prospect of Eton College" (1747). Gray's conclusion about forcing children to confront knowledge about darker sides of life is expressed in these famous lines:

> Yet ah, why should they know their fate?
> Since sorrow never comes too late,
> And happiness too swiftly flies.
> Thought would destroy their paradise.
> No more; where ignorance is bliss,
> 'Tis folly to be wise. (ll. 96–100)

But whether the issue surfaces now or comes to us from the eighteenth century, most adults are torn between protecting children from the truth and knowing that they will never properly mature unless they face the truth at some point in time. The question is, *what* point in time? In "The Grave," however, it is not adults who educate Paul and Miranda but circumstances, and the lessons being taught, especially for Miranda, are beyond her powers of present understanding. But as she says with great intensity, she wants "to *see*," and we, as vicarious participants at her moment of introduction to the momentous issues of procreation and death cannot help but accept with both sorrow and gladness her eagerness to understand the mysteries that bring us into this world and that also take us out.

Watching Miranda as she tries to see and understand is a solemn moment. It is a homely moment, certainly, but perhaps all the more solemn for being homely. To see the certainty of death may bring sadness, but not to see it cements us in shallowness. To see the certainty of *our own* death, rather than to acknowledge it as some distant abstraction, is to reach a milestone in human awareness; it brings us to the threshold of personal maturity. Prolonged innocence—Peter Panism—is not a natural or desirable condition once past childhood. It is stultifying at best, pathological at worst. Acceptance of our own death does not put every other issue in life in its proper place of course, but at least we will, once past that point of acceptance, be better prepared to separate what is serious from what is trivial.

Separating the serious from the trivial is a skill we may never exercise infallibly, but the vicarious experience of being with young minds that are taking shape in such a crucible of connotations not only shapes the children but also potentially shapes the reader. When Miranda says, "I know, like kittens. I know, like babies" (¶14), she has come as far in her understanding as she can, and she is, to our admiration, not silly, frivolous, or self-centered about it. She is intently trying to see the situation for what it is; she wants to *know*, not escape. As readers privileged to be present at this spectacle of nine-year-old bravery, we find it hard not to bond affectionately and sympathetically to this young scholar of life.

The description of Miranda's fear when at age twenty-nine she suddenly remembers this day, her brother Paul, the hot cemetery, and the dead rabbit, vividly evokes in us our own recollection of what life feels like when an abstraction that we have long *known* suddenly becomes a fact we now *feel*. When the Indian vendor unexpectedly places before Miranda the tray of tiny sugar animals that look like the rabbit fetuses that she and Paul examined twenty years earlier, her abstract knowledge suddenly maps onto her deep feelings with a profound existential wrenching. The fear she feels is like the fear we might experience when we step blindly off the curb into the path of an onrushing bus and then jump back just in time to save ourselves. The pulse spikes upward, the heart pounds, the mouth dries, the breath races: for a moment we *feel* what we know. Miranda is for a moment, "reasonlessly horrified" (¶15).

We are invited as readers to participate in Miranda's realization as if it were our own. It *is* our own. It is everyone's. Most of us, even if we are much older than Miranda, keep our mortality in the file labeled "to deal with later." What T. S. Eliot says about literature in particular also applies to story in general—or at least to many stories, Porter's included—in that "it may make us from time to time a little more aware of the deeper, unnamed feelings which form *the substratum of our being, to which we rarely penetrate*; for our lives are mostly a constant evasion of ourselves, and an evasion of the visible and sensible world" (149; emphasis added). But the style of this story invites us to pause in our pattern of avoidance and, like Miranda at nine, to *see* and, like Miranda at twenty-nine, to *feel* how the truth of mortality applies not just to others and not just to narrative characters, but to us.

The Ethics of Narrative Technique

Porter constructs the narrator's voice in this story to operate as much as possible like a transparent pane of glass. The narrator tries to show us the characters without calling any attention to her act of throwing over them the special coloring that comes from her narrator's tone and narrative angle of vision. This pose of transparency is itself an artifice, of course, and a powerful technique of influence. It invites readers to impute a kind of inevitability or naturalness to the story's events. Things seen through a transparent pane don't *look* staged (even if they are). The technique of apparent narrative transparency helps secure both emotional and intellectual assent, in other words, and is therefore not neutral in its *overall* effects but it certainly works hard to appear neutral in its *local* effects (from one sentence to the next).

Compare Porter's narrative voice, for example, to the richly nuanced narrator of Jane Austen's novels, who is arguably the most important character *in* her novels; or to Hemingway's narrators, whom Hemingway keeps in the shadows as much as possible; or to Faulkner's narrators, constantly calling attention to themselves by their anguished tone, historical reach, and highly stylized stream of consciousness; or to Dickens's vivid narrators, who by turns thunder from pulpits of moral indignation and reach for many different variations of emotional extremes. Compared to these, Porter's narrator in "The Grave" calls no particular attention to herself at all. The narrator creates the impression of staying out of action's way, which greatly intensifies the force of her invitation to see the story as something natural rather than constructed, as a representation of something permanent rather than contingent, as something true rather than false.

The most unusual feature of narrative technique in this story is the span of twenty years that goes completely unnarrated. It is not even summarized in a general way, and yet the gap is spanned so quietly, so smoothly, and so effectively that it is hardly noticed. The total time in real life covered by the story cannot be more than two or three hours, at the most, in the afternoon of the day when the rabbit is shot, and no more than a moment or two at the end, when Miranda suddenly endures her intense recollection. Thus the gap of twenty blank years is incalculably larger than *all* the represented actions in the story, yet it is not experienced as a blank at all by the reader. The action begun on the afternoon in the graveyard finds its completion in the afternoon in the market, and spans the twenty-year gap between the two by a narrative device as simple as "Miranda . . . thought about the whole worrisome affair with confused unhappiness for a few days. Then it sank quietly into her mind and was heaped over by accumulated thousands of impressions, for nearly twenty years" (¶15). In the next sentence it *is* twenty years later, and Miranda is in the Indian market.

The Story's Ethical Vision

Precisely speaking, the ethical vision of "The Grave" is not part of its formal art. Rather, the story's ethical vision is composed of those broad views about human nature, human flourishing, good and bad action, suffering and joy, and good and evil spread out by the author as the narrative soil from which the story grows. Together, these issues color all the story's artistic strategies like an electric charge that may not be much noticed but that energizes everything it touches.

There is nothing particularly novel or intellectually challenging about the ethical vision of Katherine Anne Porter's "The Grave." If a story's *effects* rest on an ethical vision that can be unpacked as a few fundamental assumptions, its *value* is largely a function of how it invites us to see and understand the *relevance* of those assumptions. The relevance of the ethical vision of "The Grave" derives from the story's foundational ethical value that *it is a good thing for human beings to see and understand the interplay of life and death*, and a good thing to be able to apply that understanding concretely to their own lives. Implicit in the story's representation of Miranda and her confrontation with both her femaleness and her mortality is the deep ethical assumption that Miranda's stepping up to *meet* this confrontation rather than avoiding or denying it is a *good* thing, a brave thing. The story leads us to the judgment that in facing this truth Miranda is stepping into her human birthright as a more mature and fully developed person than she would be if she had run away, screamed "icky," or had a meltdown with her eyes covered. The fact that it is a fictional experience on the part of a fictional person does not change the relevance or the structure of the underlying values.

An additional component of this ethical vision is Porter's assumption that growth in life requires the risk of *openness* to experience rather than self-protective resistance. Porter reveals this part of her ethical vision by naming the girl Miranda, a name that calls to mind the fresh and innocent Miranda of Shakespeare's *The Tempest,* who says admiringly of the first human beings she has ever seen besides her father, "What brave new world, / That has such people in't" (V, i). Shakespeare's wide-eyed Miranda neither rejects nor flees the changes in her world brought by strangers, nor does Porter's wide-eyed Miranda resort to stereotypical childish evasions when faced with the dead rabbit's fetuses. This takes courage, which Miranda finds in her heart and which Porter passes to us, her readers.

Finally, Porter's ethical vision assumes that anyone's moment and terms for dealing with fundamental conditions of living will always be colored and informed by historical circumstances of time and place. To contemporary urbanites of the twenty-first century, the sight of two children, ages nine and twelve, roaming about the countryside with loaded guns and shooting small animals might seem downright bizarre. Most urbanites today tend to associate guns with crime, not with hunting, and take it for granted that children should not be associated with guns at all. Yet it is the culturally specific features of this particular time and place, backwoods Texas in 1903, that set the scene for Miranda's initial confrontation with her own personal relationship to issues of life, death, and birth. Nowhere in this story does Porter *say* that all such confrontations will occur within a context established by the particularities of time and place, but this assumption is embedded everywhere in the concreteness with which this story's context is evoked: the family history, the strong grandmother, the injured son, the headstrong sister Maria, the old corncob-pipe–smoking woman with gummy eyes, and the children's familiarity with dead animals killed either at slaughtering time or on hunting trips. The details of the story suggest that in order to move toward self-consciousness and completion, human beings must be alert, attend to nuances, and avoid routine. Porter's story could be said to extend Henry James's dictum about novelists to a general dictum about all of us, namely that we should "try to be one of the people on whom nothing is lost" (441). In our respectful and thoughtful attention to detail lies our best strategy for not missing out on growth and maturity.

Having said all of this, does it follow that Porter's story is preachy, that it is written "to do us good" like an evangelical tract or a Sunday school lesson? Not at all. On the other hand, "The Grave" is not written as if it either wants to be or could be an object of such smooth aesthetic surfaces that it lacks all traction on the real world. "The Grave" is written to be as good a story as Porter could make it, presumably, but she neither could nor did make it out of nothing, and she neither could nor did make it entirely out of aesthetic strategies. The aesthetic strategies and the ethical vision unfold inside each other like flower petals; they mutually support and sustain each other. They bear the same relation to each other as the idea of a sentence to the words of the sentence. The ethical assumptions of the story constitute Porter's vision of what is important in human life combined with a set of aesthetic strategies that embody her vision.

As readers, if we are attentive, we take it *all* in—vision and aesthetics, ethical notions and artistic strategies—and doing so is like ingesting any other complex, rich substance. Insofar as the substance gets digested and internalized, it becomes part of us, and insofar as it becomes part of us we become different from what we were before, and insofar as we are different from what we were before, the story can be said to have exerted an ethical effect on us because it has changed the configuration and content of our ethos. Whether this is good or bad for us depends on the nature of the invitations and how deeply we accept them, or on the reasons we deploy for rejecting them, but we cannot pretend that we have not been invited to change, and we cannot pretend that whether we accept or deny those invitations, we *do* change.

꒰꒱꒰꒱

CHAPTER EIGHT

Ethics of Narrative in a Practical Vein Once More

Invitations to Misogyny in James Thurber's "The Catbird Seat"

Many academics and intellectuals view ethical judgments about art, especially *negative* judgments, as nothing but a scolding discourse conducted by fat-fingered bourgeoisie or dogmatic religionists who, according to the academic stereotype, leaf furiously through novels or storm noisily out of movie theaters just so they can foam at the mouth about the "dirty" parts in the hope of getting a two-second sound bite on the eleven o'clock news. It is not clear what academics thought would happen to ethical criticism when they began to abandon it at the end of the nineteenth century, an abandonment that left it in the hands of those who used it mainly as a tool for promoting doctrinaire agendas, but the truth is that all of us *do* ethical criticism all the time. If you have ever winced at the representation of objectionable attitudes in a novel, movie, or TV program because you felt, even vaguely, that such representations give the objectionable views currency and credibility, then you are doing ethical criticism. If you are among those, for example, who agree it was probably a bad idea for President Nixon to watch the movie *Patton* over and over, as he did, during the Vietnam War, then you are operating as an ethical critic. And if you have ever proffered to a friend or relative or offspring certain kinds of criticism—for example, "you know, Frank, you can't really base so many of your views about romance (or about work, money, friends, success, or whatever) on reruns of *Seinfeld* (or *Friends* or *Sex in the City* or whatever) without being unfair to women"—then you are not only taking the perspective of an ethical critic but performing the warning task that sometimes falls to the ethical critic.

When practiced in a spirit of intellectual give-and-take, the particular mode of warning used by responsible ethical critics produces discussion and argument, not dogmatic assertion. Moralizing shuts topics down. Ethical criticism powers them up. The point to performing a piece of practical negative criticism is neither to bully works of art nor to foreclose further discussion. The responsible ethical critic assumes that the ethical issues raised by stories are complex, subtle, thorny, and best analyzed within a community of thinkers who all agree about the importance of ethics in general but who do not necessarily make the same ethical judgments about particular narratives. And since we don't all agree, discussion is needed, *not* in order for one view to win out over all others but in order for us to learn what we think is important.

To illustrate this particular function of negative ethical criticism, I have chosen a short story to analyze, one of the most well-liked and most frequently anthologized short stories in the history of American fiction, James Thurber's "The Catbird Seat."[1] "The Catbird Seat," beloved by many generations of school children and college students, is just the kind of story that few people would criticize in ethical terms because so many have found it *vastly* entertaining. "The Catbird Seat" is funny and therefore precisely the kind of story that people call "mere entertainment," usually with the unspoken assumption that "mere entertainment" could never do harm.

Nevertheless, the analysis I offer here of "The Catbird Seat" shows that the ticket of assent with which readers purchase their entertainment from this story is paid for by a sacrifice of ethical values that many of them would not willingly spend if they were thinking critically—and ethically—about what they were reading. I cannot desire for any first-time reader of this story to approach it antagonistically, but once the story is read, reflection will show (or so goes my thesis) that "The Catbird Seat" disguises with highly polished comic art an invitation for all readers to feel contempt for women both as women and as human beings. Misogyny, in my view, constitutes the ethical vision—or, if you like, the *un*ethical vision—that saturates "The Catbird Seat." The critique I offer here about "The Catbird Seat" is designed to show how negative ethical criticism can work responsibly and intellectually without getting shrill and sanctimonious. My analysis merely shows *that*—and *how*—objectionable and damaging ethical invitations may be disguised as brilliant strokes of art. But, first, the story.

THE CATBIRD SEAT

by James Thurber

1. Mr. Martin bought the pack of Camels on Monday night in the most crowded cigar store on Broadway. It was theater time and seven or eight men were buying cigarettes. The clerk didn't even glance at Mr. Martin, who put the pack in his overcoat pocket and went out. If any of the staff at F & S had seen him buy the cigarettes, they would have been astonished, for it was generally known that Mr. Martin did not smoke, and never had. No one saw him.

2. It was just a week to the day since Mr. Martin had decided to rub out Mrs. Ulgine Barrows. The term "rub out" pleased him because it suggested nothing more than the correction of an error—in this case an error of Mr. Fitweiler. Mr. Martin had spent each night of the past week working out his plan and examining it. As he walked home now he went over it again. For the hundredth time he resented the element of imprecision, the margin of guesswork that entered into the business. The project as he had worked it out was casual and bold, the risks were considerable. Something might go wrong anywhere along the line. And therein lay the cunning of his scheme. No one would ever see in it the cautious, painstaking hand of Erwin Martin, head of the filing depart at F & S, of whom Mr. Fitweiler had once said, "Man is fallible but Martin isn't." No one would see his hand, that is, unless it were caught in the act.

3. Sitting in his apartment, drinking a glass of milk, Mr. Martin reviewed his case against Mrs. Ulgine Barrows, as he had every night for seven nights. He began at the beginning. Her quacking voice and braying laugh had first profaned the halls of F & S on March 7, 1941 (Mr. Martin had a head for dates). Old Roberts, the personnel chief, had introduced her as the newly appointed special adviser to the president of the firm, Mr. Fitweiler. The woman had appalled Mr. Martin instantly, but he hadn't shown it. He had given her his dry hand, a look of studious concentration, and a faint smile. "Well," she had said, looking at the papers on his desk, "are you lifting the oxcart out of the ditch?" As Mr. Martin recalled that moment, over his milk, he squirmed slightly. He must keep his mind on her crimes as a special adviser, not on her peccadilloes as a personality. This he found difficult to do, in spite of entering an objection and sustaining it. The faults of the woman as a woman kept chattering on in his mind like an unruly witness. She had, for almost two years now, baited him. In the halls, in the elevator, even in his own office, into which she romped now and then like a circus horse, she was constantly shouting these silly questions at him. "Are you lifting the oxcart out of the ditch? Are you tearing up the pea patch? Are you hollering down the rain barrel? Are you scraping around the bottom of the pickle barrel? Are you sitting in the catbird seat?"

4. It was Joey Hart, one of Mr. Martin's two assistants, who had explained what the gibberish meant. "She must be a Dodger fan," he had said. "Red Barber announces the Dodger games over the radio and he uses those expressions—picked 'em up down South." Joey had gone on to explain one or two. "Tearing up the pea patch" meant going on a rampage; "sitting in the catbird seat" meant sitting pretty, like a batter with three balls and no strikes on him. Mr. Martin dismissed all this with an effort. It had been annoying, it had driven him near to distraction, but he was too solid a man to be moved to murder by anything so childish. It was fortunate, he reflected as he passed on to the important charges against Mrs. Barrows, that he had stood up under it so well. He had maintained always an outward appearance of polite tolerance. "Why, I believe you like the woman," Miss Paird, his other assistant, had once said to him. He had simply smiled.

5. A gavel rapped in Mr. Martin's mind and the case proper was resumed. Mrs. Ulgine Barrows stood charged with willful, blatant, and

persistent attempts to destroy the efficiency and system of F & S. It was competent, material, and relevant to review her advent and rise to power. Mr. Martin had got the story from Miss Paird, who seemed always able to find things out. According to her, Mrs. Barrows had met Mr. Fitweiler at a party, where she had rescued him from the embraces of a powerfully built drunken man who had mistaken the president of F & S for a famous retired Middle Western football coach. She had led him to a sofa and somehow worked upon him a monstrous magic. The aging gentleman had jumped to the conclusion there and then that this was a woman of singular attainments, equipped to bring out the best in him and in the firm. A week later he had introduced her into F & S as his special adviser. On that day confusion got its foot in the door. After Miss Tyson, Mr. Brundage, and Mr. Bartlett had been fired and Mr. Munson had taken his hat and stalked out, mailing in his resignation later, old Roberts had been emboldened to speak to Mr. Fitweiler. He mentioned that Mr. Munson's department had been "a little disrupted" and hadn't they perhaps better resume the old system there? Mr. Fitweiler had said certainly not. He had the greatest faith in Mrs. Barrows's ideas. "They require a little seasoning, a little seasoning, is all," he had added. Mr. Roberts had given it up. Mr. Martin reviewed in detail all the changes wrought by Mrs. Barrows. She had begun chipping at the cornices of the firm's edifice and now she was swinging at the foundation stones with a pickaxe.

6. Mr. Martin came now, in his summing up, to the afternoon of Monday, November 2, 1942—just one week ago. On that day, at 3 P.M., Mrs. Barrows had bounced into his office. "Boo!" she had yelled. "Are you scraping around the bottom of the pickle barrel?" Mr. Martin had looked at her from under his green eyeshade, saying nothing. She had begun to wander about the office, taking it in with her great, popping eyes. "Do you really need *all* these filing cabinets?" she had demanded suddenly. Mr. Martin's heart had jumped. "Each of these files," he had said, keeping his voice even, "plays an indispensable part in the system of F & S." She had brayed at him, "Well, don't tear up the pea patch!" and gone to the door. From there she had bawled, "But you sure have got a lot of fine scrap in here!" Mr. Martin could no longer doubt that the finger was on his beloved department. Her pickaxe was on the upswing, poised for the first blow. It had not come yet; he had received no blue memo from the enchanted Mr. Fitweiler bearing nonsensical instructions deriving

from the obscene woman. But there was no doubt in Mr. Martin's mind that one would be forthcoming. He must act quickly. Already a precious week had gone by. Mr. Martin stood up in his living room, still holding his milk glass. "Gentlemen of the jury," he said to himself, "I demand the death penalty for this horrible person."

7. The next day Mr. Martin followed his routine, as usual. He polished his glasses more often and once sharpened an already sharp pencil, but not even Miss Paird noticed. Only once did he catch sight of his victim; she swept past him in the hall with a patronizing "Hi!" At five-thirty he walked home, as usual, and had a glass of milk, as usual. He had never drunk anything stronger in his life—unless you could count ginger ale. The late Sam Schlosser, the S of F & S, had praised Mr. Martin at a staff meeting several years before for his temperate habits. "Our most efficient worker neither drinks nor smokes," he had said. "The results speak for themselves." Mr. Fitweiler had sat by, nodding approval.

8. Mr. Martin was still thinking about that red-letter day as he walked over to the Schrafft's on Fifth Avenue near Forty-sixth Street. He got there, as he always did, at eight o'clock. He finished his dinner and the financial page of the *Sun* at a quarter to nine, as he always did. It was his custom after dinner to take a walk. This time he walked down Fifth Avenue at a casual pace. His gloved hands felt moist and warm, his forehead cold. He transferred the Camels from his overcoat to a jacket pocket. He wondered, as he did so, if they did not represent an unnecessary note of strain. Mrs. Barrows smoked only Luckies. It was his idea to puff a few puffs on a Camel (after the rubbing-out), stub it out in the ashtray holding her lipstick-stained Luckies, and thus drag a small red herring across the trail. Perhaps it was not a good idea. It would take time. He might even choke, too loudly.

9. Mr. Martin had never seen the house on West Twelfth Street where Mrs. Barrows lived, but he had a clear enough picture of it. Fortunately, she had bragged to everybody about her ducky first-floor apartment in the perfectly darling three-story red-brick. There would be no doorman or other attendants; just the tenants of the second and third floors. As he walked along, Mr. Martin realized that he would get there before nine-thirty. He had considered walking north on Fifth Avenue from Schrafft's to a point from which it would take him until ten o'clock

to reach the house. At that hour people were less likely to be coming in or going out. But the procedure would have made an awkward loop in the straight thread of his casualness, and he had abandoned it. It was impossible to figure when people would be entering or leaving the house, anyway. There was a great risk at any hour. If he ran into anybody, he would simply have to place the rubbing-out of Ulgine Barrows in the inactive file forever. The same thing would hold true if there were someone in her apartment. In that case he would just say that he had been passing by, recognized her charming house and thought to drop in.

10. It was eighteen minutes after nine when Mr. Martin turned into Twelfth Street. A man passed him, and a man and a woman talking. There was no one within fifty paces when he came to the house, halfway down the block. He was up the steps and in the small vestibule in no time, pressing the bell under the card that said "Mrs. Ulgine Barrows." When the clicking in the lock started, he jumped forward against the door. He got inside fast, closing the door behind him. A bulb in a lantern hung from the hall ceiling on a chain seemed to give a monstrously bright light. There was nobody on the stair, which went up ahead of him along the left wall. A door opened down the hall in the wall on the right. He went toward it swiftly, on tiptoe.

11. "Well, for God's sake, look who's here!" bawled Mrs. Barrows, and her braying laugh rang out like the report of a shotgun. He rushed past her like a football tackle, bumping her. "Hey, quit shoving!" she said, closing the door behind them. They were in her living room, which seemed to Mr. Martin to be lighted by a hundred lamps. "What's after you?" she said. "You're as jumpy as a goat." He found he was unable to speak. His heart was wheezing in his throat. "I—yes," he finally brought out. She was jabbering and laughing as she started to help him off with his coat. "No, no," he said, "I'll put it here." He took it off and put it on a chair near the door. "Your hat and gloves, too," she said. "You're in a lady's house." He put his hat on top of the coat. Mrs. Barrows seemed larger than he had thought. He kept his gloves on. "I was passing by," he said. "I recognized—is there anyone here?" She laughed louder than ever. "No," she said, "we're all alone. You're as white as a sheet, you funny man. Whatever *has* come over you? I'll mix you a toddy." She started toward a door across the room. "Scotch-and-soda be all right? But say,

you don't drink, do you?" She turned and gave him her amused look. Mr. Martin pulled himself together. "Scotch-and-soda will be all right," he heard himself say. He could hear her laughing in the kitchen.

12. Mr. Martin looked quickly around the living room for the weapon. He had counted on finding one there. There were andirons and a poker and something in a corner that looked like an Indian club. None of them would do. It couldn't be that way. He began to pace around. He came to a desk. On it lay a metal paper knife with an ornate handle. Would it be sharp enough? He reached for it and knocked over a small brass jar. Stamps spilled out of it and it fell to the floor with a clatter. "Hey," Mrs. Barrows yelled from the kitchen, "are you tearing up the pea patch?" Mr. Martin gave a strange laugh. Picking up the knife, he tried its point against his left wrist. It was blunt. It wouldn't do.

13. When Mrs. Barrows reappeared, carrying two highballs, Mr. Martin, standing there with his gloves on, became acutely conscious of the fantasy he had wrought. Cigarettes in his pocket, a drink prepared for him—it was all too grossly improbable. It was more than that; it was impossible. Somewhere in the back of his mind a vague idea stirred, sprouted. "For heaven's sake, take off those gloves," said Mrs. Barrows. "I always wear them in the house," said Mr. Martin. The idea began to bloom, strange and wonderful. She put the glasses on a coffee table in front of a sofa and sat on the sofa. "Come over here, you odd little man," she said. Mr. Martin went over and sat beside her. It was difficult getting a cigarette out of the pack of Camels, but he managed it. She held a match for him, laughing. "Well," she said, handing him his drink, "this is perfectly marvelous. You with a drink and a cigarette."

14. Mr. Martin puffed, not too awkwardly, and took a gulp of the highball. "I drink and smoke all the time," he said. He clinked his glass against hers. "Here's nuts to that old windbag, Fitweiler," he said, and gulped again. The stuff tasted awful, but he made no grimace. "Really, Mr. Martin," she said, her voice and posture changing, "you are insulting our employer." Mrs. Barrows was now all special adviser to the president. "I am preparing a bomb," said Mr. Martin, "which will blow the old goat higher than hell." He had only had a little of the drink, which was not strong. It couldn't be that. "Do you take dope or something?" Mrs. Barrows asked coldly. "Heroin," said Mr. Martin. "I'll be coked to the gills

when I bump that old buzzard off." "Mr. Martin!" she shouted, getting to her feet. "That will be all of that. You must go at once." Mr. Martin took another swallow of his drink. He tapped his cigarette out in the ashtray and put the pack of Camels on the coffee table. Then he got up. She stood glaring at him. He walked over and put on his hat and coat. "Not a word about this," he said, and laid an index finger against his lips. All Mrs. Barrows could bring out was "Really!" Mr. Martin put his hand on the doorknob. "I'm sitting in the catbird seat," he said. He stuck his tongue out at her and left. Nobody saw him go.

15. Mr. Martin got to his apartment, walking, well before eleven. No one saw him go in. He had two glasses of milk after brushing his teeth, and he felt elated. It wasn't tipsiness, because he hadn't been tipsy. Anyway, the walk had worn off all effects of the whiskey. He got in bed and read a magazine for a while. He was asleep before midnight.

16. Mr. Martin got to the office at eight-thirty the next morning, as usual. At a quarter to nine, Ulgine Barrows, who had never before arrived at work before ten, swept into his office. "I'm reporting to Mr. Fitweiler now!" she shouted. "If he turns you over to the police, it's no more than you deserve!" Mr. Martin gave her a look of shocked surprise. "I beg your pardon?" he said. Mrs. Barrows snorted and bounced out of the room, leaving Miss Paird and Joey Hart staring after her. "What's the matter with that old devil now?" asked Miss Paird. "I have no idea," said Mr. Martin, resuming his work. The other two looked at him and then at each other. Miss Paird got up and went out. She walked slowly past the closed door of Mr. Fitweiler's office. Mrs. Barrows was yelling inside, but she was not braying. Miss Paird could not hear what the woman was saying. She went back to her desk.

17. Forty-five minutes later, Mrs. Barrows left the president's office and went into her own, shutting the door. It wasn't until half an hour later that Mr. Fitweiler sent for Mr. Martin. The head of the filing department, neat, quiet, attentive, stood in front of the old man's desk. Mr. Fitweiler was pale and nervous. He took his glasses off and twiddled them. He made a small, bruffing sound in his throat. "Martin," he said, "you have been with us more than twenty years." "Twenty-two, sir," said Mr. Martin. "In that time," pursued the president, "your work and your—uh—manner have been exemplary." "I trust so, sir," said Mr. Martin. "I

have understood, Martin," said Mr. Fitweiler, "that you have never taken a drink or smoked." "That is correct, sir," said Mr. Martin. "Ah, yes," Mr. Fitweiler polished his glasses. "You may describe what you did after leaving the office yesterday, Martin," he said. Mr. Martin allowed less than a second for his bewildered pause. "Certainly, sir," he said. "I walked home. Then I went to Schrafft's for dinner. Afterward I walked home again. I went to bed early, sir, and read a magazine for a while. I was asleep before eleven." "Ah, yes," said Mr. Fitweiler again. He was silent for a moment, searching for the proper words to say to the head of the filing department. "Mrs. Barrows," he said finally, "Mrs. Barrows has worked hard, Martin, very hard. It grieves me to report that she has suffered a severe breakdown. It has taken the form of a persecution complex accompanied by distressing hallucinations." "I am very sorry, sir," said Mr. Martin. "Mrs. Barrows is under the delusion," continued Mr. Fitweiler, "that you visited her last evening and behaved yourself in an—uh—unseemly manner." He raised his hand to silence Mr. Martin's little pained outcry. "It is the nature of these psychological diseases," Mr. Fitweiler said, "to fix upon the least likely and most innocent party as the—uh—source of persecution. These matters are not for the lay mind to grasp, Martin. I've just had my psychiatrist, Dr. Fitch, on the phone. He would not, of course, commit himself, but he made enough generalizations to substantiate my suspicions. I suggested to Mrs. Barrows when she had completed her—uh—story to me this morning, that she visit Dr. Fitch, for I suspected a condition at once. She flew, I regret to say, into a rage, and demanded—uh—requested that I call you on the carpet. You may not know, Martin, but Mrs. Barrows had planned a reorganization of your department—subject to my approval, of course, subject to my approval. This brought you, rather than anyone else, to her mind—but again that is a phenomenon for Dr. Fitch and not for us. So, Martin, I am afraid Mrs. Barrows's usefulness here is at an end." "I am dreadfully sorry, sir," said Mr. Martin.

18. It was at this point that the door to the office blew open with the suddenness of a gas-main explosion and Mrs. Barrows catapulted through it. "Is the little rat denying it?" she screamed. "He can't get away with that!" Mr. Martin got up and moved discreetly to a point beside Mr. Fitweiler's chair. "You drank and smoked at my apartment," she bawled at Mr. Martin, "and you know it! You called Mr. Fitweiler an old windbag

and said you were going to blow him up when you got coked to the gills on your heroin!" She stopped yelling to catch her breath and a new glint came into her popping eyes. "If you weren't such a drab, ordinary little man," she said, "I'd think you'd planned it all. Sticking your tongue out at me, saying you were sitting in the catbird seat, because you thought no one would believe me when I told it! My God, it's really too perfect!" She brayed loudly and hysterically, and the fury was on her again. She glared at Mr. Fitweiler. "Can't you see how he has tricked us, you old fool? Can't you see his little game?" But Mr. Fitweiler had been surreptitiously pressing all the buttons under the top of his desk and employees of F & S began pouring into the room. "Stockton," said Mr. Fitweiler, "you and Fishbein will take Mrs. Barrows to her home. Mrs. Powell, you will go with them." Stockton, who had played a little football in high school, blocked Mrs. Barrows as she made for Mr. Martin. It took him and Fishbein together to force her out of the door into the hall, crowded with stenographers and office boys. She was still screaming imprecations at Mr. Martin, tangled and contradictory imprecations. The hubbub finally died out down the corridor.

19. "I regret that this has happened," said Mr. Fitweiler. "I shall ask you to dismiss it from your mind, Martin." "Yes, sir," said Mr. Martin, anticipating his chief's "That will be all" by moving to the door. "I will dismiss it." He went out and shut the door, and his step was light and quick in the hall. When he entered his department he had slowed down to his customary gait, and he walked quietly across the room to the W20 file, wearing a look of studious concentration.

The Ethics of Style

Style is the main vehicle of this story's ethical vision. Thurber is deft in his management of plot and narrative technique, but in "The Catbird Seat" he relies mainly on heightened uses of language—his metaphors, descriptions, images, tone, diction, and so on—to shape the reader's likes and dislikes, hopes and gratifications. The whole effect of "The Catbird Seat" turns on the reader's desire for meek Mr. Martin to triumph over the loud, obnoxious, and threatening Mrs. Ulgine Barrows. The story can gratify our desire for Mr. Martin's triumph, obviously, only if we feel sympathy for Mr. Martin and antipathy for Mrs. Barrows. This means that Thurber has given himself the task of showing that each character possesses traits that merit the "right" responses—his desired placement of readers' sympathy or antipathy—that allow the story to work. And Thurber knows exactly how to generate the responses he wants. In a tour de force of brilliant characterization primarily created by stylistic heightenings, Thurber manages to make Mrs. Barrows completely unsympathetic, while adroitly avoiding the attribution of any traits to Mr. Martin that usually compel a reader's admiration or respect.

Mr. Martin is a type: the modern functionary, the bureaucrat in modern government or business whose main and perhaps only interests in life revolve around the minute procedures of his work in a large organization. Never mind that his own role is tiny; it still defines his whole existence. It works for him because his existence is tiny. Mr. Martin has no identity beyond the system he keeps running, and no critical interest in assessing whether that system is good, bad, or improvable. (Perhaps the most brilliant satire on the stupid reverence of system-as-system is Dickens's inspired excoriation of the Circumlocution Office in *Little Dorrit,* that bureau of government that has completely mastered the science of "how not to do it.") The functionary bureaucrat is often satirized but seldom used as a conventional fictional hero, yet Thurber manages brilliantly to make Mr. Martin seem sympathetic and courageous: he takes a major risk and triumphs utterly. How does Thurber manage to gratify us with his triumph?

He manages this feat by pitting Mr. Martin against an antagonist whom he represents as so extraordinarily obnoxious in every respect that readers are willing, presumably, to sympathize with *anyone* who opposes her. Thurber knows that everyone is attracted by an oddity, and Thurber shows Mr. Martin "opposing" Mrs. Barrows by plotting her murder, a mode of opposition that piques our interest because of the odd discrepancy between the violence of the act, the ostensible meekness of Mr. Martin's bureaucratic exterior, and the interior passion with which he decides he must "rub out" Mrs. Barrows in order to protect the filing system of F & S. Plotting to murder someone whose only crime is being obnoxious is not a surefire way to purchase readerly sympathy, however, unless the obnoxious victim is obnoxious in some particularly heinous way that persuades us, somehow, that she *merits* being whacked.

The story's "somehow," its means of persuasion, lies in its linguistic heightenings, and these make clear what heinous crimes Mrs. Ulgine Barrows is guilty of. *She is guilty of not being a human being, she is guilty of being bestial, and, most of all, she is guilty of being an "uppity" woman in a man's world.* Mrs. Barrows is—gasp—*unfeminine,* a threat to men and their precious systems. Her being unfeminine is part and parcel of her being threatening. In the first place, Mrs. Barrows's name is itself a condemnation, a brilliant stylistic stroke on Thurber's part. It is impossible to say "Ulgine"—and it is especially impossible to read it on the page—without seeing and feeling the anagram-like reference to "ugly." Having planted the notion of the character's ugliness by means of her name, Thurber then gives her a surname that turns her into a pig.

In the swine world, a "barrow" is a castrated boar. Using "barrow" to insult a "masculine" woman is an allusion that undoubtedly sails past many of today's readers completely unnoticed. Most contemporary urban readers' knowledge of pigs comes from *Charlotte's Web* or from plastic-wrapped packages of pork in supermarkets. "Barrow," however, is a deliberate sneer from Thurber, who went to an agricultural university, Ohio State, in the early years of the twentieth century and whose general audience in that day would have much more readily recognized agricultural allusions than any general audience today. Thus in one brilliant stylistic hit, Thurber robs Mrs. Barrows not only of her humanity but of her sex as well.[2] She's not a woman, but she's not a man either. She's an unnatural monster. As an ugly pig, Mrs. Barrows is not even an ugly *female* pig, a sow. Instead, she is a boar without the anatomical equipment that defines a boar. Thus, before we know anything else about her conduct, opinions, or character, Mrs. Ulgine Barrows stands before the reader saturated in the unpleasant associations of her name.

But "ugly castrated boar" is just the beginning. The stylistic assault continues. Thurber's descriptions of Mrs. Barrows continue to focus brilliantly, relentlessly, and maliciously on collapsing the boundaries between her human nature and animal nature. Mrs. Barrows is also portrayed as a duck and an ass—"her quacking voice and braying laugh" (¶3)—as well as a horse, a cow, a donkey, and a frog: "even in [Mr. Martin's] own office,

into which she romped now and then like a circus horse" (¶3); "Mrs. Barrows snorted and bounced out of the room" (¶16); "'Well, for God's sake,
look who's here!' *bawled* Mrs. Barrows, and her *braying* laugh rang out
like the report of a shotgun" (¶11; emphasis added); and two references to
the frog-like appearance of Mrs. Barrows's "great popping eyes" (¶6).

All in all, Thurber's style bestializes Mrs. Barrows so thoroughly and
dramatically that it is nearly impossible to see her as a human being. Represented as a series of obnoxious animals, Mrs. Barrows deserves only
our contempt. Besides being bestial, Mrs. Barrows is also a destroyer, one
who wields a crude, male tool: "She had begun by chipping at the cornices
of the firm's edifice and now she was swinging at the foundation stones
with a pickaxe. . . . Mr. Martin could no longer doubt that the finger was
on his beloved department. Her pickaxe was on the upswing, poised for
the first blow" (¶5–6). This is brilliant stuff. It has worked on generations
of readers who for more than sixty years have hated the horsy, donkey-
like, piggy, froggy, ugly, castrated Mrs. Barrows, and who have rooted for
meek-and-mild Mr. Martin to put her in her place, to triumph over her
so completely that she will never again emerge as a threat.

The Story's (Un)Ethical Vision

But what ethical vision informs Thurber's artistic brilliance, and what
are my justifications for calling it mean-spirited? Am I committing the
besetting crime of so much bad ethical criticism of the past? Am I being
dour, puritanical, and humorless, denouncing as immoral what I don't
like and then trying to position my prejudices beyond reproach by labeling my criticisms as "morally sensitive"? Doesn't Thurber have as
much right as other authors to satirize any target of his choice—and of
any gender—among the world's vast array of obnoxious people? Chaucer pokes fun at the Wife of Bath and is praised for it. Charles Dickens
and Jane Austen are praised for poking fun at Sairy Gamp and Lady
Catherine de Bourgh, so why should Thurber be condemned by me for
belittling Mrs. Barrows? The problem cannot be that Mrs. Barrows is
a woman and Thurber is a man. Everyone knows that in both life and
literature some women *are* as obnoxious as some men, so the claim that

Thurber's picking on a woman is an ethical failure on his part because men should never satirize an obnoxious woman would be illogical.

The problem with Thurber's treatment of Mrs. Barrows is not that he stands chivalry on its head, but that he ridicules Mrs. Barrows's character not by portraying an obnoxious character who happens to be a woman, but by relying on ready-made anti-woman stereotypes as the grounds of his criticism. He doesn't work to *earn* our antipathy. Instead, he draws brilliantly but with intellectual laziness and ethical malice on many centuries of standing antipathy toward "uppity" women. Thurber does not satirize the stereotypes he employs—he exploits them—and by exploiting them reinforces their credibility. In doing so, Thurber's ethical vision in "The Catbird Seat" invites readers to feel contempt not just for Mrs. Barrows, but for all women who are strong enough and driven enough to be called "uppity" by those who want all women to meet traditional expectations of subservience.

Chaucer's satirical portrayal of the Wife of Bath, unlike Thurber's portrayal of Mrs. Barrows, is not anti-woman as such. The Wife of Bath's lust for sex and life is portrayed as a broadly human appetite, and Chaucer does not criticize the Wife's sex games because he thinks that women are not allowed to play the same sex games that men play; he criticizes her sex games because she is as dishonest and manipulative as men in the way she plays them. Dickens's ridicule of Sairy Gamp is based primarily not on her gender failings, but on her human failings: her self-rationalizations, her self-indulgence, her self-serving dramatizations. Austen doesn't invite us to despise Lady Catherine because she is a woman but because of her broadly human ethical failings: she is proud, unfeeling, cold, selfish, and egotistical. That these portraits of ridicule happen to be portraits of women does not constitute an invitation on Chaucer's or Dickens's or Austen's part to conclude that all women share the vices of these particular characters, or, to put it the other way 'round, they are not invitations to feel that these characters have their particular vices merely because they are women.

But this *is* precisely the kind of invitation that Thurber makes to his readers about Ulgine Barrows. It is a highly telling moment in "The Catbird Seat," for example, when Mr. Martin observes that "the faults of the woman *as a woman* kept chattering on in his mind like an unruly witness" (¶3; emphasis added). Part of the (un)ethical vision of this story, in other words, is that Mrs. Barrows's sins are not sins because people in general are wrong when they are loud, aggressive, and opinionated, but because *women* in particular are wrong when *they* are loud, aggressive, and opinionated (especially in the company of men).

This story's ethical vision says that Thurber's characterization of Mrs. Barrows as a beast of company confusion and personal aggressiveness is funny *if and only if*—and it leads readers to desire her punishment *if and only if*—we accept the story's implicit invitation to believe that women *as women* should never behave like Mrs. Barrows, and that when they do act like Mrs. Barrows, they deserve to be put in their place, their place being, of course, outside a man's world. Simply put, Thurber's ethical vision in this story invites us to accept the view that unfeminine, unsubmissive women deserve to be punished. In relation to such women, it is ethically excusable for men to manipulate them, lie to them, and harm them. At the very least such women deserve public humiliation.

What Thurber takes for granted and—especially important for my inquiry here—what he invites *the reader* to take for granted as a plausible description of what a woman looks and sounds like when she is behaving badly draws on a long history of destructive, anti-woman stereotypes. Thurber goes for laughs at Mrs. Barrows's expense by relying on the same kinds of stereotypes that a homophobic author might employ to ridicule a gay man by portraying him as effeminate, or the way a racist author might ridicule a black man by portraying him as a Step 'n' Fetchit. No one who aspires to any responsible level of intellectual thoughtfulness or ethical sensitivity excuses anti-gay or Step 'n' Fetchit portrayals on the grounds that they are "mere entertainment," yet generations of high school and college students have been encouraged to assent to the stereotypical contempt that Thurber heaps on Mrs. Barrows because the story is "so entertaining." Thurber does not really show his readers that Mrs. Barrows behaves badly as a *person*, only that she does not behave the way Mr. Martin, James Thurber, and, presumably, other right-thinking persons think *women* ought to behave.

The difference between Thurber's use of stereotypes and the stereotypes of more thoughtful authors can be seen by comparing Thurber's

simplistic demonization of Mrs. Barrows to the complexly dehuman-
ized and at the same time complexly humanized portrait of Shylock in
The Merchant of Venice. Even Shylock, one of the most maligned characters in literature, is given several moments of genuine humanity in
Shakespeare's play, culminating, of course, in the "Doth not a Jew bleed"
speech (III, i). But Thurber's ethical imagination is not so generous as
Shakespeare's, nor is his artistic vision sufficiently keen to see defining
particularities. Shakespeare draws on anti-Jew stereotypes, but still sees
the man inside the stereotype. Thurber, however, is so eager to see an aggressive and threatening woman humiliated that he gives Mrs. Barrows
not one moment of genuine humanity, not one shred of identity apart
from the stereotypes out of which he conjures the witch. The game is
fixed against Mrs. Barrows from the story's first word through its last.

That Mrs. Barrows is a study in stereotypes can be tested by imagining how the story would be changed if Mrs. Barrows were *Mr.* Barrows.
A male version of Mrs. Barrows would stand a much better chance of
not being despised *merely* because he is obnoxious. Our culture *allows*
powerful men to be obnoxious. If a Mr. Barrows were found contemptible, he would be judged this way because *people* with these traits are
contemptible, and the competition between *Mr.* Barrows and Mr. Martin
would be about power only, not about "perverted" (castrated) feminin-
ity. If his rival were male, Mr. Martin's underhanded lying and scheming
would tell against *his* character, not against his opponent's character. If
Mr. Martin's rival were *Mr.* Barrows, the joke would then consist of Mr.
Martin's revealing himself to be a lying little sneak. He is triumphant in
his scheming and lying only because Thurber's ethical vision invites us
to take for granted that it is permissible to use scheming and lying—not
to mention character assassination—if that's what it takes to punish an
overreaching woman. Nothing in the story suggests that Thurber has
anything but complacent confidence that his readers will overwhelmingly agree with his misogynistic, mean, belittling joke. It would be
humiliating for Mr. Martin to have to revise his beloved filing system
because he lost a battle for influence to a *Mr.* Barrows, but it would be
doubly humiliating for him to lose to *Mrs.* Barrows, an aggressive and
forceful woman. But Thurber is there to protect Mr. Martin from Mrs.
Barrows, as well as to reclaim Mr. Fitweiler from the "monstrous magic"

that has misled him, and to direct the reader's antipathies against Mrs. Barrows—and any other woman—who might make the mistake of acting as if she knows more than men.

I wish to conclude by discussing the vexed question of how to apply ethical criteria to aesthetic choices. I am particularly interested in how to assess formal brilliance in relation to ethical obtuseness. In the course of my conclusion, I will refer to such artistic features of Thurber's story as narrative technique and plot. Given what I have just said about "The Catbird Seat," you can see that an important question has been raised about narratives in general: *Is it still possible to admire the formal features of a work of art even if it is precisely these formal features that make its questionable ethical vision seem compelling?* If "The Catbird Seat" invites us to feel hostility and contempt not only for Mrs. Barrows but for aggressive and forceful women in general, how do we judge those brilliant strokes of narrative technique, style, and plot that make the invitation to contempt seem compelling?

One answer to this question says that art is one thing and morality is another, but this response is facile. To say that we must evaluate the art of "The Catbird Seat" exclusively on artistic grounds puts us in the curiously illogical and indefensible position of saying something like this: bigotry may be condemnable, but if the strategies by which bigotry gets advanced are brilliant art, then we may still condemn the bigotry but not the art. Karen Hanson, a philosopher analyzing Hume's views on taste, agrees with me in objecting to this sophistical argument.

> In identifying bigotry and superstition as the spoilers of art, [Hume] effects a point of contact with those of us who are attracted to the case for the moral evaluation of art, but who grant the excellence of some art whose morality we deplore. For bigotry and superstition, as Hume understands them, are exactly the opposite of cogent thought and genuine deliberation. Thus, art marked by bigotry and superstition is art deprived, to that extent, of power and grace. This is not to deny that bigotry and superstition can be powerfully conveyed and inculcated by means of art. It is to insist that *bigotry in art, patently weak thought, and intellectual confusion count as artistic, as aesthetic, flaws.* The work is, as art, worse for their presence, and we should find

unredeemed displeasure in the surfacing of these defects. ("How Bad
Can Good Art Be?" 221; emphasis added)

If you discovered that I were slipping poison into your dinner every
night, you would not only view the raw act itself as condemnable, but you
would be especially horrified by any special skills I might possess—social,
rhetorical, stylistic, presentational, representational, and so on—to make
you *want* the poisoned food. You would judge that the more skill I em-
ployed in making you want my poison, the guiltier I would be. Or, to use
a much more common example (I am thinking of anti-Semitic websites),
if I were a vicious anti-Semite who knew how to cloak my anti-Semitism
in educated language, if I knew how to use seemingly relevant historical
examples and anecdotes, and how to make myself *seem* reasonable and
thoughtful rather than bigoted or pathological, am I more or less dangerous than the anti-Semitic bigot who screams at you with insane eyes and
spews spit from his mouth? If I am James Thurber, can I get high marks
for the "art" of my sophisticated misogynistic bigotry?

It is not a satisfactory solution to the problem of art and ethical vision in "The Catbird Seat," or any other story, to give Thurber an A for
art and an F for ethical vision. As James Woods says, "the reality of fiction must also draw its power from the reality of the world. The real,
in fiction, is always a matter of belief" (xiii). And if Thurber makes me
believe, or reinforces an uncritical prejudice I already hold, namely, that
"unfeminine" women are contemptible both as women and as human
beings, then he has foisted on me and reinforced for the rest of the world
a belief that makes our world a worse place than it has to be, and that
makes me a worse person than I should be.

Thus I cannot exculpate Thurber for being good at the art of a story
whose high artistic polish invites us to desire the punishment of "unfeminine" women. I note, for example, the skill with which Thurber constructs his plot. The movement begins with initial instabilities on two
fronts: instabilities in the company of F & S introduced by Mrs. Barrows
and instabilities in the discrepancy between Mr. Martin's meek demeanor
and his intention to commit homicide. These instabilities are complicated
by Mr. Martin's realization in Mrs. Barrows's apartment that he cannot
possibly commit murder by means of physical violence (it is interesting

to note also that his change of mind is *not* a change of heart). I acknowledge the skill with which these instabilities are brought to a swift climax
by Mr. Martin's realization that he may be able to defeat Mrs. Barrows not
by killing her body but by assassinating her character and, by lying, to
completely humiliate and discredit her. I note that while the *moment* of
this climactic realization is made known to the reader, the actual *content*
of the plan is not revealed, thus creating a forward thrust of desire on the
reader's part to see the actual nature of Mr. Martin's plan. And I admire
the skill with which the plot is resolved as Mrs. Barrows is punished and
Mr. Martin rewarded.

I note all this skill, all this art, and I admire the technical proficiency
of the artist, but in the end my approval of the art of the story is under-
mined by my realization that to yield to this art is to yield to the misogynistic message unfolding inside it. In everyday life the influence of one
story will be diluted by the influence of other stories. On the other hand,
there is a major river of anti-woman stories running like a poisonous
current through many of the world's dominant cultures, and it is clear
that Thurber is doing what he can to swell this current by throwing his
widow's mite of misogyny into the flow. He and his story deserve to be
called to account because both its ethical and its political effects are potentially malicious.

Ethical discourse is not the only kind of critical discourse we should
engage in, however, nor are its judgments final. As readers speak up who
might think that I am unfair to Thurber and "The Catbird Seat," a conversation ensues in which both they and I might learn something. The only
thing I will insist on is crediting ethical criticism for opening up space
within critical discourse where we can discuss how consumers are influenced by stories as they make choices that determine the way they live.

The same may be said of other works as well. The moral and ethical
difficulties in *The Merchant of Venice* do not go away because Shakespeare is a great artist. In a work of art the aesthetic components of which
are as skillfully kneaded together as they are in "The Catbird Seat"—or in
The Merchant of Venice or in thousands of other stories in many different
forms—art and ethical vision are inseparable. The ethical vision and the
aesthetic strategies unfold inside each other; they do not speak to each

other in muted tones across a broad field. As M. H. Abrams says, with regard to any work of literature that really "works,"

> Our appreciation of the matters it presents is not aloofly contemplative, but actively engaged. We are not disinterested, but deeply concerned with the characters and what they say and do, and we are interested in a fashion that brings into play our entire moral economy and expresses itself continuously in attitudes of approval or disapproval, sympathy or antipathy. And though the poet is not concerned to persuade us to take positions outside the poem, it is his constant concern to persuade us to concur with the common-sense and moral positions presupposed by the poem. . . . The skillful poet contrives which of our beliefs will be called into play, to what degree, and with what emotional effect. (17)

It remains an indefensible position, then, to argue that representational art should be evaluated *exclusively* in artistic and technical terms. This view is often used as a shield by writers, movie directors, TV executives, and song lyricists who find it too complicated, irksome, or costly to think about the invitations to belief, feeling, and judgment buried in the powerful invitations of their art. In the end, however, this view remains merely an ethical evasion, not an ethical vision.

CHAPTER NINE

ぴふらメをみ

Ethical Engagements Over Time

Reading and Rereading

David Copperfield *and* Wuthering Heights

In chapters 7 and 8, respectively, I have shown how up-close and detailed ethical criticism can yield both positive and negative judgments. In this chapter I show how up-close and detailed ethical analysis can yield mixed judgments based on an account of how an auditor's perceptions of an artwork can change over time. The contents of this chapter also develop the thread of argument introduced in previous chapters, namely, that issues raised by ethical criticism are often profoundly personal. In this chapter I demonstrate that the personal influence stories sometimes exert on ethos is not limited to whatever effects end when the story ends, but are sometimes effects that change every time the story is revisited. Given that the development of an ethos is organic, not mechanistic, it may be the case that while a given story can exert a *persistent* influence on us, it may not always exert the *same* influence, especially over long periods of time.

How each of us learns from narratives that we encounter many times over many years is a complicated process, one worthy of its own narrative. In what follows, I will explore as case studies my ongoing ethical engagement with two narratives, Charles Dickens's *David Copperfield* and Emily Brontë's *Wuthering Heights*. My claim is not that all readers will or should respond to these stories as I have done, but that my experience offers one version of a more general phenomenon with stories that I believe other story lovers will recognize. One's ongoing interactions with a given story are certainly not a once-and-for-all thing like a brass casting.[1] Ongoing interactions with any narrative may mean that an auditor is, at one point in time, especially open to the story's ethical vision, but that at other points in time he or she may be especially susceptible to misreading that vision or seeing it through a glass darkly. My story illustrates several facets of this general phenomenon, and more.

Ethical Vision in *David Copperfield* and Its Usefulness to Me

Many of Dickens's most passionate readers first discovered him when they were children, but I did not. My personal relationship with *David Copperfield* began when I discovered Dickens's novels as a twenty-four-year-old graduate student at the University of Chicago. In a bright Chicago autumn in a class taught by the great scholar Morton Dauwen Zabel, I discovered the banquet table of Dickens's novels, and I devoured one after another as rapidly as I could. I strode around my tiny married-student apartment reading to the walls the speeches from different characters, laughing my head off at Vincent Crummles's story of the circus pony in *Nicholas Nickleby*, whose mother, says Crummles, "ate apple-pie at a circus for upwards of fourteen years, and went to bed in a nightcap; and, in short, took the low comedy entirely" (286); was brought nearly to tears in *Little Dorrit* over the sadness of Arthur Clennam's childhood, which Clennam remembers as "a legion of Sundays, all days of unserviceable bitterness and mortification, slowly passing before him" (30); or raged bitterly with Dickens against the callous neglect of the poor as the narrator of *Bleak House* responds to Jo's death with his thunderous denunciation, "Dead, your Majesty. Dead, my lords and gentlemen. Dead, Right Reverends and Wrong Reverends of every order. Dead, men and women, born with Heavenly compassion in your hearts. And dying thus around us every day" (649).

I can just hear the disapproval of some of my readers. "Laughter and tears? How gauche! How naïve! How unprofessional!" Yes, these responses are all gauche, naïve, and unprofessional. I plead guilty on all counts. But I also remain unrepentant on all counts. My responses were naïve and unprofessional because they were not responses I cooked up for the sake of looking good in Zabel's class or for the sake of teaching my own Dickens classes later. (As for having responses that I might later publish in a book, I would at that time have considered this possibility no more likely than writing the Great American Novel on the back of a napkin.) My responses, naïve and raw, came directly from the heart of Dickens's ethical visions to my own heart, which was intensely hungry for an ethical vision of life more generous, compassionate, humane, thoughtful, connected, and nourishing than the ethical vision of Protestant fundamentalism and parental meanness foisted on me in my childhood.

Since my discovery of Dickens's novels during that bright autumn of my graduate school years, the components of Dickens's ethical vision have woven themselves like living threads into the warp and woof of my life. They form an active part of my personal history. The Dickens novel that has had the greatest effect on me is *David Copperfield*, at the heart of which lies an ethical vision of nurturing versus destructive relations between children and adults: an ethical vision of how some kinds of child/adult relations create the foundations for human flourishing, and how other kinds of child/adult relations create weakness, self-absorption, self-loathing, and stymied development.

When I first read *David Copperfield*, I especially vibrated in sympathy to the way the history of my own young life mirrored the history of Davy's young life, primarily because my own father shared many features of character with Mr. Murdstone. My own Murdstone father was my biological father, not my stepfather. Like Mr. Murdstone, he was egotistical, tyrannical, and rigid and had a short fuse that could explode into sudden violence, mostly directed at me and nearly always delivered behind the mask of self-righteous, pious, Murdstonean ideologies like "spare the rod and spoil the child," and "discipline is good for the soul," and (the most infuriating piety of all) "this hurts me worse than it hurts you."[2] David Copperfield's description of the character assumed by both his new stepfather and his odious sister, Miss Murdstone, also fits my own father:

> Firmness, I may observe, was the grand quality on which both Mrs. and Miss Murdstone took their stand. However I might have expressed my comprehension of it at that time, if I had been called

upon, I nevertheless did clearly comprehend in my own way, that it was another name for tyranny; and for a certain gloomy, arrogant, devil's humor, that was in them both. The creed . . . was this. Mr. Murdstone was firm; nobody in his world was to be as firm as Mr. Murdstone; nobody else in his world was to be firm at all, for everybody was to be bent to his firmness. (49)

It was also that case that my own mother, like Davy's, was fearful, weak, easily dominated, and weepily ineffectual—a world-class expert at living in withdrawal and denial—and thus offered me no protection from my Murdstone father. At the age of twenty-four, when I first read *David Copperfield,* I had not processed—indeed, I was still at that time unable even to see—the bruising dynamics of having been raised in a family of highlight-reel dysfunctionality, but you can imagine how sympathetically I responded to Davy's childhood sufferings. I never bit the hand that caned me, but even though I was in my twenties when I first encountered this scene in *David Copperfield*, I received a major jolt of vicarious pleasure in the payback.

The value of such vicarious experience, however, surely lies not in the enjoyment of petty paybacks. If the value of reading about Davy biting Murdstone were merely vicarious payback, I'm sure that I would have soon outgrown the novel. The *value* of this narrative experience for me, and, presumably, for others, lies not in its cementing of petty emotions, but in its ethical invitation to deepen my understanding of both my past and my present, and thus to acquire a different ethos from the person I would have been as merely the victim of that past. Even at the unreflective age of twenty-four, I could see more clearly in Davy's life than I could see in my own life certain consequences of having been raised under tyranny, namely, the way a tyrannized child tends to respond both too uncritically and too eagerly for his own good to any crumb of support and sympathy from an outside source, as Davy responds too eagerly and loyally to Steerforth's careless and manly but elegant attentions.[3] I could see in Davy's case that the no-nonsense support of Betsy Trotwood, who expected reciprocal support from Davy, modeled for Davy a more mature ethos than he would have had if he had received the kind of compensation for childhood suffering that every suffering child wants: unlimited sympathy.

But I could only see these things, of course, because they were there to be seen, because they form part of the ethical vision of Dickens's novel. Seeing the history of David Copperfield's relationship to Mr. Murdstone helped me place my relationship with my own father before me as an object to be apprehended and *thought* about, not just felt. I don't want to overstate the case and say that the scales fell from my eyes on my first reading, but the novel affected me deeply, and in so doing it prepared me to see more objectively my relationship with my own father.

Claiming that this story helped me see things more clearly contradicts Plato's claim that imitations only confuse our hearts and muddle our thinking, but Plato is so often right in this claim that contradicting him requires taking a moment for explanation. It won't do to dismiss Plato as if his claim were always and on principle wrong. Plato sees clearly that many imitations—stories, to us—do indeed invite us to think shallowly, self-interestedly, and unclearly about life. Who would argue that Broadway musicals, Disney movies, pornography, and most TV soap operas and sitcoms help us see life whole and see it more clearly? Plato was dead right—even though he didn't have *All My Children* or Andrew Lloyd Webber musicals or *The Little Mermaid* to point to— when he claimed that a lot of narratives pander to fantasy (in the worst sense of losing ourselves in ego wish fulfillment), pride, ambition, and unearned fulfillments. Where Plato loses the best thrust of his argument is in its overextension, his assumption that there are no distinctions to be made between the clarifying representations of Homer and Sophocles, on the one hand, and the poetry of mindless repetition he hated from the rhapsodists. Dickens helped me see my own life more clearly not by pandering to my self-pity but by showing me how Davy's defects of character are *not* solely rooted in Mr. Murdstone's abuse, but also grow from Davy's maudlin self-pity, his sentimental emotionalism, and his excessive trust in self-styled authority figures. *David Copperfield* did not pander to my own excesses; it challenged them, and it helped me see them more clearly, thus helping me establish an ethos of greater maturity and generosity than I would have been able to establish without its guiding models and informative presence.

A relevant distinction here (and an additional point) is a distinction between ethical models that we might wish to emulate and ethical models that assist or enrich our understanding. Davy's biting attack on

Murdstone decidedly did not give me a useful model to emulate. This episode did not make me wish to bite my father's hand, and biting it would not have solved anything anyway. Reading that scene did, however, prepare me to understand better some of my childish resentments and also my childish tendency, even in young adulthood, to unwittingly exaggerate the extent of my father's power and authority over both me and others.

Two other passages generated by this novel's ethical vision have carried great weight for me, both when I first read *David Copperfield* and throughout my many years of rereading it. My relationship to these two passages has been changing and variable, more like the dynamic relationship one has with a lifelong friend than the static relationship one has with a toaster or an automobile (see Booth, "The Way I Loved" and *Company*). The passage early on in which young Davy portrays himself in his tiny attic bedroom, reading and rereading the delightful cache of novels that he has discovered there as a kind of secret legacy from his dead father struck me with great force because it so mirrored my own youthful reading. In the chapter called "I Fall into Disgrace," a condition into which both Davy and I were frequently cast by our father figures—a condition which goes far to explain why we both spent much solitary time in our rooms reading—Davy describes himself in the following passage, which I have considerably shortened:

> My father had left a small collection of books in a little room upstairs, to which I had access. . . . From that blessed little room, Roderick Random, Peregrine Pickle, Humphrey Clinker, Tom Jones, the Vicar of Wakefield, Don Quixote, Gil Blas, and Robinson Crusoe, came out, a glorious host, to keep me company. . . . It is curious to me how I could ever have consoled myself under my small troubles (which were great troubles to me), by impersonating my favorite characters in them—as I did. . . . I have been Tom Jones . . . for a week together. I have sustained my own idea of Roderick Random for a month at a stretch, I verily believe . . . and for days and days I can remember to have gone about my region of our house, armed with the centerpiece out of an old set of boot-trees—the perfect realization of Captain Somebody, of the Royal British Navy, in danger of being beset by savages, and resolved to sell

his life at a great price. . . . When I think of it, the picture always rises in my mind of a summer evening, the boys at play in the churchyard, and I sitting on my bed, *reading as if for life.* (55–56; emphasis added)

I, too, as a boy, spent a good deal of time roaming the areas where my family lived, usually rural areas, pretending I was a character from one of my latest-read novels. But the significance of the "reading as if for life" passage has not meant the same thing to me over the years. At the time I first read it, I had not yet dealt with the painful truths of my upbringing, but the image of young Davy escaping from family troubles and trying to avoid further disgrace by retreating into a world of imagination and readerly experiences elicited responses from me that were warm and sympathetic, although fairly mushy and muddled. My reaction was partly formed, I believe now, out of unacknowledged self-pity and a sense of kinship with any young child to whom reading was not only the means of escaping a forbidding and frightening father but indulging in a private pleasure beyond anyone else's dismissal or contempt.

Now, however, many years later, this "reading as if for life" passage is still important to me, but in a quite different way. Instead of evoking a vague dissatisfaction with my lot and awakening in me a childish self-pity about my abusive upbringing, it evokes for me the satisfying realization that my youthful reading, no matter what unhappy pressures may have been partly responsible for it, ultimately yielded more benefits and advantages for me than almost anything else I have ever done, second only in importance and benefits to the wife and daughters who grace my life. I can look back now on "reading as if for life" and think, "Yes, I did read not merely *as if* for life but in a way that has made reading a way of life in itself. I have kept on reading for life and can't imagine another or a better one."

The second passage that has greatly assisted me over the years in my pursuit of a stable personal identity (Eldridge, Eakin, Ricoeur) is the opening sentence of *David Copperfield*: "Whether I shall turn out to be the hero of my own life, or whether that station will be held by anybody else, these pages must show" (1). This sentence has been a touchstone for me in times of confusion and uncertainty, helping me return to a clearer and more purposeful sense of myself. It has played this role in my life because it plays this role in the ethical vision of the novel, which is nothing if not an ethical vision of how David Copperfield becomes an independent and self-knowledgeable ethical agent instead of the frightened lump of self-pitying weakness that he was programmed to be.

But children such as Davy Copperfield and I don't *easily* discover or travel the path to independent agency. For many years "whether I shall turn out to be the hero of my own life" nearly haunted me. I knew intuitively that it did not refer merely to masculine daring—firing the torpedoes, winning the game, or saving the child—but instead to something more like internal integrity, self-direction, and self-knowledge. I knew that being the hero of my own life meant believing that I could become something like a "best version" of myself despite not having been properly nourished and supported as a child. But I also knew intuitively, and this intuition troubled me greatly, that I could not be the hero of my own life unless I broke free from the emotional insecurities of having been a child who was forever and forever "falling into disgrace."

One of the many dangers of being an unloved and powerless child is that such children tend to resist rather than embrace personal agency and personal responsibility. Unloved children too often become adults who never see failures as their own fault, but as the fault of those who should have cared for them more and loved them better. *Unloved and powerless children have great trouble embracing the truth that being unloved does not let them off the hook for being responsible agents in the world.* They tend to think at the very least that the trade-off for suffering ought to be *not* being held responsible. They never say this to themselves explicitly, but it is a perspective on themselves that they find easy to maintain. I wanted agency for the obvious reason that autonomy is a superior mode of life compared to slavery, but I also resisted it because it meant not only that I would have to become responsible for my own life, but that I would have to give up nursing my childish angers and resentments. For many children these angers and resentments can become lifelong habits of their adult hearts.

M. M. Bakhtin's analysis of novelistic discourse offers a useful model for the kind of ongoing relationship with a novel that I am describing here. Bakhtin's conception of the dialogic relationship among multiple voices within novels invites an analogy to the dialogic relationship that can develop between novels and their readers over time. In Bakhtin's words,

The way in which the word conceptualizes its object is a complex act . . . and into this complex play of light and shadow the word enters. . . . If we imagine the *intention* of such a word, that is, its *directionality toward the object*, in the form of a ray of light, then the living and unrepeatable play of colors and light on the facets of the image that it constructs can be explained as the spectral dispersion of the ray-word . . . in an atmosphere filled with the alien words, value judgments and accents through which the ray passes on its way toward the object; the social atmosphere of the word, the atmosphere that surrounds the object, makes the facets of the image sparkle. (277; emphasis in original)

Adapting this image so that the object becomes the reader and the word becomes the novel—but preserving Bakhtin's insight into the nature of dialogic interaction—captures the sense of my own historical relationship with the ethical vision of *David Copperfield*. This work, this novel-as-word, entered my life like a ray and established a dynamic relationship with something alien to it, something not itself—that is, my consciousness and the facts and conditions of my life—such that I, as the object of the word, came under the influence not of a passive word but of an interactive discourse, what Bakhtin has just called "the spectral dispersion of the ray-word." Dickens's ethical vision of what it might mean to "become the hero of my own life" threw light on my ambition, my deep impulse, to liberate myself from Murdstone-like oppression. Along with other influences, the light of ethical vision in *David Copperfield*–as-word helped me see the possibilities of my own life in a new way and, in helping me see it, helped midwife my emergence into maturity. Stories are often a kind of midwife to character, but unlike physical children who get born only once, character is always *being* born, shaped out of the ongoing choices we make. As an ongoing thing of emergence, then, rather than a one-time fixed thing, character is susceptible to enduring dialogical relationships with a great many influences, including stories, as *David Copperfield* has been to me.

For me the relationship with my father acted as a lens that focuses sharply on certain representations in *David Copperfield*—namely Davy's relationship with Murdstone—but it is easy to imagine that other readers—women, for example—might have typical experiences of fe-males in a patriarchal society that invite them to focus not on Dickens's depth of psychological insight into Murdstone's pathologies, but on his shallowness of psychological insight into the possibilities for female ful-fillment. I can imagine that many if not most women could not be happy having to choose between the clichéd silliness of Dora Spenlow or the clichéd saintliness of Agnes Wakefield.

Limitations of Ethical Vision in *Wuthering Heights*

In contrast to the instant bond I felt with the ethical vision of Dickens's novels, I have had an up-and-down relationship with the ethical vision at the heart of *Wuthering Heights*, and it is precisely this history of up-and-down interactions that makes an account of my relations with this story useful to the present discussion. Here I focus primarily on who I was when I first read *Wuthering Heights* and who I was when I engaged in subsequent rereadings of this novel at different points in time, and how the differences in who I was at each point in time both influenced my reading and was influenced *by* my reading.

- I first read *Wuthering Heights* when I was in high school, deeply steeped in all of my family's dysfunctional turbulence.
- The second time I read *Wuthering Heights* I was in college, where my budding intellectual development and my distance from home allowed me to read the novel less pressured by family dynamics.
- The third time I read *Wuthering Heights* I was in graduate school, where my reading was driven primarily by growing skills of technical analysis, especially narrative technique, and this change in reading technique led me to a total reevaluation of the novel's ethical vision.[4]
- The fourth time I read *Wuthering Heights* was in the spring of 2004, thirty-five years after graduate school, as part of my preparation for writing this chapter.

Only my last and most recent rereading of *Wuthering Heights* occurred at a far distant time and in a vastly different psychic space from all entanglements with my family's dysfunctionality. My first painful confrontations with this dysfunctionality had occurred when I was thirty, which was also my age when I finished my doctorate, when I had finished the first three years of my professional career, and when I had just experienced the thrill of my first daughter's birth, the catalytic event that led me, finally, to face my family's sad pathologies. Each planetary tilt of my responses to *Wuthering Heights* has been produced by an interactive dynamic between the gravitational pull of the novel's ethical vision and my own ethical quest for autonomy and self-knowledge as I orbited around it.

It speaks to the educational power of story in general to say that, in my view, the greatest contribution to this quest was made by story, not by desire. In the first place, to describe myself as engaged in a "quest for autonomy and self-knowledge" is not something I could have said before reading *David Copperfield* and *Wuthering Heights*. Reading these novels did not do all of the work for me, but they positioned me *closer* to this kind of self-awareness than if I had never read them at all. In the second place, while it would not be smart to underestimate the motivational power of human desire, the truth is that desire by itself, no matter how intense, doesn't necessarily produce progress or generate light. In order to grow toward autonomy and self-knowledge I needed more than desire. I needed ideas, concepts, images, and models to work with—in short, I needed food for thought—and this I found in abundance in the novels I was reading.

My High School Reading of *Wuthering Heights*:
Heathcliff and the Ethic of Power

In my powerlessness and lack of agency in high school, at age fifteen, what most attracted me about the ethical vision of *Wuthering Heights* was Heathcliff's power, or, more precisely, his *rise* to power from an early position of abuse and deprivation. Heathcliff in his youth was precisely all the things that I was in my youth at the time I first encountered him in the pages of Brontë's novel. He was psychologically battered and physically beaten, unappreciated, and treated unfairly, with no one to turn to for redress (after the death of old Mr. Earnshaw). After Heathcliff left

Wuthering Heights and returned to it a few years later as a man, however, he showed that he had become all the things that I was not and that, in truth, I could not at that time even imagine becoming. Heathcliff returned as a man who was independent, certainly, but most of all he returned as someone powerful—powerful enough to place himself beyond the injustice and pain inflicted on him by those who had delighted in mistreating him when he was young.[5]

Most significant of all, Heathcliff generated the energy and the means for his rise to power—somehow—out of his own internal resources. For neither Heathcliff nor me was there a deus ex machina in the form of a king, God, Saint George, a magistrate, or the Cheeryble brothers to help us out or to right our wrongs. But Heathcliff, unlike me, tapped sources of internal power and righted his wrongs for himself, a spectacle that was for me highly charged. I took care (unconsciously) not to identify with these feelings with any precision, for I had good reason to know in my relations with my father, as Heathcliff knew in his relations with Hindley, that it was dangerous to reveal either verbal or physical signs of rebellion. But underneath—in those murky regions of the human heart where nascent intentions are often disguised by the smoke of passion—Heathcliff's ethic of power fed my rising spirit of rebellion.

Reading *Wuthering Heights* this way meant that there were many facets of Heathcliff's ethical character that I simply failed to take into account: that Heathcliff uses his power not merely to protect himself from others' abuse but to seek revenge (and to seek it in out-of-scale ways); that Heathcliff shows profound disrespect for others by his willingness to use them as tools; that Heathcliff takes out his spite on innocent creatures like Isabella's spaniel, whom he hangs, and on Catherine Linton, who is not entirely innocent but who has never wronged Heathcliff in any way that merits the hatred he bears her; that Heathcliff cruelly enjoys inflicting pain; that Heathcliff is willing to sacrifice (by force) others' happiness, not to mention their very well-being, to serve his avarice; and that Heathcliff is not just deficient in charity but *devoid* of charity (as well as fellow-feeling, generosity, civility, and compassion) not only toward anyone who ever wronged him, not only toward anyone who is innocently *associated* with anyone who ever wronged him, but to some people who have *never* wronged him, such as Lockwood.

The abused, deprived, and needy frame of mind in which I read *Wuthering Heights* when I was fifteen prevented me from seeing these facts in their proper light. I hurried over these uncomfortable facts and squeezed them into the background of my attention. Because I was so tightly riveted to the spectacle of Heathcliff's rise to power, I failed to see the totality of his character, even though the data about Heathcliff's character is clearly laid out in the text. In trying to save Isabella from certain misery in forming an attachment to Heathcliff, Catherine Earnshaw says clearly—and as the only person who loves Heathcliff, her condemnation carries both veracity and force—that Isabella must not "imagine that [Heathcliff] conceals depths of benevolence and affection beneath a stern exterior! He's not a rough diamond . . . he's a fierce, pitiless, wolfish man" (89–90). On the other hand, it is a curious feature of the ethical vision of this novel as mediated by a skillful narrative technique that I and all other readers of *Wuthering Heights* are *invited*, despite the explicitness of Catherine's characterization and Heathcliff's own actions, to make, if not an incomplete assessment of Heathcliff's character, as I did, then a more ethically benign assessment than the novel's own evidence, viewed merely as data, calls for.

Brontë skillfully pulls off this interesting, ethical sleight-of-hand primarily by employing two storytelling strategies that nearly always work when an author or movie or TV director wants to cement her audience's sympathy for a character of dubious ethical nature. First, just as Thackeray makes us sympathize with Becky Sharp during the first half of *Vanity Fair* (1848), despite giving us plenty of evidence of her heartlessness—by showing Becky as *comparatively* better (in an ethical sense) than those around her or at least as no worse (and a whole lot more entertaining)—Brontë works for the same kind of amelioration of judgment by surrounding Heathcliff with people who, especially in his youth, are clearly just as fierce, wolfish, and pitiless, if not more so, than Heathcliff himself, and who have physical power over Heathcliff that they exploit to Heathcliff's disadvantage and pain. Second, in his youth, Heathcliff's physical courage and his attachment to Catherine give him a better-seeming character, comparatively, than those around him. Third, Brontë coerces leniency of judgment from her audience toward Heathcliff, as authors and storytellers have been doing forever, by showing him wrongfully abused, a technique that is especially effective if the abused character is a child. If all of the different kinds of evidence for and against Heathcliff's character are given full consideration, no careful reader could conclude that *Wuthering Heights* fails to give him or her all the data needed for seeing the wolfish and pitiless character whom Catherine accurately describes, but the strategies I have just cataloged also invite readers, even careful ones, to lean sympathetically in Heathcliff's direction and allow Brontë to have her narrative cake and eat it too. As a youthful reader I was wrong to focus so narrowly on Heathcliff's rise to power—wrong for letting the lens of my life obscure my clear view of the novel's own data—but Emily Brontë plays a calculating game as narrator in making such a misreading easier for me (and for any other reader as well) than if she had given her readers the ethical skinny about Heathcliff's character in a more straightforward manner.

But of course Brontë is right to tell her story in her own way. She's a novelist, not my moral babysitter, and as long as she doesn't deliberately contradict the terms of her own representation, which she doesn't, what she achieves by means of her novel's ethical vision of complex rights and wrongs is a layered portrayal of the multidimensional context in which ethical character emerges and in which ethical judgments are generated. She shows clearly that the interplay between ethical character and ethical judgments is messy, complicated, always susceptible to corruption from the play of self-interest, and highly prone to error because of human beings' limited ability to draw correct ethical inferences from others' concrete conduct. But she also shows equally clearly that nothing is more important than sustaining an energetic effort, despite its difficulties, to get it right: to understand what ethical character is and to see clearly the criteria by which to judge it.

My College Reading of *Wuthering Heights*: Embarrassing Credulity about Nelly

When in my third year of college I read *Wuthering Heights* for the second time, my increased skills of analytical reading led me to see Heathcliff's villainy of character more clearly than I had before. The more I thought about Heathcliff in this new light, the more it became apparent to me that

Heathcliff did not represent the kind of power I wanted for fending off my father's injustices. Now I saw Heathcliff's wolfish pitilessness as just another version of my father. Since even in my abused youth I longed for power primarily as a means of self-protection, not self-aggrandizement, my now clearer view of Heathcliff's villainy led me as a reader to a highly uncritical acceptance of the only person in the novel, Nelly Dean, who persistently articulates explicit judgments against Heathcliff's character. As a college reader I was still allowing the dynamics of my troubled family relations to guide my reading of *Wuthering Heights* in ways that continued to obscure my understanding. What I failed to see on this second reading, of course, was all the evidence that Nelly Dean is often an unreliable narrator and is always a self-serving narrator. As I attempted in my college reading to correct my high school fascination with Heathcliff's power by now distancing myself from his villainy, I used Nelly's platitudinous judgments as my means of doing so.

I cringe to admit that Nelly's platitudes became my platitudes. When Nelly smugly tells readers that "I went about my household duties, convinced that the Grange had but one sensible soul in its walls, and that lodged in my body" (103), my too-credulous college-reader self (*mea culpa!*) believed her. And when she responds with a pious cliché to one of young Heathcliff's many angry claims that he will one day work his revenge on Hindley—"'For shame, Heathcliff!,' said I. 'It is for God to punish wicked people; we should learn to forgive'" (57)—I took her to be prescribing civilized and sensible medicine for the cure of Heathcliff's bitterness. On the face of it this *is* what Nelly is doing, of course, but prescribing generic medicine that fails to take the patient's circumstances into realistic account is not actually a help. It's just moralizing for the sake of moralizing.

But there are instances when Nelly's judgments are sufficiently shrewd, insightful, and ethically satisfying that inattentive or inexperienced readers such as I was in college can be lulled into lowering their critical guard and taking everything else that Nelly says at face value, including her sentimental elevation of all the novel's "nice" characters and her exaggerated depreciation of the "not nice" characters. Inattentive readers can also be led to accept the persistently self-serving commentary that Nelly uses to justify her control over the flow of domestic information in her employers' homes. Acting as a kind of information gatekeeper,

Nelly sometimes deletes information, sometimes alters it, almost always spins it, and sometimes just makes it up. But despite these questionable ethical practices—questionable on the ethical fronts of honesty, respect, integrity, compassion, and sometimes just plain kindness—Nelly buys a vast deal of credit for herself with the few arrows of criticism that fly dead center to her target, as when she deftly delivers a slitty-eyed rejoinder to Catherine's complaint that she is always having to baby Edgar's and Isabella's feelings. Nelly shoots back, "'You're mistaken,' Mrs. Linton,' said I. 'They humor you. . . . You can well afford to indulge their passing whims, as long as their business is to anticipate all your desires'" (86). Readers who delight in the dead-on accuracy of this insight, and a few others that Brontë strategically salts throughout her tale, are tempted to view all other insights by Nelly as having equal authority. The only problem is, they *don't* all have equal authority. I simply failed to see this fact in my college-level reading of *Wuthering Heights*.

My Grad School Reading of *Wuthering Heights*:
Whiplash Judgments about Nelly

When I reread *Wuthering Heights* in graduate school at the University of Chicago, however, I nearly gave myself intellectual whiplash from the force of my rebound interpretation of Nelly Dean's status as an ethical judge and social commentator. Having developed my reading skills exponentially since college, and having just read Wayne Booth's *The Rhetoric of Fiction*, as well as having taken classes in literary criticism from Booth, Ronald Crane, and Elder Olson, I walked to the batter's box on my next rereading of *Wuthering Heights* fully prepared not to swing at any sucker pitches. Nelly Dean, stuck with her script, naturally, threw all of the same explanations and judgments that had sailed right by me in earlier years like those low inside pitches that hitters who like high outside balls never see. Now, however, armed with all kinds of major league skills for hitting spitball pitchers who try to slide platitudinous, unreliable curve balls over my narrative plate, I knocked poor Nelly off the pitching mound by line-driving all her meddling, dishonest, trimmed, shaved, and trumped-up information right back at her.[6]

As you can doubtless infer from my batting metaphors, I certainly felt intellectually virtuous and highly professional in having learned how to do this sort of reading, and now I had an even greater problem with *Wuthering Heights'* ethical vision than I did with Nelly Dean as narrator. I especially disliked what I perceived—and continue to perceive—as the novel's championing of an ethical vision that favors undisciplined, rampant Romanticism: a configuration of rights and wrongs that asks readers to admire intensity of feeling for its own sake, no matter how self-indulgent or irrational or harmful, and that asks readers to be fascinated with near-mad emotionalism, as if such emotional extremity constitutes an obviously higher mode of existence than everyday soberness and judicious thought.

Wuthering Heights honors not just fiercely intense emotions but fiercely intense emotional*ism*, a state of being in which one is addicted to extreme feelings in the same way that Duke Orsino is a man addicted to being in love with love. This kind of emotionalism for its own sake was all too similar to the anti-intellectual emotionalism of the Protestant fundamentalism I had been raised in, and I knew all too well how easily it could mask limitless forms of self-aggrandizement, selfishness, and cruelty. When Heathcliff makes histrionic utterances such as "The moment [Catherine's] regard ceased [for Linton], I would have torn his heart out, and drank his blood!" or "[Linton] couldn't love as much in eighty years as I could in a day" (125–26), I'm convinced that Brontë wants all of her readers to feel that the energy, the vigor, the masculine power, and the brutal assertion of self-interest so honestly portrayed is a good thing—or at least a good thing in comparison with the mealy-mouthed piety of Linton. Heathcliff's contempt for Linton seems to be Brontë's contempt as well, the product of an ethical vision all aswoon over Romantic intensity.

The novel's over-the-top melodrama ethically repelled me even in my graduate school days. Catherine's violent response to Edgar's anger about Heathcliff is a good example: "There she lay dashing her head against the arm of the sofa, and grinding her teeth, so that you might fancy she would crash them to splinters!" "Good," was my reaction, "I hope she hits wood and knocks some sense into her head." I was even unhappier with the novel's rip-off of Ophelia's mad scene in which she distributes the flowers to the Elsinore courtiers[7] and the later rip-off of Keats's "Ode to a Nightingale."[8] If I had thought that Brontë was using these rip-offs to satirize excessive and irrational emotionalism, I might have appreciated their deft appropriateness in revealing Catherine's character, but it seemed to me then—and still seems to me now—that Brontë uses these rip-offs not to satirize the characters but to show that despite their social and psychological pathologies they enjoy a more intense and therefore superior kind of existence to that of everyone else.

Nothing separates the ethical vision of Brontë's ersatz, immature Romanticism from the ethical vision of mature Romanticism better than a contrast with the near ending of Keats's "Ode to a Nightingale," which is also a literary representation about escaping bodily constraints and living in some golden realm where bodies do not shatter and feelings do not shred. But Keats, unlike Brontë, is enough of a hardheaded realist to accept facts rather than indulge in fantasies. "The fancy cannot cheat so well," he admits. The fancy, in other words, cannot provide real escape from the built-in conditions of human existence. In the end, the bird's song, which throughout the poem has symbolized a transcendent avenue of escape from the mundane, *simply goes away*—"Adieu! adieu! thy plaintive anthem fades"—leaving human beings positioned where they are always positioned: negotiating their existence in the context of a thousand competing desires and conditions, but never escaping their muddled, mixed state as creatures of innumerable contraries.

If an ethical vision either in a narrative or in a life serves any concrete end at all, it provides the resources for making or not making the kind of call that Brontë's ethical vision avoids and that Keats's ethical vision embraces. Brontë seems intent on ordering the rights and wrongs of her fictional world in such a way that, at least for Heathcliff and Catherine, escape really is possible. In the end, Brontë tries to pass off this bogus notion to her readers, initially through Lockwood's vision of Catherine's ghost at the beginning of the novel, and subsequently through Heathcliff's visions of that same ghost as he becomes more and more distractedly entangled with it, such that he can neither eat nor sleep, until he dies, at which point he and Catherine are joined together, presumably, forever.

Yawn. This is an ethic of escapism, not an ethic of generosity or kindness or self-control or honesty or compassion. In short, it is not an ethic that has anything to do with *ethics* as principles to which we might appeal for assistance in living a deliberate life in which, at the very least, we do no harm, or a life in which, at the most, we might actually make life for us and our companions better than it would otherwise be. This is a humble enough ethical vision, to be sure—there's nothing grandly heroic about doing no harm or trying to create the conditions in everyday life that encourage human flourishing—but who can deny that an ethical vision based on honesty, justice, kindness, self-control, generosity, compassion, and the capacity to feel shame when we have done wrong would make the world more hospitable to human happiness than the ethic of *Wuthering Heights*, an ethic that honors the selfish assertion of fiercely intense emotionalism above all other ethical qualities.

Rereading *Wuthering Heights* After Thirty Years: Coming to Terms

But perhaps Brontë is more subtle than I have just described her to be. Perhaps she is not simply out to honor the selfish assertion of fiercely intense emotionalism but, in fact, after larger, different, and more interesting game.[9] An alternative way of understanding the ethical vision of *Wuthering Heights* is to see it as a critique of middle-class power, middle-class niceties, middle-class sentimentality, and, above all, middle-class hypocrisy. Viewed in this way, the ethical vision of *Wuthering Heights* positions Thrushcross Grange as a kind of miniature kingdom dominated by middle-class values, and existing in direct opposition to Wuthering Heights as a kind of miniature kingdom dominated by *anti*–middle-class values.

From this perspective, both kingdoms are places where power matters most but where the typical power of each kingdom manifests itself in radically different ways. The power at Thrushcross Grange is socially legitimate, historically traditional, and massively patriarchal—God the father above all, King the "sire" above all subjects, men above women, husbands above wives, fathers above children, masters above servants—and is accompanied by all the behaviors that traditionally identify and reinforce middle-class power: going to church, getting educated, observing proprieties, paying lip service to the pieties, using a refined accent, dressing like other middle-class persons, observing traditional gender roles, and, above all, sticking with class peers in all matters of tension, competition, or trouble between middle-class persons and the lower orders, especially about matters of sexual tension in which persons threaten to blur class lines by falling in love and getting married across class boundaries.

This is a more interesting hypothesis about the ethical vision at the center of *Wuthering Heights* than my earlier hypothesis about rampant Romanticism because it makes Brontë's ethical vision in support of the intense emotionalism at Wuthering Heights a means to an end, not an end in itself. From this perspective, Brontë's ethical vision is designed to make us see the corrupt ethics of middle-class power—typified by the configuration of rights and wrongs in the kingdom of Thrushcross Grange—for what it really is. Its end, in other words, is to expose a kind of velvet-hammer middle-class oppression, and its means is to show us what that oppression looks and sounds like when it drops the velvet hammer and picks us the ax and pitchfork, when oppressiveness asserts itself in the most raw, selfish, callous, undisciplined, unguarded, unfeeling, and unkind ways possible, which are the ways that it typically expresses itself in the kingdom of Wuthering Heights.

Throughout her novel Brontë exerts persistent pressure on middle-class ideals and values. She keeps smashing at them the way Heathcliff smashes at the windows and locks of Thrushcross Grange, and Heathcliff and Catherine are her main smashing tools. Of Isabella, whose love for Heathcliff seems based on a middle-class archetype of the blunt-man-with-a-gruff-exterior-who-turns-out-to-be-honorable-and-loving-underneath-the-surface, Heathcliff says, once Isabella's eyes are opened to reality, "I don't care who knows that the passion was wholly on one side, and I never told her a lie about it. She cannot accuse me of showing one little bit of deceitful softness" (127). His speech of contempt about Linton's love for Catherine is even more explicit in its attack on middle-class notions of decency, decorum, and rightness: "And that insipid, paltry creature attending [Catherine] from *duty* and *humanity*! From *pity* and *charity*! [Edgar] might as well plant an oak in a flowerpot, and expect it to thrive, as imagine he can restore [Catherine] to vigor in the soil of his shallow cares!" (129; emphasis in original).

There's no middle-class gallantry here, and no middle-class niceness, but there is an honesty of contempt. Surely Brontë is right to suggest that contempt is also present in many middle-class relations, only in *those* relations contempt is masked by middle-class charms, conventions, and well-bred smiles. If this is what Brontë hates, she does a good job of showing what its real nature looks like once its middle-class garb is removed and it stands naked before us in all of its self-interested ugliness. But if Brontë wants readers to infer that honestly expressed oppression is to be preferred, especially on ethical grounds, over middle-class hypocritical oppression, I can only say to her, "ask the victims whether it really matters or not." The distinction between middle-class modes of hypocritical oppression and honestly raw self-interested oppression is a nicety unimportant to victims.

An ethical vision that only tears down what we hate cannot help us build up what we love. If Thrushcross Grange represents middle-class values and conduct and Wuthering Heights represents *anti*–middle-class values and conduct, what this ethical vision seems unable to comprehend is that an anti–middle-class ideology is not a program for living—or, if Brontë does comprehend it, she seems to have boxed herself in with a story that cannot go beyond it. The ethical vision of *Wuthering Heights* expresses objections to human diminishment but includes no theory of human flourishing. If Brontë thinks, as she apparently does, that an anti–middle-class ideology can be substituted for a positive theory of life, then perhaps she has not departed very far, after all, from the Romantic escapism I earlier accused her of indulging in. Having used Catherine and Heathcliff to critique middle-class hypocrisy, but having no view of how they might actually construct a positive life together in the mundane realm, the best that Brontë seems to be able to offer them is that bogus life-after-death, which posits that they live for the remainder of eternity wandering the moors together as ghosts.

Ethical Vision and Human Flourishing

Is it fair to hold Brontë, or any other storyteller, to the criterion of advancing an ethical vision that includes "a theory of human flourishing"? Certainly not—not in any abstract, absolute, deductive sense. But it is certainly not *un*fair to point out in an inductive way that *this* story or *that* story does *not* include such an ethical vision—and that *David Copperfield* clearly does.[10] I have no desire to position Emily Brontë at some precise spot on a bogus continuum that runs from "lesser" storytellers up to "greater" storytellers. But it is legitimate for me to bare the grounds of my prejudice in favor of stories that have theories, so to speak, over those that merely have objections.

This means that, for me at least, I feel a profounder resonance with stories that include an ethical vision of how life might be put together than with stories whose ethical visions limit themselves merely to attacking the failures of some other ethical vision. There were lots of things in Dickens's world that *he* objected to—and few writers could voice their objections with the same rhetorical force as Dickens—but Dickens's ethical vision that in a single stroke bound my heart to his works in graduate school, and that still binds me to them today, is not just his *objections* to Murdstone's cruelty, Steerforth's selfishness, and Uriah Heep's meanness, but his positive theory about the kinds of human relations that make everyday life—the place where we all really live—not just bearable but joyful and productive.

Dickens, like Keats, ultimately tries to be a realist. He is certainly unrealistic in some ways, most notably in his limited understanding of romantic relations between young men and women, but his grasp of such ethical principles as *justice, kindness, honesty, compassion,* and *the capacity for shame* is both strong and sure. Dickens knows goodness versus oppression and compassion versus cruelty when he sees them, but he never longs for a transcendent realm of bogus escape. His ethical vision asserts powerfully that the quality of people's lives is created not by the ideologies they applaud in the abstract, but by the ethical choices they make in the concrete world of everyday social interactions at business, in the street, at table, and when people need help or are called upon to give help. And he knows how to contrast nourishing and productive ethical choices with those that are demeaning, destructive, selfish, cruel, and self-interested.

As Dickens's novels show and as *Wuthering Heights* does not, we really can live better lives if we shape them in accordance to an ethical vision that encourages us to live up to everyday standards of decency, honesty, justice, and compassion. The economic system of energy and values that Brontë depicts in *Wuthering Heights*, however, suggests that life is too compressed, too thin, and too competitive ever to provide the resources for human flourishing. Once old Earnshaw brings Heathcliff home, there isn't enough love to go around any more. Hindley and Cathy are placed outside the orbit of the old man's concern. No matter where we turn in this novel we see insufficiencies. Even the cold stone floors and drafty windows and dark walls repel all approaches of human softness and warmth. There is especially an insufficiency of primitive ethical virtues and resources—concern, compassion, kindness, justice—such that everyone at Wuthering Heights grows up not only cold and lonely but stunted, deprived, manipulated, manipulative, and misshapen.

In everyday life these kinds of consequences are not determined by the huge abstractions that we like to blame for them (which has the dubious benefit of letting us off the moral hook for other people's unhappiness and pain), abstractions such as the "forces of history" or "economic laws" or "the depravity of humankind." In everyday life, our failures of ethical responsibility and sensitivity are created or avoided *not* by these huge abstractions, but by the day-by-day, moment-by-moment choices we make in our social and ethical relations with other people. Dickens sees this. He knows that any attempt to see Murdstone as merely the product of original sin, or as a product of the pressures of a commercial society, or as a product of misguided Puritanism misses the fact that Murdstone could have behaved differently if he had been possessed of a different ethical vision of life, one that is clearly available to him because other people who are equally vulnerable to original sin and the pressures of a commercial society and misguided Puritanism do *not* behave as Murdstone behaves.

In analyzing the origin of pathologies in either fictional or real-life persons, we may talk the language of politics, power, ethnicity, gender, race, class, economics, nationalism, tradition, custom, mores, and so on. All of this talk is highly relevant to an understanding of our circumstances as embodied, historically situated agents. I am not claiming that ethical visions are *not* embodied and historically situated—they are—but I am claiming that ethical visions are not so much the *products* of history and culture as they are the elemental human *orientations* that make culture and history possible.[11]

Dickens's ethical vision taps into rock-bottom human orientations. His vision is simple but goes deep, and for this reason I will always hold

Dickens's works more closely to my heart than Brontë's works, though I want to emphasize that the point of ethical criticism is not to rank novelists and their novels on some simple scale, but to engage in complex ways with the ethical visions they offer. In this regard, I have found many rewards over a forty-year period of reading and rereading *Wuthering Heights* because the struggle I have had in weighing its values over time has taught me to think productively about the very ideas I have discussed in this chapter. I could never have written this chapter without the education I have acquired in my rereadings of *Wuthering Heights*. I value the instructiveness of this engagement almost as much as I value the ways in which *David Copperfield* has been a touchstone for me.

For all of us, a lifetime of engagements with the ethical visions of stories becomes a major component in the construction of our ethical vision of life. Engaging with new stories and reencountering old ones generate a dynamic composed of both energy and matter, desire and substance. The actions, attitudes, and judgments we see in stories become the actions, attitudes, and judgments we put together in life, and these, cumulatively considered, turn us into persons we become. Surely this not only explains but justifies a deep concern to understand, compare, and evaluate stories' ethical visions. We weave together the stories *in* our life into a pattern that ultimately becomes the story *of* our life. Learning to understand, compare, and evaluate stories' ethical visions becomes a way to understand ourselves: not only who we are and what we want, but who we ought to be and what we should want.

CHAPTER TEN

Postscript

Toward an Ethical Theory

Where Do Ethical Criteria Come From?

Up to this point I have dealt mainly with what philosophers would call moral psychology rather than moral theory. I have built a case about how stories exert influence on the development of ethos based mainly on people's need to learn, to enlarge their stock of experiences, to enlarge their range of human companionships, to acquire information beyond their firsthand lives, and to find models for how to put together a whole life. I have also focused on the use we make of such cognitive powers as the vicarious imagination, and on the kinds of aesthetic strategies in stories that hook our feelings, beliefs, and judgments. The upshot of the argument I have made can be schematically summarized in the following way. (Such a summary leaves out all the nuances but captures the basic structure of the argument.)

1.   Because human beings are born incomplete and undeveloped and have no inevitable agenda of development or completeness programmed into them, they must acquire the arts and skills for becoming more or less developed and complete through learning.

2. Human beings learn from many sources and are influenced by many agents—families, churches, teachers, peers, ideas, and firsthand experience, to name only a few of the most important—and under the influence of that learning they make the choices that construct a life.

3. One of the important sources whose depth of influence is persistently underrated by most people is stories—narratives—regardless of whether they come to us from traditional literary forms such as short stories and novels or from narrative poetry, computer games, movies, TV programs, histories, biographies, autobiographies, radio talk shows, parables, legends, children's games, gossip, travelogues, jokes, sermons, fairy tales, song lyrics, or other sources.

4. Human beings are eager for the influence from stories because stories' invitations to *feel* in certain ways, to *believe* in certain ways, and to *judge* in certain ways—invitations that we almost always accept—give us deep pleasure and also operate as paradigms and models that we can use as guides for generating the steady stream of firsthand emotions, beliefs, and judgments that we must deploy in order to deal with events and people in real life. Our eagerness for fictional pleasure and paradigms, not to mention the nearly ceaseless engagements we have with narratives, cannot help but render us vulnerable to their influence.

5. Because everyone's everyday life is saturated with stories, and because of stories' role in shaping ethos, it is both logical and, indeed, imperative that everyone who values autonomy of personhood and independence of mind should develop supple, thoughtful, nuanced, and interrogative modes of ethical criticism (as opposed to dogmatic assertion or condemnation) for assessing whether the narrative influences we invite into our lives should be wholeheartedly embraced, examined at an arm's distance, thoroughly rejected, or examined in a way that combines some or all of these responses.

As I summarize my argument in this way, you may notice something important that I have not done. There is something missing. If you were students in my class on literary theory and had just finished reading the first nine chapters of this book, what I would now want you to say to me is, "Dr. Gregory, what is the theory that defines what 'good for us' and 'bad for us' really means? Where do we get the criteria that generate and justify these kinds of judgments?" I would like to hear this question not because it's the easiest question to answer—in fact it's the hardest question so far—but because it's the smartest and most important question.

I hope at various points as I have made claims about stories' invitations to ethical response, you have wanted to ask me where I get my criteria. I have shown that accepting Invitations A, B, and C from any given story might entail Alterations D, E, and F in our ways of feeling, believing, and judging, and I have made clear my conviction that whatever influences us in these ways is an *ethical* influence simply because our typical ways of feeling, believing, and judging just *do* constitute our ethos. But I have not shown (yet) the location, or the source, of the criteria that allow us to construct an argument about why this or that altered feeling, belief, or judgment is good or bad for us. How do I know—how do any of us know—what qualities of ethos we should most desire for ourselves and others?

This question is easy to answer in small tribal societies or in peasant societies where the pervasive agreement among socially cohesive group members about the criteria for good and bad provides little need for thinking analytically about the underlying assumptions on which those criteria are based. *Tradition* rather than analysis provides the criteria, and the authority of moral criteria is reinforced by priests, shamans, elders, and so on. No one is invited to think critically, much less to challenge, ethical standards in such societies, where separating "good" from "bad" merely seems like common sense, transparent in meaning and unproblematic in content.

But in pluralistic and complex societies, people who make ethical judgments with the air of having said what is only common sense are often seen by others as making wrong or prejudiced judgments, not uttering common sense, and wrong at two levels: wrong about the intrinsic logic of the positions they espouse, and wrong about the degree to which they assume that other people share their views. It is common practice for politicians and pastors, for example, merely to employ a quick-reference, brown-and-serve method of making ethical judgments supported with little or no analysis and argument. Pastors and politicians mainly want *agreement* from their constituencies, not intellectual independence and not critical argument. Such modes of ethical evaluation describe *most* public discourse about ethics in contemporary society. In contemporary American society, ethical positions mostly get asserted, not argued, or they get graphically associated in political ads or in editorial cartoons with versions of the opponents' views that make the opponents look callous, selfish, deceitful, moronic, or homicidal.

But it is a highly significant clue to the way human beings are built that no matter how often serious ethical argument gets evaded or caricatured, and no matter how often they say that they are cynical about ethical standards, *people never cease evaluating each other's conduct in moral and ethical terms.* We never stop *judging* people as bad or good, honorable or dishonorable, honest or deceitful, cruel or kind, callous or compassionate, stingy or generous, fair or unfair, and so on. People find themselves particularly attached to ethical standards when they become the object of some unethical action such as the theft of their wallet or the unfaithfulness of a spouse or a betrayal by a friend. No matter how remote or incoherent ethics may have seemed before, the moment someone "does us wrong," as we say, ethics comes roaring back into relevance: we want justice, we want fairness, we want redress, and sometimes we even want payback.

Honesty provides a good example of the hardiness of ethical standards in general. Hardly anything is more common in society than dishonesty. Every day wallets are stolen, spouses cheat, friends betray, and politicians lie. But here's the odd thing: despite the pervasiveness of dishonesty and despite our expectation about its persistence, we never collectively give up on honesty either as an ideal, as a criterion, or as a practice. Honesty remains our default expectation for other people *despite the common experience of deceit.* The fact that we don't use our daily experience of deceit to reformulate our ethical criterion of honesty says something deeply important about human nature. It says that we are built *for* honesty rather than not: honesty is not a discretionary value for us as a species. Individuals may treat it as a discretionary value with respect to certain goals of their own, but as a species we cannot survive without the cooperation among ourselves that is supported and facilitated by honesty.

Nor, despite its commonness, is *dis*honesty allowed free rein. We may lack the means in many cases to *dis*allow it, but if I catch the thief who steals my wallet, everyone will congratulate me. They will not wonder why I bothered about a thing so common as a stolen wallet. Furthermore, honesty as an ethical standard still has teeth. Lying to a jury will get you imprisoned, lying to your boss will get you fired, and lying to your spouse (about certain issues) will get you divorced. Moreover, we never cease to be hurt, disappointed, sad, or angry when we find that we have been deceived, especially by a family member or a friend. In short, ethical standards may not have the authority or scope that we sometimes wish they had, but they still have bite, and no one ever proposes that we just forget about ethics altogether while we each concentrate on pursuing our own self-interests in any way possible. Why is this?

Why Do We Hold to Ethical Standards with Such Tenacity?

All of us spend much of our life's energy trying to decide "the right thing" to do. As the narrator in Jane Hamilton's *The Book of Ruth* says, there are "certain rules about human beings. . . . We're dying to follow directions perfectly, even for the simple tasks, *so we can do remarkably well*" (228; emphasis added). In the curiously economical and vivid way that good art has for clarifying important truths of the heart, this homely statement touches two deep truths with wonderful deftness. The first truth is that no matter how liberal, tolerant, or relativistic we are, none of us ever gives up completely on the intuition that there are indeed some "rules about human beings." We may not believe in a great many rules, perhaps, and we might be uncertain about how many of our "rules" really possess universal authority, but, despite these uncertainties, we all believe in a few rules that no one can argue us out of. I offer some examples two paragraphs below.

The second deep truth the quote points to is that all of us do indeed want to do "remarkably well." While we may concede that some people seem to exhibit a kind of perverse pleasure in doing ill, most of us not only don't wish to do ill but do indeed wish to be competent, not just at skills but at life. Most of us most of the time really do want to do "the right thing." Whether we know how to launch arguments about "the right thing," we all think that in everyday life *virtue counts*. I am defining *virtue* here as actually *doing* the right thing rather than just wanting to or just talking about it. Regardless of whether we expect the right thing to be done by ourselves or others, its actually getting done or not done in everyday life *matters*. It matters to all of us if the person who finds our wallet returns it to us with the money still in it, if the politician who says he will help us really does (or does not), and if our spouse's vow of fidelity can be counted on (or not).

Our intuitions about fairness constitute an example as robust as my example about honesty. It is a "rule" of human relations, we feel, that we should not be treated unfairly: that we should not be physically or psychically assaulted at the whim or mere self-interest of others; that we should not be ridiculed or despised when we have done nothing to deserve it; that we should not be allowed to starve when other people have plenty to eat; that we should not be betrayed by those who have vowed fidelity to us; that we should not be deprived of due process; that we should not be passed over for rewards or recognition that we have earned; that we should not be falsely defamed or misrepresented; that we should not be discriminated against because of our physical "givens," such as gender, sexual orientation, or skin color; that our children should not be vulnerable to other people's carelessness or hostility, and so on. We may be a bit vague about the sense in which these expectations actually constitute a "rule," but whether we shrink from calling fairness a rule or not, we are not about to give up being outraged if we find ourselves starving in the midst of others' plenty or find our spouse having a sexual affair with our best friend behind our back.

Here are other examples. We feel guilty if we lie to a spouse or friend; we feel angry if we find that they have lied to us. We feel guilty even if we *unintentionally* hurt a friend's feelings, and we apologize for even our unintentional blunders. We think fortunate people should respond compassionately to other people's suffering and bad luck. Teachers enforce codes of honesty among students, some of whom exhibit little guilt about cheating but many of whom would not cheat no matter how much they might gain from it. Most teachers grade all students fairly, even the ones they don't like. Scientists everywhere are outraged at the occasional stories of colleagues who fabricate or alter their data. Survey after survey reveals that Americans think that most politicians lie as a matter of routine, yet politicians caught lying often lose both the respect of their constituencies and their seats of office. If they lie about sexual affairs with teenagers or about their taxes, they may even go to jail. Most of us never steal anything even when we have the opportunity. Parents insist on truthfulness from their children, and are hurt and outraged when children tell lies instead, *despite the fact that all children sometimes lie.* Some employers use job reviews for personally vindictive or manipulative purposes, but this fact never convinces us that such purposes are ethically justifiable. Examples could go on and on.

Some people's commitment to principles of ethical relativism never undercuts their commitment to ethical standards. No one uses relativism to excuse the two fathers in tonight's news who killed their own infant children, one in order to take revenge on his wife, and the other in a drunken rage. Doing the right thing—or the wrong thing—doesn't just count for us only when our personal interests are at stake. Generally speaking, we think that doing the right thing should always count *even if we also think that it is seldom a primary motive in most people's conduct.* In the words of Pascal Boyer, "our moral intuitions suggest to us, from the youngest age, that behaviors are right or wrong *by themselves,* not depending on who considers them, or from what point of view" (189).

An especially vivid example of the tenacity of moral standards can be seen in the conduct of people whose *theories* deny the authority of moral standards, but who still hold strongly to moral standards in practical affairs. During the seventies and eighties, for example, when a certain elaborate and high-pitched theory that denied the existence of anything resembling objective truth and stable meaning reigned supreme in my own academic discipline (the theory of deconstruction), the deconstructionists who espoused those theories never, in fact, allowed those theories to guide their concrete interactions with students and colleagues. In everyday interactions, the deconstructionists behaved just like everyone else. They asked for evidence when their colleagues made arguments about departmental policy. They were unembarrassed about using terms that should have been outlawed by their theories such as *decency, fairness, right,* and *wrong.* They insisted on a fair and impartial evaluation of the credentials of their junior colleagues who were applying for tenure and promotion. They were scandalized if they caught a student cheating. They observed scrupulous truth telling in making reports about their research budgets, and so on. In short, even among self-conscious thinkers whose formal notions of truth were so relativistic that moral standards, in theory, *must* be tossed out along with all notions of stable linguistic meaning, these folks quite inconsistently showed in their conduct the same stubborn commitment to ethical standards that the rest of us also show.

One thing this stubborn commitment suggests is not that they always work but that we simply cannot do without them. Ethical judgments remain in the forefront of all social life because they are nondiscretionary. We can *think* our way around ethical standards, perhaps, as the deconstructionists attempted to do, but we cannot *live* our way around them. Since human beings cannot have any life apart from groups, it follows that certain features of living that support the stability and persistence of group dynamics—such as sharing, cooperation, and empathy—have been selected for by evolutionary pressures operating over thousands of generations.[1] Group living cannot be made manageable—much less be made productive, stable, and pleasant, or anything like a context for human flourishing unless, to put it simplistically, we behave ourselves. Unless most of us most of the time exercise impulse control, helpfulness, orderliness, sharing, honesty, and empathy, group living cannot endure. Despite the fact that ethical standards fail to regulate 100 percent of everyone's conduct 100 percent of the time, we still hold to whatever standards support group living *because the standards are more important to our survival than the deviations from them.*

Not that our "holding" to ethical standards is a rational or calculating process. Evolutionary pressures seem to have selected certain cooperative dispositions among the members of our species, but our *experience* of these dispositions is one of *feelings* rather than of reasons. Most of the time, we don't avoid dishonest actions that might serve our self-interest because we perform a cost-benefit analysis, but, because, as we say, it would just make us *feel awful* to steal from a friend or refuse to leave a tip or mug an old lady—even when we know that we could get away with these actions quite handily (Boyer, 174–91).

The fact is that most of us *do* behave ourselves most of the time, and that society goes on in a fairly stable way despite the destabilizing influence of persistent violations of moral standards. *We exaggerate the prevalence of ethical violations precisely because we are shocked at them,* and we fail to notice—because we take them so much for granted—that no matter how many terrible violations of moral standards occur, those violations still remain only a tiny fraction of all the ongoing cooperative human interactions that remain uncounted. Only an infinitesimal percentage of the population runs red lights or shoots other people. Most of us go on green and stop on red and avoid violence and hold the door open for the person behind us and give customers the right change without thinking much about it. The *proof* of these ongoing cooperative interactions is that group life continues to endure. It endures because most of us most of the time are cooperating with each other to make sure that it does. We are stuck with ethics because our nature as social creatures requires it. If you think ethics is a superficial tissue of issues created mainly by social prudes, inhibited introverts, and religious dogmatists, just consider briefly the horrendous consequences that occur in societies under the kind of stress that really does make most ethical standards disappear, as in societies ripped apart by revolution, war, or natural disaster.[2]

Ethical Theory and Narrative Art

What does all of this ethical theory have to do with stories? Some of the resources we deploy as we negotiate the everyday ethical thickets and conundrums of life—namely stories—are quite different from the resources that we think of first in any catalog of ethically instructive influences: our parents and communities, our religious creeds (if we believe in any), our intuitions, the laws of our country and community, and the ethical lessons embodied in a few often repeated ethical formulas such as "the golden rule" ("do unto others as you would have them do unto you") or "the Kantian imperative" ("always treat other people as ends, never as means"). The way in which stories are different is that we usually think of ourselves as interacting with stories in order to be entertained, not in order to receive ethical instruction. The way in which stories are *exactly* like these other resources, however, is that we do in fact go to stories to receive ethical instruction whether we *think* of ourselves as doing so or not.

No one has written more insightfully about the invitations to virtue offered by art, including narrative art, than Iris Murdoch, whose depth of thought about this issue merits quoting at length.

> These arts [i.e., the representational arts], especially literature and painting, show us the peculiar sense in which the concept of virtue is tied on to the human condition. They show us the absolute pointlessness of virtue while exhibiting its supreme importance; *the enjoyment of art is training in the love of virtue.* The pointlessness of art is not the pointlessness of a game; it is the pointlessness of human life itself. . . . Good art reveals what we are usually too selfish and too timid to recognize, the minute and absolutely random detail of the world, and reveals it together with a sense of unity and form. This form often seems to us mysterious because it resists the easy patterns of the fantasy, whereas there is nothing mysterious about the forms of bad art since they are the recognizable and familiar rat-runs of selfish day-dream. Good art shows us how difficult it is to be objective by showing us how differently the world looks to an objective vision. . . . Art transcends selfish and obsessive limitations of personality and can enlarge the sensibility of its consumer. It is a kind of goodness by proxy. Most of all it exhibits to us the connection, in human beings, of clear realistic vision with compassion. The realism of a great artist is not a photographic realism, it is essentially both pity and justice.
>
> Herein we find a remarkable redemption of our tendency to conceal death and chance by the invention of forms. Any story which we tell about ourselves consoles us since it imposes pattern upon something which might otherwise seem intolerably chancy and incomplete. However, human life is chancy and incomplete. It is the role of tragedy, and also of comedy, and of painting to show us suffering without a thrill and death without a consolation. Or if there is any consolation it is the austere consolation of a beauty which teaches that nothing in life is of any value except the attempt to be virtuous. . . . The great deaths of literature are few, but they show us with an exemplary clarity the way in which art invigorates us with a juxtaposition, almost an identification, of pointlessness and value. The death of Patroclus, the death of Cordelia, the death of Petya Rostov. All is vanity. The only thing which

is of real importance is the ability to see it all clearly and to respond to it justly which is inseparable from virtue. (85–87; emphasis added)

This view of life is subtle, challenging, disturbing, and deep. In her echo from Ecclesiastes 1:2—"all is vanity"—Murdoch is not asserting that everything is meaningless. She is not uttering a philosophy of despair. She is saying, rather, that *whatever meaning exists we create by the ethical stance we assume in life* because life is all we are ever sure of and we are only sure of it in the brief moments that we are actually conscious enough to claim it. In that brief moment between a sleep and a forgetting, to borrow Wordsworth's famous phrase, and *only* in this brief moment, do human beings have the chance to create the persons they become. The ethical project of creating an ethos for ourselves by the choices we make is the most important project we ever embark on. Apart from the benefits or afflictions of luck, everything else we do and create is a consequence of our ethical project, creating a self.

The words that follow "all is vanity" in Ecclesiastes are "What profit hath a man of all his labor which he taketh under the sun? One generation passeth away, and another generation cometh" (1:3–4; King James Version). This view says that none of the energy, effort, and achievement that people work for in life achieves permanency. Death and time consume everything. Two questions arise from an honest confrontation with this view. First, what's the point of virtue in a world where nothing lasts? Murdoch's answer is that virtue's point is not its good effects in the future but in its good effects *now*: the practice of virtue (or not) creates the quality of everyone's everyday world. Second, how do human beings manage in their brief moment of sun to become creatures of dignity and wisdom within themselves, and creatures of comfort and support to their fellow beings? Murdoch's answer is two-tiered: people accomplish these aims, first, by trying to see their circumstances devoid of fantasy and evasion, and second, by responding to the common human predicament of uncertain chance and certain mortality with fairness and compassion toward others.

These observations overlap with the ethical criticism of narratives because what we learn from stories and how we respond to them—the yeses and noes that help create our moral ethos—help determine the extent to which we become persons who are willing to see life without relying on fantasy and evasion, and who treat each other with justice and compassion (or not). Narratives can help us learn how to think more clearly about two issues—first, about moral criteria, and, second, about the notion of virtue itself.

Virtue: Different Kinds, Most Valuable Kind

In the following discussion of four basic human virtues, I am using "virtue" in the first three cases in its etymological root sense ("virtue" derives from the Latin term *vir*, meaning "strength," specifically, the strength required to accomplish a particular aim). This sense of "virtue" is still preserved in such contemporary locutions as "in *virtue* of the argument you have just made, I am persuaded to change my mind." Only in the last part of this discussion do I use "virtue" to mean "goodness." My reason for employing "virtue" in all four cases is to clarify several different ways in which contemporary discourse reflects fundamental confusions about what a virtue is and how ethical goodness is or is not connected to other forms of human talent and achievement.

On my own map of virtues, or strengths, the four important ones most useful in both our real-life and narrative evaluations of people are the following: *physical virtues, intellectual virtues, social virtues,* and *ethical virtues.* What's at stake in making these distinctions is the usefulness of separating the first three kinds from the last. When ethical virtues are conflated with physical, social, or intellectual virtues, as they often are, confusion about the line between ethics and talent or ethics and charm or ethics and beauty or ethics and intelligence always follow. Also at stake is our ability to recognize clearly that certain kinds of stories not only maintain these basic distinctions but embed them in concrete representations that show how these virtues actually work in the everyday world of conduct.

Physical Virtues

The preeminent physical virtues, or physical strengths, clearly, are good physical and mental health. Possessing good bodily health yields a fairly sizeable complement of virtues that even if not well developed are at least attainable: strength, stamina, and vitality. Possessing good mental health yields a mind that can learn and emotional moods that support creative engagements with the world. Other physical virtues include beauty of form and countenance, grace of movement, and complete functionality of parts (a one-armed person may have good health but still be impaired with respect to the missing limb).

Are physical virtues in the original sense of strength connected at all with virtue in the alternative sense of goodness? Sometimes yes, sometimes no: the physical virtues are not nearly so important to the moral virtues as other kinds of strengths, but our bodies are in the vanguard of all of our interactions with other people and intertwine themselves throughout those interactions, adding and subtracting not just emphasis and value but significance to all that we do or say. For example, the kind of eye contact we make with others, the brightness or darkness of our countenance, our body language, the tone of our voice, our gestures, our smiles and frowns: in these and many other physical ways our bodies give others their first set of clues about what kind of ethical agents we are.

The interesting thing about physical virtues is that anyone possessing several of the physical virtues all together—vitality, good looks, stamina, and grace, for example—stands a good chance of being uncritically credited with ethical goodness by the rest of us because we are all drawn to vitality, beauty, and grace. We always *want* to believe that impressive physical advantages are aligned with impressive goodness, even though we know that in truth there *is* no such necessary alignment. Those who possess physical charisma especially receive uncritical credit. Consider the awe and reverence given to movie stars, rock singers, revival evangelists, the occasional politician, and premier athletes, when in fact the people who feel awe struck know nothing about the ethical character of the charismatic, vital persons they so industriously admire.

Storytellers have always known that the slippage between physical and ethical virtues allows for powerful plots (as well as the same slippage in reverse: the denial of ethical credit to good people who are physically disfigured or ugly). The beauty of the serpent in the Garden of Eden and the hideousness of Frankenstein's monster are two classic examples. The serpent uses his beauty to gain initial acceptance and then to deceive, making Adam and Eve his dupes. Victor Frankenstein's monster seeks acceptance from others but is denied because of his ugliness. In both cases it is the presence or absence of physical virtues that sets up the entire story that follows. Estella's beauty disguises for Pip the coldness of her heart (in *Great Expectations*), and Captain Dobbin's lack of flair disguises for Amelia Sedley his moral superiority to George Osborne (in *Vanity Fair*). The dynamics of physicality is an endless source of complication in narratives because they are an endless source of confusion in life.

Intellectual Virtues

Intellectual virtues refer to strengths of cognition, understanding, and intellect: not just *potential* strength of mind but *cultivated* strength of mind—the kind of cultivation acquired by education, reading, and knowledge of the world larger than the community of one's origins— and therefore includes one's aesthetic taste. Cognitively, the intellectual virtues generally show themselves as the capacity for clear thinking; critical thinking; the ability to deal with abstractions and concepts; the ability to use language fluently, persuasively, and precisely in both written and spoken form; the ability to employ analysis, synthesis, induction, deduction, and logic; the ability to see fallacies and weak reasoning; the ability to recognize at least some of the "big ideas" important as cultural currency among people of education and reading; the ability to listen closely and accurately; and, finally, the skills of argumentation.

    Story writers employ the representation of intellectual virtues (or their absence) in a great variety of ways, but they seem more concretely aware than most people that the possession of intellectual virtues is not synonymous with ethical goodness, as we can see in stories that go back as far as Plato's account of Alcibiades in the *Symposium* and come up to the present in a series of movies about the brilliant but evil Dr. Hannibal Lecter in *Silence of the Lambs* (1991), *Hannibal* (2001), and *Red Dragon* (2002).

    Surely it is right to think of intellectual virtues as important *adjuncts* to moral goodness rather than as necessary to it. The depth and breadth of examples of intellectually skilled persons who use their brainy superiority for self-interested or evil ends is too vast to support the notion that one cannot be a good person unless one is also an intellectually cultivated person. On the other hand, it is clear that anyone trying to think his or her way through life's ethical conundrums will be better able to do so if with a cultivated intellect than without one.

Social Virtues

The social virtues include the knowledge of how to behave in company: being competent in the conventions of manners and conduct, knowing how to adjust one's forms of public speech and expression according to different social occasions, knowing how to recognize a group's emotional currents by picking up on people's tones of voice and their body language, being sensitive to others' expectations and especially their approval or disapproval, knowing when and in what ways it might be appropriate to speak one's true feelings or thoughts and when to remain silent, knowing how to dress for different social events and occasions, knowing what demeanor of conduct and body language to employ on different social occasions and among different social groups, and so on. In their most brilliant and developed form the social virtues lead to charisma, especially if combined with physical gifts of beauty and grace.

Much of our knowledge of social virtues is acquired so early in life and is embedded so deeply within our socialized self that we often fail to think of it as *knowledge* because we don't remember ever having worked to acquire it. Nor are we likely to think of social knowledge as subtle or sophisticated, but it is, despite the fact that we make our adjustments more or less automatically. Social virtues are not only deeds we *perform*, but deeds that others *expect*. Most of the time, these expectations cannot be violated with impunity. Violate social expectations in a job interview or in a marriage proposal, and you don't get the job or the girl. Talk too loudly in a movie theater, and angry patrons will tell you to pipe down. Light up a cigar in the nonsmoking section of a restaurant, and someone is likely to douse your cigar in your water glass. Social virtues regulate social occasions precisely to keep them *social* rather than allowing them to lapse into the individualistic pursuit of uninhibited self-expression or blatant self-interest.

Nevertheless, mastery of social virtues is a highly unreliable index of moral goodness, although many of us are so swayed by socially skilled persons that we persistently confuse ourselves on this front. It is precisely the human tendency to conflate social suavity and moral goodness that gives swindlers their operational domain. Successful con men and other flim-flam artists succeed precisely because they know how to exercise the social virtues with insincerity. People who assume that such social mastery is a reliable index of ethical character often find to their chagrin just how naive that assumption can be.

On the other hand, the exercise of social virtues is not *necessarily* unconnected to ethical character, and may in fact give us the only real clues to other people's goodness or villainy that we have. At least social interactions, unlike thoughts, can be seen. They are the parts of others' conduct most visible to us. People's mastery of social virtues doesn't give us *certain* knowledge of anyone's character, but it at least provides us with a first set of clues about them, to be revised, perhaps, as deeper information becomes available.

On the other *other* hand, *not* having mastery of the social virtues is also not a reliable index of moral character. People with an inadequate social education or excessive levels of personal insecurity may fail to give the expected responses to established social cues and thus have their ethical character judged negatively by others, when in fact they may be merely socially inept but not ethically crude or malicious. Behind their social ineptitude they may be persons of great good will, benevolence, and consideration (once you get to know them). How many movies have been made about the generally scorned nerd or the inarticulate prostitute who turns out to have a heart of gold?

The complex dynamics among people created by sincerity or insincerity and by the polished or crude exercise of social virtues has always provided story writers with an inexhaustible source of human interactions ripe for narrative representation. The number of positions that people can occupy along a sliding scale of mastery versus nonmastery of social virtues and sincere exercise versus insincere exercise of social virtues—not to mention people's accurate or mistaken insight into other people's motives as expressed or hidden by their manipulation of social skills—is infinite. Being taken through all of the possible combinations and permutations of social relations as represented in stories (regardless of the medium) constitutes a vastly wider education in social possibilities than we could ever acquire by relying on firsthand experience alone.

Ethical Virtues

The term "ethical virtues" refers to the fundamental components of *character*. One of the few examples of this word used in its original sense in today's mass media occurs in the phrase, "the character issue," which refers to a politician's personal integrity. The ethical virtues refer to the presence or absence of fundamental traits of ethical goodness, but what are these? In the contemporary world, ethical discourse has been translated so often into the terms of other discourses, especially psychological and economic discourse, that reclaiming a straightforward ethical vocabulary tends to hit many people's ears with an old-fashioned, perhaps corny sound. Yet these straightforward ethical terms are the ones that people reach for when issues of agency get urgent: when we need things from other people such as help or truth, and when others need things from us such as generosity or comfort. In such moments the fundamental vocabulary of moral agency reasserts its authority and relevance. What terms make up that vocabulary?

The obvious and most important ethical virtues are identified by precisely the terms you have been using all of your life: kindness, compassion, generosity, honesty (both to others and to one's self), fairness, humility, self-control, and the capacity for shame. There are a number of quasi-ethical virtues such as loyalty and courage, but their moral status, unlike compassion and kindness, is contingent on the moral status of the causes they serve.

It is important in everyday living and in everyday reading (or however we consume stories) not to conflate ethical virtues with intellectual and social virtues. When ethically vicious persons have the social, intellectual, and physical virtues to make themselves seem not only generous and decent but highly attractive, their trickery can be positively dangerous. The unreformed Scrooges of this world may crush others when they can, but they seldom mislead. How many of us are likely to be fooled by an out-and-out Scrooge? It is characters like the charming Steerforth of *David Copperfield* and the talented Edmund of *King Lear* and the brilliant serpent of *Paradise Lost* who mislead people, for the Steerforths, Edmunds, and other snakes-in-the-grass of the world know how to use their intellectual and social virtues as masks for their corruption and viciousness (and they are often *self*-deceiving as well as other-deceiving). One of the most useful functions of art in contemporary society—*especially* in contemporary society, since so few places in contemporary society are capable of creating a sustained discourse about ethical issues—is to remind us of the relevant distinctions among the practical vices and virtues, and to present us with plausible representations of how these *work* in everyday life.

Hardly any story can make headway without employing the distinctions I have laid out here. Even in a story as simple as "The Three Little Pigs," the very structure of the story requires us to see that the problem with the first two little pigs is primarily a deficiency of intellectual virtue—an inability to calculate realistically the dangers of a world where wolves with porcine appetites roam freely—laced with a dollop of ethical deficiency as well, revealed by their self-indulgent desire to spend their time dancing and singing (foolish little porkers) rather than working hard and building sturdy homes. In contrast, pig number three is sufficiently self-disciplined to defer singing and dancing until he has built himself a wolf-proof house. On the other hand, we are also made to see that, comparatively speaking, the ethical deficiencies of the first two pigs are nothing compared to the ethical viciousness of the wolf, who, despite the intellectual virtue he reveals both in his trickery and in his manipulation of catchy rhythms and rhymes, shows himself as an ethical rotter of the first order by wanting to eat pork instead of vegetables and pasta. Within the ethical boundaries of the story, the pigs are not perfect creatures—they exhibit flaws of both intellectual and moral virtues—but they are comparatively innocent. They only want to dance, sing, and play, activities that everyone views as essentially innocent unless, as the first two pigs show, they are excessively indulged, while the wolf—not a real wolf with an ecological "right" to prey on other animals, but a surrogate for all surly predators of the human spirit—is ethically depraved in both his desires and his actions. Moral: even (supposedly) simple stories require us to make fairly subtle distinctions among the different kinds of virtues and vices that are relevant to everyday living, and we all *do* make these distinctions. We make them, moreover, at lightning speeds distorted by the lumbering slowness of my analysis. The point of my account is to show that we mostly do such analysis without being much aware of it.

Virtue in Jane Austen's Novels

Among authors of complex and sophisticated stories, Jane Austen is notable for the clarity with which she uses and thus illustrates the relevance of subtle distinctions among the intellectual, social, ethical, and physical virtues (and vices) of her characters. Few storytellers are as clear as Austen about the difference between being smart, clever, accomplished, and socially polished, or even charismatic (Willoughby in *Sense and Sensibility*, Wickham in *Pride and Prejudice*, and Emma in *Emma*), on the one hand, and being *good* on the other hand.

Austen in novel after novel echoes Philip Sidney's distinction between well-knowing and well-doing. At the end of *Pride and Prejudice,* for example, she has Darcy, as he engages in a retrospective review of the good reasons why Elizabeth turned down his first proposal of marriage, evaluate his own character in the following terms: "I have been a selfish being all my life, in practice, though not in principle. As a child I was taught what was *right,* but I was not taught to correct my temper. I was given good principles, but left to follow them in pride and conceit" (369). In short, Austen has Darcy articulate the view that *knowing* what is right (an intellectual virtue) is not enough in itself to make one want to *do* what is right (an ethical virtue). Darcy's comment also shows the value of the capacity to feel shame as well. By means of intellectual virtue we can *note* or even *analyze* our ethical violations (as does Edmund in *King Lear*) until the cows come home, but in the absence of the capacity for shame, we have no motive to apologize, offer redress, or otherwise make things right. The capacity for shame is the one virtue that *mobilizes* all the others.

As Darcy has come to realize, the principles of virtue must be internalized as active and shaping principles of everyday conduct, not merely stored up as static, inert slogans the way students give rote test answers. Austen is clear that if our principles do not shape our conduct, then no amount of brilliance among our intellectual and social virtues will compensate for vices of selfishness, self-indulgence, callousness, pride, and deceit.

At the end of *Mansfield Park,* Sir Thomas Bertram muses ruefully on the active internalization of principles as he reflects on the upbringing of his own daughters, who, like Darcy, have been given the right instruction, but only as a matter of abstract precept, not of concrete conduct. With respect to the ethical education of Sir Thomas's two daughters, Maria and Julia Bertram, both of whom have disgraced themselves and one of whom, Maria, has brought real harm to her family, Sir Thomas can only conclude that

> something must have been wanting *within*. . . . He feared that principle, active principle, had been wanting, that they had never been properly taught to govern their inclinations and tempers, by that sense of duty which alone can suffice. *They had been instructed theoretically in their religion, but never required to bring it into daily practice.* To be distinguished for elegance and accomplishments—the authorised object of their youth—could have had no useful influence that way, no moral effect on the mind. *He had meant them to be good, but his care had been directed to the understanding and manners, not the disposition;* and of the necessity of self-denial and humility, he feared they had never heard from any lips that could profit them. (463; emphasis added)

And in *Persuasion,* a story in which every reader desires that Anne Elliot should acquire a comfortable home of her own where she is properly valued, far away from her father's home where she is persistently *not* valued, we all see, as does Lady Russell, the many ways in which a proposal from Anne's cousin, Mr. Elliot, the heir presumptive to the seat of her father's baronetcy, Kellynch Hall, would be a good match. But despite the unquestionable eligibility of Mr. Elliot's position, and despite his unquestionable cultivation of both mind and manners, there still remains the more important—the essential—issue of his character, which *is* questionable. Anne says of Mr. Elliot that

> though they had now been acquainted a month, she could not be satisfied that she really knew his character. That he was a sensible man, an agreeable man,—that he talked well, professed good opinions, seemed to judge properly and as a man of principle,—this was all clear enough. He certainly knew what was right, nor could [Anne]

fix on any one article of moral duty evidently transgressed; but yet she would have been afraid to answer for his conduct. . . . She saw . . . that there had been a period of his life (and probably not a short one) when he had been, at least, careless on all serious matters; and, though he might now think very differently, who could answer for the true sentiments of a clever, cautious man, grown old enough to appreciate a fair character? . . .

Mr. Elliot was rational, discreet, polished,—but he was not open. . . .

Mr. Elliot was too generally agreeable. Various as were the tempers in her father's house, he pleased them all. He endured too well,—stood too well with everybody. He had spoken to her with some degree of openness of Mrs. Clay; had appeared completely to see what Mrs. Clay was about, and to hold her in contempt; and yet Mrs. Clay found him as agreeable as anybody. (160–61)

In other words, Mr. Elliot is everything anyone could wish on the surface—his mastery of social virtues is adroit and comprehensive—but Austen knows that character is a matter of integrity that goes all the way down, not a mastery of mere surface conventions, and that when inner integrity is missing, then the question arises, as it does in this passage, whether the social and intellectual virtues are not only to be looked through, so to speak, but to be criticized for masking a corrupt agency. In Anne Elliot's view, a cultivated mind and polished manners are positively damnable if they disguise that most important feature of anyone's agency, his or her status as an ethical or unethical character.

Finally, the whole story of *Emma* is the story of how the headstrong Emma Woodhouse starts down the path of possible disgrace and harm like Maria Bertram but, unlike Maria, learns to know herself in relation to active ethical principles in time *not* to do real harm, or at least in time to repair what real harm she has done. Emma's source of good advice and instruction throughout the story is Mr. Knightley, who takes Emma to task each time she deceives herself about right conduct. At the Box Hill picnic, for example, when Emma humiliates Miss Bates by publicly ridiculing her garrulity, Emma is being intellectually clever and socially brilliant, but she is not being good. Mr. Knightley reproves her behavior in just these terms as they leave Box Hill to return home. He accuses Emma of at least four forms of dishonesty:

- deceiving herself about the real harm done to Miss Bates's social standing
- deceiving herself about the selfishness and unkindness of her ridicule (sacrificing another person's well-being in order to display her intellectual virtues and social preeminence)
- deceiving herself about her act as a crude display of pride (placing her own desire to lead and rule ahead of respect and duties due to others)
- deceiving herself about her lack of compassion (insufficient feeling for the vulnerability of a weak and defenseless person)

While the whole speech that Mr. Knightley makes *is* a kind of sermon, it does not come off *as* a sermon, at least not in the sense of abstract moralizing or pontification. Mr. Knightley grounds everything he says on the concrete realities of the social and ethical context of the characters' everyday lives. He talks not about abstract precepts but about concrete conduct, the social and moral *practices* (not just theory) that give Highbury its distinct ethical and social texture, a place in which the weak, the vulnerable, and even the garrulous, such as Miss Bates, may be nourished by a collective commitment to the importance of specific ethical virtues.

> "I cannot see you acting wrong with wrong, without a remonstrance. How could you be so unfeeling to Miss Bates? How could you be so insolent in your wit to a woman of her character, age, and situation?— Emma, I had not thought it possible."
>
> Emma recollected, blushed, was sorry, but tried to laugh it off.
>
> "Nay, how could I help saying what I did?—Nobody could have helped it. It was not so very bad. I dare say she did not understand me."
>
> "... Were she your equal in situation—but, Emma, consider how far this is from being the case. She is poor; she has sunk from the comforts she was born to; and, if she live to old age, must probably sink more. Her situation should secure your compassion. It was

badly done, indeed! . . . to have you now, in thoughtless spirits, and the pride of the moment, laugh at her, humble her—and before her niece, too—and before others, many of whom (certainly *some,*) would be entirely guided by *your* treatment of her." (374–75)

This last passage highlights the virtue I have termed "the capacity for shame." You may prefer alternative phrases such as "the capacity for repentance" or "the urge to seek forgiveness." However we name this virtue, it operates as the energizing component that makes the other virtues active rather than passive. None of us goes through life without making mistakes, but if our response to mistakes, errors, transgressions, and wrongdoings is simply to recognize them, or, like Emma, to laugh them off, neither of these is a sufficient motive to make us modify our future conduct along more ethically sensitive lines. Our virtues will never work *actively* until we have the capacity to be *ashamed* of ourselves when we violate them. And not until we can independently subject our conduct to this kind of ethical scrutiny can we begin to make claims about being good.

From this point of view, the key words in the passage just quoted that keep us tied to the reality of Emma's goodness and our hopes for her improvement are the words "Emma . . . was sorry" in the second paragraph. The fact that Emma immediately registers shame at what she has done is the only thing that keeps her good as well as highly bred, good as well as smart and clever. Throughout the whole novel, in fact, Austen gives us access to the inner workings of Emma's shame and repentance each time she violates one of the moral virtues, and it is this sustained insight into a character that is flawed—but that can feel ashamed of its flaws and that wants to be and to do better—that keeps our sympathies tied to Emma during the period of her repeated failings and her annoying capacity for rationalizing away those same failings.

Story as Ethical Discourse

What I have really been discussing here is story's capacity to create a special kind of ethical discourse. *Emma* and *Mansfield Park* are novels, not philosophy, but in them the representation of human actions and especially the evaluation of the worthiness or culpability of those actions is clearly *based* on an ethical theory that Austen forthrightly deploys as the touchstone for her judgments about her characters' ethical agency. To see these judgments worked out, to participate in them as readers, and to recognize them as active principles of everyday conduct rather than as yes-or-no answers to Sunday school questions about "how to be good" is to receive the kind of practice at moral deliberation that all of us need if we are to be liberated from the clichés, prejudices, catchwords, and knee-jerk reactions of everyday society. In the words of Martha Nussbaum,

> literary forms call forth certain specific sorts of practical activity in the reader that can be evoked in no other way. . . . We need a story of a certain kind, with characters of a certain type in it, if our own sense of life and of value is to be called forth in the way most appropriate for practical reflection. . . . This practical conception is most adequately expressed . . . in texts that have a complex narrative structure. . . . Those narratives are also the texts best suited to evoke in the reader the moral activities associated with this conception [which Nussbaum defines as] the human importance of a fine-tuned responsiveness to complex particular cases and of a willingness to see them *as* particular and irreducible to general rules. (290)

Nussbaum's comment helps us see that to accompany Jane Austen through the representations of and judgments about her fictional characters is to participate in the kind of vital analysis of ethical issues that determines the texture and quality of all of our social interactions, no less than Mr. Knightley's vital analysis of Emma's conduct helps establish the quality of the ethical and social life in Highbury. Surely Jane Austen helps us see not only the existence of important ethical categories but, equally important, their relevance to everyday life. If, to paraphrase and adapt St. Paul, these four virtues abide—physical, intellectual, social, and ethical—then the greatest of these are the ethical virtues, for it is they which motivate us to go through life neither envying nor puffed up, rejoicing not in iniquity, not easily provoked, and rejoicing in the truth (see 1 Corinthians 13). For the many to whom this biblical language possesses too much moralism and too little psychology, the moral virtues are important because they motivate us to go through life with empathy for others and humility about ourselves, and thus allow us to lead socially productive and psychologically integrated lives. Both versions mean the same thing. Stories contribute to our understanding of what the right thing is, give us models of how the right thing might be done, and show us how things look when the wrong thing is done. Stories of course cannot *make* us be good any more than religion or the law or the Ten Commandments can, but if we are ever to make ourselves better by seeing ourselves and the issues of life more clearly, more comprehensively, and in greater depth, then it follows that stories—at least some kinds of stories—are qualified to provide us with assistance that is vital, vivid, and irreplaceable.

Stories and the Nutritional Analogy

Nutritionists like to say "we are what we eat," a thumbnail way of saying that our habitual diet is foundational to our overall health. My argument throughout this book has been similar. I have been saying that readers' habitual imaginative diet—the consistent consumption of narrative scenarios—is foundationally important for our ethical health (or ill health). This analogy leads to two extensions, one dealing with further implications for the story consumer, the other dealing with the role of the nutritional specialist—the ethical critic.

Nutritionists deal with exercise in addition to diet. They know that our bodies become what they are not only because of what we take in, but also because of how we exercise. Kenneth Burke throws light on this issue of ethical exercise. In a chapter that he calls "Literature as Equipment for Living," Burke lays down an argument—sketchy but pregnant—asserting that fiction "names" the situations of life we respond to, and, moreover, helps us adopt attitudes toward these situations that define our own ethical agency. By representing these situations in all of their concrete embeddedness, and by helping us "adopt an attitude," stories provide us with models, Burke argues, for how to deal with life's situations.

> The main point is this: A work like *Madame Bovary* (or its homely American translation, *Babbitt*) is the strategic naming of a situation.

It singles out a pattern of experience that is sufficiently representative of our social structure . . . for people to "need a word for it" and *to adopt an attitude toward it*. . . . Art forms like "tragedy" or "comedy" or "satire" would be treated as equipments for living that size up situations in various ways and in keeping with correspondingly various attitudes. (296–304; emphasis added)

In adopting attitudes we create ethos. The assumption behind the nutritional analogy (reinforced by Burke's comment) is that while our diet of stories can never be *all*-determinative of character, we uncritically underrate the ethical influence of our narrative diet in general (see Gregory, "Character Formation"; Gregory, "Sound of Story").

Ethical criticism helps ordinary readers, parents, teachers, and others find ways of saying what is valuable about the love they feel for some great stories. William Kennedy recalls his initial confusion when, as an undergraduate at the University of Virginia, he first heard William Faulkner talk in class about literature's ability to "uplift" the human heart.

This uplift business baffled me. I was reading and rereading *The Sound and the Fury, Sanctuary, Light in August, The Wild Palms* and *Absalom, Absalom!*—tales of incest and whoring and rape and dying love and madness and murder and racial hate and miscegenational tragedy and idiocy—and saying to myself, "This is uplift?"

But I kept reading and found I couldn't get enough; I had to reread to satisfy the craving, and came to answer the question in a word: yes. I felt exalted by the man's work, not by reveling in all the disasters, but by learning from his language and his insights and his storytelling genius how certain other people lived and thought. I was privileged to enter into the most private domains of their lives and they became my friends or people I'd keep at least at arm's length or people I pitied, feared or loved. This was truly an uplifting experience, something akin to real friendship, and I began to understand the process by which writing reaches into another person's heart.[3] (35)

The nutritional analogy suggests to the ethical critic a proper function: assisting others to think more clearly about the relationship between stories and ethos. No nutritionist worth his professional degree would ever let a client get by with the shabby argument that, after all, chocolate cake is "mere entertainment," or is subject to a variety of nutritional interpretations, or is composed of nutritionally unstable perspectives, or is nutritionally indeterminate, or must be viewed in its historical nutritional context, or is the favorite dessert of the English faculty at Yale, Harvard, and Duke. Without being diverted by such self-serving and diversionary rationalizations, but also without arrogating or even *desiring* the authority to *force* the client to forgo chocolate cake, the responsible nutritionist would nevertheless be aggressive in presenting the most reasonable and carefully thought-out arguments he could muster *for* healthy food and *against* rich desserts. No ethical critic who has really thought about the complexity of the relationship between ethos and stories has such faith in the infallibility of her judgment that she would even want, much less attempt, to exercise the power to *coerce* other people to consume only the stories that she likes best. Those who *do* wish to enforce their views on writers or libraries or readers or movie lovers are not ethical critics but dogmatists. The two should not be confused.

Wrapping Up: Who Do We Wish to Become?

Nothing should be clearer by now than my passionate belief that we do ourselves an injustice not to think hard and evaluate carefully the potential ethical influence of the stories we put into our hearts and heads because, like any other form of nutrition, their contents nourish us either richly or poorly. Surely it is not a violation of aesthetic purity—a bogus notion to begin with—and obviously it is not a call for censorship to encourage us to prefer stories that richly reinforce the interplay between the physical, intellectual, social, and ethical virtues, an interplay that determines the quality of everyone's everyday lives. Stories that pretend that there are no such virtues or that attack such virtues reflect a view of life that will not stand up to the kind of argument about the inescapability of ethical standards that I have offered in previous chapters of this book.

Most of the stories that I disapprove of are not stories that deliberately undermine people's efforts to live effective, full, or responsible lives.

The kinds of stories whose influence I deplore, and invite you to deplore as well, are not deliberately malicious stories but are mostly *thoughtless* stories that eagerly reflect, mostly for commercial reasons, the leading clichés and prejudices of any given cultural moment. In times of war, for example, when patriotism is being called for by governmental officials, some movie makers, TV programmers, and story writers are sure to start creating stories that fit the moment almost as if their stories were being made to order. But whether the issue du jour is a new call for patriotism, a trendy new therapy, celebrity high jinks, holiday sentimentality, or some other tidbit that creates a moment of cultural froth, some stories invite us to participate in the prejudices of culture and the clichés of the moment with a breathless sense of being in the know, while other stories help us see culture's prejudices and clichés for what they are and also challenge us to reach for an understanding of perennial issues that lie at the core of human existence. Always, the issues at the core of human existence will have an ethical valence, an understanding of which—or at least thoughtfulness about which—is essential to anyone wishing to live a life of autonomy, reflection, and good judgment.

My point is not that the prejudices of culture and the clichés of the moment are always and necessarily wrong. My larger point is that stories trafficking in prejudices and clichés anesthetize our ability to *think* about the very issues they pretend to illuminate. The stories themselves are thoughtless, and they issue powerful invitations to their consumers also to become thoughtless. In my view, any influence that anesthetizes our ability to think—whether that influence comes from stories or from anywhere else—is an influence that diminishes our grasp on autonomy and freedom. Surely we have a right to ask the stories we consume to help us critique the terms of our existence, not to cement us in whatever transitory values happen to dominate the moment. To be whipped around by transitory cultural values, to accept invitations from stories or from any other source to map our own ethos onto whatever "they" or "everyone" is thinking or doing, the farther away from autonomy, freedom, and thoughtfulness we move.

Ethical criticism challenges all of us steeped in stories—in other words, it challenges all of us—to consider whether we not only have a right but whether we have an obligation, not to any external agent or agency but to ourselves, to ask whether the stories of our culture help us along the path toward autonomy, freedom, and thoughtfulness, or whether they place obstacles in the way of our deeper forms of understanding, feeling, and judgment. It is in the interests of marketers, manufacturers, and other powerful people to make us think that our uncritical acceptance of the status quo is the same thing as freedom itself. But when the stories we consume in movies, in novels, and on TV operate on us like commercials, then we have a right to object—not by making proposals for censorship (which never work and carry more evils than the disease), but by engaging in vigorous ethical discourse about who we want to become and about the kinds of influences that help or hinder our progress. In that vigorous ethical debate, which should occur on a great many fronts, one of the most interesting and important questions that arises is how to evaluate the potential ethical influence of the stories that swirl around us with the omnipresence of air. This book has been an attempt to help us conduct that ethical evaluation in ways that avoid dogmatism, sectarianism, and bullying, while simultaneously respecting our right and our need to raise unembarrassed ethical questions. At stake is nothing less than our ethos: the issue of how we turn into the persons we become.

NOTES

CHAPTER ONE
Reading for Life

1. For my birthday a few years ago a good friend of mine, having read this chapter in an early draft, presented me with a copy of *Smoky the Crow*, which he purchased from an online company specializing in hard-to-find and out-of-print books. Those of you who share with me vivid recollections of your first reading experiences can imagine my pleasure at seeing this simple and innocent little book again after all these years, its institutional green cover with black and white illustrations looking exactly as I remembered it from my childhood. In rereading *Smoky*, however, I was chagrined to see how much of the book's contents I had forgotten over the decades.

CHAPTER THREE
For Good or Ill

1. The New York commuter who hops on the subway every day is not much different in this regard from the Amazon hunter who takes his bow and poison-tipped arrows into the jungle every day to make a living. Both lives, and everyone else's as well, are mostly a matter of doing the same things today that we did yesterday and mostly in the company of the same people.

CHAPTER FOUR
Stories and the Ethics of Experience

1. I'm not failing to recognize that the characters in stories are very often disorganized, disoriented, and sometimes mad. It is not stories' *characters*

who convey to us an image of unity, but the work of narrative art itself: a good story about boring people is not a boring story, and a good story about haplessly disorganized schlemiels is not thereby a haplessly disorganized story.

CHAPTER FIVE
Judgment that Bites, Assent that Risks

1. According to some of the prevailing theories in literary criticism, we were facing a nonproblem. Deconstruction (first advanced by the French philosopher Jacques Derrida) was new in 1973 but already gaining great steam, and from Derrida's point of view the signifiers (words and phonemes) making up the texts in Mellie's anthology were in constant motion, never coming to rest, and no determinate meaning could therefore be attributed to or derived from the story. According to deconstruction, then, we had no worry as parents about what our daughter might take these (objectionable) stories to mean, for they didn't, and couldn't, "mean" anything at all. Needless to say this view—highly exciting at the time to intellectuals doing rarified theory-talk at literary conferences far removed from children's nurseries—didn't seem helpful to us as parents trying to solve a perennial problem in practical psychology. At another level deconstruction seemed, frankly, untrue, but its truth status is not the issue here.

If our problem was a nonproblem to deconstructionists, it was also a nonproblem to advocates of certain versions of reader response theory, who, like deconstructionists, were also insistent on the indeterminacy of textual meanings. In these theories, however, nonmeaning is not a function of the indeterminate properties of language (as in deconstruction), but a function of the emotional needs of the reader. This is an interesting proposition. According to this view, readers reconstitute, or rewrite, texts according to their emotional needs. A reader's emotions "take over" a text in imperial ways, colonizing it with whatever meanings the reader "needs." Basically this view says that readers simply rewrite each text more or less in their own image *as* they read. The text has no objective reality about it and thus exerts no demands on the reader. Therefore Mellie would make out of the text whatever she wanted to make—not to worry. But since we wanted Mellie to grow up able to read a textbook or a newspaper or a Shakespeare play and see something besides her own reflection, reader response theory seemed no more helpful than deconstruction.

Two other versions of contemporary literary criticism supported our view that we had a problem, but we did not like the solutions these theories offered us. Certain feminist theories, for example, offered a solution succinctly defined five years later by Judith Fetterley in a book called *The Resisting Reader* (1978). The idea here is that women readers should approach every literary text with their antagonistic defenses powered up like some kind of force field in a science fiction movie. The point to women reading this way is to resist being molded into traditional female roles and attitudes by the reigning patriarchal values subtly advanced in American fiction. This resistant force field, by placing readers in an adversarial relationship with the text's patriarchal ideology from word one to word last, would prevent infection by effectively blocking any affective bonding with the characters and events in any story. But to my wife and me as parents, pre-Fetterley feminists seemed of no more help than deconstructionists or reader response theorists because, simpleminded as we might be thought by our professional colleagues, we actually wanted our daughter to *like* reading, not to view it as a hostile, suspicious activity. To take Fetterley's kind of approach meant that we would work hard to deny our daughter the delights of literary assent—not only the delights, but the education—of being taken to other worlds and learning about other people by saying yes to story's invitations.

On another front, contemporary literary criticism based on the writings of Michel Foucault, another French philosopher, certainly agreed with us that literary texts trafficked in oppressive stereotypes and are therefore a problem, but the Foucauldian solution was only a stronger version of the feminist notion of the resisting reader. Foucauldian criticism basically advised us to view literary texts as malicious agents of an overarching power system designed to keep the sheep of society deluded with the illusion that their imprisoning pen is really a domain of freedom. To take Foucault seriously meant that we would be committed to teaching our daughter to view literary authors as slavish pencils writing master scripts of oppression designed to maintain the status of society's top-dog power groups. Talk about taking the fun out of reading! Jane Austen and Emily Dickinson as agents of social oppression! This was not exactly the view of story we wanted to give our daughter.

2. "The willing suspension of disbelief" is directly contrary to the "hermeneutics of suspicion" recommended by postmodern criticism, which tends to turn the act of interacting with narratives into a hectoring, scolding activity focused mostly on artists' failures of political correctness.

CHAPTER SIX
Story as Companionship

1. For an interesting take on this issue, see Bellah et al., *Habits of the Heart*.

CHAPTER EIGHT
Ethics of Narrative in a Practical Vein Once More

1. The phrase appears to have originated in the American south, although the date and circumstances are uncertain. There's certainly an association with the sport of baseball, and most of the early citations of the phrase mention the game. That includes the first mention of it in print, in James Thurber's *55 Short Stories from The New Yorker*, November 1942: "She must be a Dodger fan. Red Barber announces the Dodger games over the radio and he uses those expressions. . . . 'Sitting in the catbird seat' means sitting pretty, like a batter with three balls and no strikes on him" (http://www.phrases.org. uk/meanings/87600.html).

2. By saying that Thurber's choice of a suggestive name for Mrs. Barrows is brilliant I do not mean to say that Thurber's strategy is unique. Choosing names that praise characters or condemn them or reveal something about their character or conduct or profession is as old as Sophocles, who named Oedipus "lame footed" because his father drove a nail through his feet when he was born; and Shakespeare, who named his dull constable Anthony Dull, his sprightly inn owner Mistress Quickly, and his bellows mender Francis Flute; and Dickens, who named his brutish schoolmaster M'Choakumchild, named his inexorable utilitarian ironmonger Mr. Gradgrind, and named the mad woman who kept birds Miss Flite. But no matter how common the technique is, when the name is "right," we cannot help being led by it.

CHAPTER NINE
Ethical Engagements Over Time

1. For other recent accounts of professional rereading and personal reflection see Booth, *Company*; Booth, *Modern Dogma*; Booth, *Rhetoric*; Booth,

"The Way I Loved"; Nussbaum; Nafisi, Lesser, Edmundson, and Graff (*Beyond, Clueless*).

2. I was the person my father hit, but he fought with everyone. He was a not very successful Protestant minister (for reasons of personal pathology, not perverted theology), and as he fought with those persons in our churches' social and financial hierarchy who were most powerful, he always displayed the same mean bitterness, the same cold fury, and ultimately the same inevitable failure as the white trash father in Faulkner's "Barn Burning," who fought with his landed employers.

3. See in particular Martha Nussbaum's insights into the Copperfield/ Steerforth relationship in Section V of "Steerforth's Arm: Love and the Moral Point of View" (335–64).

4. Even here, however, right in the midst of my absorption in intellectual pursuits, ethical vision played an important role, for what was motivating my intellectual efforts more than anything else was my ethical vision of not just becoming intellectually accomplished but taking on the attributes that I thought described intellectually accomplished persons: wise, gracious, and benign. The fact that I was ludicrously wrong in my naive assumption that most intellectually accomplished persons possess this kind of character doesn't diminish the ethical drive at the center of my ambition.

5. All during my childhood and youth, when we kids played the "which animal would you like to be" game, I always chose the elephant. I was forty before I realized that this choice derived directly from my desire to be a person big enough and powerful enough to repel (and punish?) all attackers.

6. I delighted in my new ability to see that when Nelly asserts to Edgar that Heathcliff's return "will make a jubilee to [Catherine]"—next to which in the margins of my college text of *Wuthering Heights* I had written "an ill-considered statement"—Nelly was *not* making merely "an ill-considered statement" but was making mischief. I was pleased to catch Nelly making mischief again when she "related [to Edgar] the scene in the court, and . . . the whole subsequent dispute" (96). This is the dispute in which Heathcliff spits out to Catherine several insults about Edgar, including the violent threat that "every day I grow madder after sending [Edgar] to heaven!" (97). But when Catherine, distraught over Edgar's angry reaction to Heathcliff's threats, supposes that Edgar knows about Heathcliff's insults because he was eavesdropping on their conversation, Nelly does not confess that she has related this conversation to Linton. "What possess [Edgar] to turn listener? [asks Catherine] Heathcliff's talk was outrageous . . . [but] had Edgar never gathered our

conversation, he would never have been the worse for it" (97). The fact that Edgar had not, indeed, *overheard* that conversation but had been gratuitously *told* of it by Nelly Dean shows Nelly to be manipulative and self-serving in ways that are truly harmful to those around her. My graduate-reader–self was determined to find every such instance (of which there are many) and to bring Nelly to the bar of narrative and ethical judgment, where I intended to sentence her to the fullest extent allowed by the laws of literary criticism. I think I may have pictured myself wearing the barrister's periwig—not a good fashion for me at any time of my life but especially ridiculous in those graduate school days when I still looked fifteen—for the ethical condemnation of Nelly Dean's meddlesome perfidy as triumphantly exposed by my graduate student skills of narrative cross-examination.

7. In the Ophelia rip-off scene, Catherine, having worked herself into a state of nearly mad distraction after the quarrel between Heathcliff and Edgar, tears open her pillowcase with her teeth and then goes into a reverie-like cataloguing of the various birds' feathers that she now begins pulling from the pillow's insides. "That's a turkey's . . . and this is a wild-duck's; and this is a pigeon's. . . . And here is a moor-cock's; and this—I should know it among a thousand—is a lapwing's. . . . I made [Heathcliff] promise he'd never shoot a lapwing" (105). This is such a close adaptation of Ophelia's mad scene that it seems little more than a substitution of feathers for flowers. Ophelia enters: "There's rosemary, that's for remembrance. Pray, love, remember. And there's pansies; that's for thoughts. . . . There's fennel for you, and columbines. There's rue for you, and here's some for me. . . . There's a daisy. I would give you some violets, but they withered all when my father died" (*Hamlet* IV, v). Brontë's working this vein of rue and poignancy on Catherine's part has never seemed persuasive to me.

8. The Keats rip-off is so blatant that it hardly seems as if Catherine's voice and character provide any kind of adequate disguise—much less a creative reworking—of it. As Catherine speaks to Nelly of her declining health, she says of her bodily prospects, "the thing that irks me most is this shattered prison, after all. I'm tired, and tired of being enclosed here. I'm wearying to escape into that glorious world, and to be always there; not seeing it dimly through tears, and yearning for it through the walls of an aching heart; but really with it, and in it. . . . You are sorry for me—very soon . . . I shall be sorry for *you*. I shall be incomparably beyond and above you all" (134). In his famous ode, Keats, apostrophizing the nightingale, longs to "Fade far away, dissolve, and quite forget / What thou among the leaves hast never

known, / The weariness, the fever, and the fret / Here where men sit and hear each other groan; / Where palsy shakes a few, sad, last gray hairs, / Where youth grows pale, and spectre-thin, and dies, / Where but to think is to be full of sorrow / And leaden-eyed despairs, / Where Beauty cannot keep her lustrous eyes, / Or new Love pine at them beyond tomorrow. / Away! away! for I will fly to thee / . . . Darkling I listen; and for many a time / I have been half in love with easeful Death / . . . Now more than ever seems it rich to die."

9. I am indebted for this suggestion to my colleague and daughter Melissa Gregory, whose views about *Wuthering Heights* as driven by Brontë's contempt for middle-class "niceness" and hypocrisy she has urged on me with great energy, persuasiveness, and perspicacity.

10. I long ago bit the bullet on my illegitimate desire—which every one of my readers shares with me—to elevate my own preferences in taste and ideas to the status of generally required standards for everyone else, and I have no wish to make myself sound as pompous or foolish as F. R. Leavis intoning that "great" novelists are "significant in terms of the human awareness they promote" or that "the adult mind doesn't as a rule find in Dickens a challenge to an unusual and sustained seriousness" (19). Nor am I eager to hear myself making some fatuous claim that Emily Brontë lacks "depth" in the way that Arnold is often quoted, *not* as a compliment, for his claim that Chaucer lacks "high seriousness" ("Study," 1257). The detailed and generous analysis of Chaucer's art that precedes Arnold's unfortunate formulation renders him much less guilty of ugly smugness than does Leavis's attitude of insufferable patronage toward Dickens, but I have no grounds for being either smug or patronizing. In any event, while R. S. Crane concedes that all critics have their prejudices, he enjoins us all "to try not to exalt our prejudices . . . into religious dogmas or to expect them to be shared by more than a reasonable number of our contemporaries" (xiii). In acceptance of the wisdom of Crane's dictum, I am willing to live within the limitations of this constraint, and I am willing to accept this limited degree of audience approval.

11. Postmodern theory turns my formulation around—embodiment precedes ethical vision: we get our visions from our historical situatedness—but this is both too simple and, ultimately, wrong, because the only kind of embodiment that postmodernists are interested in is *cultural* forms of embodiment, and cultural forms of embodiment offer no explanation for those deep forms of human orientation that are pre-cultural but not transcendent. I refer to those deeper forms of human orientation explained by evolutionary psychology and cognitive science that postmodern theory *never* takes

into account. These deeper forms of human (biological and evolutionary) orientation involve no positing of transcendental ideals—they are not Derrida's "transcendental Signified"—but neither are they created by culture. To the evolutionary psychologist there is an embodied human nature that derives not from culture but from a common human brain structure, common parameters of human perception, common systems of endocrine and hormonal flow, common requirements of brain chemistry, and so on. Indeed, from the point of view of evolutionary psychology, culture itself is rooted in these considerations—which give rise to sociability and to the need for ethical systems. (See E. O. Wilson, *Consilience*; E. O. Wilson, *On Human Nature*; J. Q. Wilson; Pinker, *Blank Slate*; Pinker, *Language Instinct*; Lakoff and Johnson, *Metaphors*; Lakoff and Johnson, *Philosophy*; M. Johnson, *Body*; M. Johnson, *Moral Imagination*; Boyer; de Waal, *Ape*; de Waal, *Good Natured*; Wrangham and Peterson; Damasio, *Feeling*; Damasio, *Looking*; Calvin; Mithen.)

CHAPTER TEN
Postscript

1. In the words of David Barash, who summarizes here an increasingly important area of ethical thought developing in biology, the problem in human conduct is that

> we need to refrain from both morally repulsive excesses of selfishness and overdoses of self-destructive altruism. One of the most powerful insights of current evolutionary theory is that although our brains have been produced by self-serving genes, these same self-serving inclinations have resulted in behavior that is often cooperative, social, and—at the level of bodies, if not genes—altruistic. . . . The more we learn about biology, the more sensible becomes the basic thrust of social ethics, precisely because—even with the meliorating effects of kin selection and reciprocity—nearly everyone, left to his or her devices, is likely to be selfish, probably more than is good for the rest of us. Seen that way, a biologically appropriate wisdom begins to emerge from the various commandments and moral injunctions, nearly all of which can be interpreted as trying to get people to behave "better"—that is, to develop and then act upon large and generous desires, to strive to be more amiable, more altruistic, less competitive, and less selfish than they might otherwise be. (B7)

2. This is not to say that organized societies do not also commit horrendous acts (wars of aggression, death squads, genocide, apartheid, and so on), but when organized societies commit such crimes, they almost always receive organized resistance and moral condemnation from other organized societies of the world that employ morally oriented language such as "crimes against humanity" as part of the organized resistance. At some point admissions of guilt and efforts at reparation, even if greatly incomplete, are called for and often made. The crimes that people commit against each other in societies where all moral standards have disappeared, however, are seldom reported, resisted, punished, or even taken into account. Victims seldom have any redress, and perpetrators are seldom brought to trial.

3. In *Love's Knowledge* Martha Nussbaum corroborates Kennedy's sense of friendship with literary characters and books in a parallel account of her own schooling:

> In my school there was nothing that Anglo-American conventions would call "philosophy." And yet the questions of this book (which I shall call, broadly, ethical) were raised and investigated. The pursuit of truth there was a certain sort of reflection about literature. And the form the ethical questions took, as the roots of some of them grew into me, was usually that of reflecting and feeling about a particular literary character, a particular novel; or, sometimes, an episode from history, but seen as the material for a dramatic plot of my own imagining. All this was, of course, seen in relation to life itself, which was itself seen, increasingly, in ways influenced by the stories and the sense of life they expressed. Aristotle, Plato, Spinoza, Kant—these were still unknown to me. Dickens, Jane Austen, Aristophanes, Ben Jonson, Euripides, Shakespeare, Dostoyevsky—these were my friends, my spheres of reflection. (11)

WORKS CITED

Abrams, M. H. "Belief and the Suspension of Disbelief." *Literature and Belief: English Institute Essays 1957.* Ed. M. H. Abrams. New York: Columbia University Press, 1958. 1–30.

———. *A Glossary of Literary Terms.* 6th ed. New York: Holt, Rinehart and Winston, 1993.

Angier, Natalie. "Scientists Mull Role of Empathy in Man and Beast." *New York Times* May 9, 1995, sec. B: 7, 9.

Arnold, Matthew. "Preface to *Poems, 1853.*" *Victorian Poetry and Poetics.* Ed. Walter E. Houghton and G. Robert Stange. 2nd ed. Boston: Houghton Mifflin, 1968. 487–94.

———. "The Study of Poetry." *English Prose of the Victorian Era.* Ed. Charles R. Harrold and William D. Templeton. New York: Oxford University Press, 1938. 1247–64.

Asher, Kenneth. "Ethics and Literature." *ALSC Newsletter* 2.2/3 (Spring/ Summer 1996): 1+.

Austen, Jane. *Emma.* 1816. *The Oxford Illustrated Jane Austen.* Ed. R. W. Chapman. 3rd ed. Vol. 4. Oxford: Oxford University Press, 1933.

———. *Mansfield Park.* 1814. *The Oxford Illustrated Jane Austen.* Ed. R. W. Chapman. 3rd ed. Vol. 3. Oxford: Oxford University Press, 1933.

———. *Persuasion.* 1818. *The Oxford Illustrated Jane Austen.* Ed. R. W. Chapman. 3rd ed. Vol. 5. Oxford: Oxford University Press, 1933.

———. *Pride and Prejudice.* 1813. *The Oxford Illustrated Jane Austen.* Ed. R. W. Chapman. 3rd ed. Vol. 2. Oxford: Oxford University Press, 1933.

Bakhtin, M. M. "Discourse in the Novel." *The Dialogic Imagination: Four Essays.* Trans. Caryl Emerson and Michael Holquist. Ed. Michael Holquist. Austin: University of Texas Press, 1981. 258–422.

Barash, David P. "The Conflicting Pressures of Selfishness and Altruism." *Chronicle of Higher Education,* Section *The Chronicle Review* 49.45 (July 18, 2003): B7+.

Bellah, Robert N., et al. *Habits of the Heart: Individualism and Commitment in American Life.* Berkeley: University of California Press, 1985.

Birkerts, Sven. *The Gutenberg Elegies: The Fate of Reading in an Electronic Age.* New York: Ballantine Books, 1994.

Booth, Wayne C. *The Company We Keep: An Ethics of Fiction.* Berkeley: University of California Press, 1988.

———. *Modern Dogma and the Rhetoric of Assent.* Chicago: University of Chicago Press, 1974.

———. *The Rhetoric of Fiction.* Chicago: University of Chicago Press, 1961.

———. "'The Way I Loved George Eliot': Friendship with Books as a Neglected Critical Metaphor." *Kenyon Review* 2 (1980): 4–27.

Booth, Wayne C., and Marshall Gregory. "The Unbroken Continuum: Booth/Gregory on Teaching and Ethical Criticism." *Pedagogy: Critical Approaches to Teaching Literature, Language, Composition, and Culture* 7.1 (Spring 2007): 40–60.

Boyer, Pascal. *Religion Explained: The Evolutionary Origins of Religious Thought.* New York: Basic Books, 2001.

Brodsky, Joseph. *On Grief and Reason.* New York: Farrar, Straus Giroux, 1995.

Brontë, Emily. *Wuthering Heights.* 1847. Ed. William M. Sale. Norton Critical Edition. New York: W. W. Norton, 1963.

Brooks, Peter. *Reading for the Plot: Design and Intention in Narrative.* Cambridge, MA: Harvard University Press, 1984.

Browning, Robert. "Porphyria's Lover." 1836. *Robert Browning's Poetry.* Ed. James F. Loucks. New York: W. W. Norton, 1979. 74–75.

Bruner, Jerome. "Life as Narrative." *Social Research* 54 (Spring 1987): 11–32.

Buford, Bill. "The Seductions of Storytelling." *New Yorker* June 24 and July 1, 1996, special fiction issue: 11–12.

Burke, Kenneth. *The Philosophy of Literary Form: Studies in Symbolic Action.* 2nd ed. Baton Rouge: Louisiana State University Press, 1967.

Calvin, William H. *How Brains Think: Evolving Intelligence, Then and Now.* New York: Basic Books, 1996.

Carey, Benedict. "This Is Your Life (and How You Tell It)." *New York Times* May 22, 2007: http://www.nytimes.com/.

Coetzee, J. M. *The Master of Petersburg.* New York: Viking Penguin, 1994.

Coleridge, Samuel Taylor. *Biographia Literaria.* 1817. *The Critical Tradition: Classic Texts and Contemporary Trends.* Ed. David H. Richter. 3rd ed. Boston: Bedford/St. Martin's, 2007. 325–29.

Crane, R. S. *The Languages of Criticism and the Structure of Poetry.* Toronto: University of Toronto Press, 1953.

Damasio, Antonio. *The Feeling of What Happens: Body and Emotion in the Making of Consciousness.* New York: Harcourt Brace, 1999.

———. *Looking for Spinoza: Joy, Sorrow, and the Feeling Brain.* New York: Harcourt, 2003.

Davies, Robertson. *What's Bred in the Bone.* New York: Viking Penguin, 1985.

Dear Author: Students Write about the Books that Changed Their Lives. Collected by Weekly Reader's *Read* Magazine. Berkeley: Conari Press, 1995.

Derrida, Jacques. "Structure, Sign, and Play in the Discourse of the Human Sciences." Trans. Richard Macksey and Eugenio Donato. *The Languages of Criticism and the Sciences of Man: The Structuralist Controversy.* Ed. Richard Macksey and Eugenio Donato. Baltimore: Johns Hopkins University Press, 1970. 247–65.

de Waal, Frans. *The Ape and the Sushi Master: Cultural Reflections of a Primatologist.* New York: Basic Books, 2001.

———. *Good Natured: The Origins of Right and Wrong in Humans and Other Animals.* Cambridge, MA: Harvard University Press, 1996.

Dickens, Charles. *Bleak House.* 1853. New York: Oxford University Press, 1948.

———. "A Christmas Carol." 1843. *Christmas Books.* New York: Oxford University Press, 1954. 7–77.

———. *Life and Adventures of Martin Chuzzlewit.* 1844. New York: Oxford University Press, 1989.

———. *Little Dorrit.* 1857. New York: Oxford University Press, 1953.

———. *Nicholas Nickleby.* 1839. New York: Oxford University Press, 1950.

———. *The Personal History of David Copperfield.* 1850. New York: Oxford University Press, 1948.

Eakin, Paul John. *How Our Lives Become Stories: Making Selves.* Ithaca, NY: Cornell University Press, 1999.

Edmundson, Mark. *Teacher: The One Who Made a Difference.* New York: Random House, 2002.

Eldridge, Richard. *On Moral Personhood: Philosophy, Literature, Criticism, and Self-Understanding.* Chicago: University of Chicago Press, 1989.

Eliot, George. *Middlemarch.* 1872. Ed. Bert G. Hornback. A Norton Critical Edition. New York: W. W. Norton, 1977.

Eliot, T. S. *The Use of Poetry and the Use of Criticism.* Cambridge, MA: Harvard University Press, 1933.

Fetterley, Judith. *The Resisting Reader: A Feminist Approach to American Fiction.* Bloomington: Indiana University Press, 1978.

Fox, Paula. "To Write Simply." *Horn Book Magazine* (September/October 1991): 552–55.

Freud, Sigmund. *The Collected Papers of Sigmund Freud.* Ed. Ernest Jones. Vol. 4. New York: Basic Books, 1959.

Frost, Robert. "Stopping by Woods on a Snowy Evening." Robert Frost: America's Poet, http://www.ketzle.com/frost/snowyeve.htm.

Frye, Northrop. *The Educated Imagination.* A Midland Book. Bloomington: Indiana University Press, 1964.

Gass, William H. *Fiction and the Figures of Life.* Boston: David R. Godine, 1971.

Goodman, Nelson. *Ways of Worldmaking.* Indianapolis: Hackett, 1978.

Gorky, Maxim. *On Literature.* Trans. Julius Katzer. Seattle: University of Washington Press, 1973.

Graff, Gerald. *Beyond the Culture Wars: How Teaching the Conflicts Can Revitalize American Education.* New York: W. W. Norton, 1992.

———. *Clueless in Academe: How Schooling Obscures the Life of the Mind.* New Haven: Yale University Press, 2003.

Gray, Thomas. "Ode on a Distant Prospect of Eton College." 1747. http://rpo.library.utoronto.ca/poem/884.html.

Gregory, Marshall. "Character Formation in the Literary Classroom." *CEA Critic* 53.2 (Winter 1990): 5–21.

———. "Humanism's Heat, Postmodernism's Cool." *CEA Critic* 57.2 (Winter 1995): 1–25.

———. "The Sound of Story: An Inquiry into Literature and Ethos." *Narrative* 3.1 (January 1995): 33–56.

Hall, Brian. "The Group: When Did Reading, Once a Solitary Pursuit, Start to Attract a Crowd?" *New York Times Book Review* June 6, 1999: 22–23.

Hamilton, Jane. *The Book of Ruth.* Boston: Houghton Mifflin, 1988.

Hanson, Karen. "How Bad Can Good Art Be?" *Aesthetics and Ethics: Essays at the Intersection.* Ed. Jerrold Levinson. New York: Cambridge University Press, 1998. 204–26.

———. "The Pleasures of Thought." *ADE Bulletin* 99 (Fall 1991): 4–7.

Havelock, Eric A. "The Psychology of the Poetic Performance." *Preface to Plato.* Cambridge, MA: Harvard University Press, 1963. 145–64.

Havill, Juanita. "Journey of a Lifetime." *The Most Wonderful Books: Writers on Discovering the Pleasures of Reading.* Ed. Michael Dorris and Emilie Buchwald. Minneapolis: Milkweed Editions, 1997. 93–97.

Helprin, Mark. *Winter's Tale.* New York: Harcourt Brace Jovanovich, 1983.

Horace. *Satires.* Trans. Naill Rudd. *The Satires of Horace and Persius.* London: Penguin, 1973.

James, Henry. "The Art of Fiction." 1884. *The Critical Tradition: Classic Texts and Contemporary Trends.* Ed. David Richter. 2nd ed. New York: St. Martin's Press, 1998. 436–47.

Johnson, Mark. *The Body in the Mind: The Bodily Basis of Meaning, Imagination, and Reason.* Chicago: University of Chicago Press, 1987.

———. *Moral Imagination: Implications of Cognitive Science for Ethics.* Chicago: University of Chicago Press, 1993.

Johnson, Samuel. "Preface." *A Dictionary of the English Language.* 1755. Johnson, Preface to the *Dictionary,* http://andromeda.rutgers.edu/~jlynch/Texts/preface.html.

———. "Preface to Shakespeare." 1765. *The Critical Tradition: Classic Texts and Contemporary Trends.* Ed. David Richter. 3rd ed. Boston: Bedford/St. Martin's, 2007.

Keats, John. "The Eve of St. Agnes." Bartleby.com, http://www.bartleby.com/126/39.html.

———. "Ode to a Nightingale." Bartleby.com, http://bartleby.com/101/624.html.

Kennedy, William. "Why It Took So Long." *New York Times* May 20, 1990: http://nytimes.com/.

Kieran, Matthew. "Art, Imagination, and the Cultivation of Morals." *Journal of Aesthetics and Art Criticism* 54.4 (Fall 1996): 337–51.

Kirkpatrick, David D. "Writing Memoir, McCain Found a Narrative for Life." *New York Times* October 13, 2008: http://www.nytimes.com/.

Kushner, Tony. "Ten Questions for Tony Kushner." *New York Times* June 4, 2004, Readers' Opinions Section: 1. http://www.nytimes.com/.

Lakoff, George, and Mark Johnson. *Metaphors We Live By.* Chicago: University of Chicago Press, 1980.

———. *Philosophy in the Flesh: The Embodied Mind and Its Challenge to Western Thought.* New York: Basic Books, 1999.

Lamarque, Peter. "How Can We Fear and Pity Fictions?" *British Journal of Aesthetics* 21.4 (Autumn 1981): 291–304.

Leavis, F. R. *The Great Tradition: George Eliot, Henry James, Joseph Conrad.* New York: New York University Press, 1963.

Lesser, Wendy. *Nothing Remains the Same: Rereading and Remembering.* New York: Houghton Mifflin, 2002.

Lewis, C. S. *An Experiment in Criticism.* Cambridge: Cambridge University Press, 1961.

Louden, Robert B. *Morality and Moral Theory: A Reappraisal and Reaffirmation.* New York: Oxford University Press, 1992.

MacIntyre, Alasdair. *How to Be a North American.* Humanities Series, Publication no. 2-88. Washington, DC: Federation of State Humanities Councils, 1987.

McCarthy, Mary. "Artists in Uniform." *Harper's Magazine* (March 1953): 41–49.

Midgley, Mary. *Can't We Make Moral Judgments?* New York: St. Martin's Press, 1991.

Miller, J. Hillis. "Narrative." *Critical Terms for Literary Study.* Ed. Frank Lentricchia and Thomas McLaughlin. 2nd. ed. Chicago: University of Chicago Press, 1995. 66–79.

Milton, John. *Areopagitica.* 1644. Ed. Roy Flannagan. *The Riverside Milton.* Boston: Houghton Mifflin, 1998.

Mithen, Steven. *The Prehistory of the Mind: A Search for the Origins of Art, Religion, and Science.* London: Thames and Hudson, 1996.

Monroe, William. *Power to Hurt: The Virtues of Alienation.* Urbana: University of Illinois Press, 1998.

Montaigne, Michel de. *Essays of Montaigne.* Trans. Charles Cotton. Ed. William Hazlitt. Vol. 3. London: Reeves and Turner, 1877.

Morton, Kathryn. "The Story-Telling Animal." *New York Times Book Review* December 23, 1984: 1+.

Murdoch, Iris. *The Sovereignty of Good.* London: Routledge & Kegan Paul, 1970.

Nafisi, Azar. *Reading Lolita in Tehran: A Memoir in Books.* New York: Random House, 2003.

Nussbaum, Martha C. *Love's Knowledge: Essays on Philosophy and Literature.* New York: Oxford University Press, 1990.

O'Faolain, Nuala. *Are You Somebody? The Accidental Memoir of a Dublin Woman.* New York: Henry Holt, 1998.

Olson, Elder. *On Value Judgments in the Arts and Other Essays.* Chicago: University of Chicago Press, 1976.

———. "Prologue to His Book." *Collected Poems.* Chicago: University of Chicago Press, 1963.

Ozick, Cynthia. *Art and Ardor.* New York: E. P. Dutton, 1983.

Paterson, Katherine. "Why Do I Read?" *The Most Wonderful Books: Writers on Discovering The Pleasures of Reading.* Ed. Michael Dorris and Emilie Buchwald. Minneapolis: Milkweed Editions, 1997. 201–4.

Percy, Walker. *The Message in the Bottle: How Queer Man Is, How Queer Language Is, And What One Has to Do With the Other.* New York: Farrar, Straus and Giroux, 1975.

Petrarch. *De sui ipsius et multorum ignorantia.* Trans. H. Nachod. Quoted in Hanna H. Gray, "Renaissance Humanism: The Pursuit of Eloquence." *Journal of the History of Ideas* 24.4 (Oct.–Dec. 1963): 497–514.

Pinker, Steven. *The Blank Slate: The Modern Denial of Human Nature.* New York: Viking, 2002.

———. *The Language Instinct: How the Mind Creates Language.* New York: William Morrow, 1994.

Pinker, Steven, and Rebecca Goldstein. "Steven Pinker and Rebecca Goldstein." *Seed Salon,* May 19, 2004: 47+.

Pinsky, Robert. "Some Notes on Reading." *The Most Wonderful Books: Writers on Discovering the Pleasures of Reading."* Ed. Michael Dorris and Emilie Buchwald. Minneapolis: Milkweed Editions, 1997. 205–10.

Plato. "Ion." *The Dialogues of Plato.* Trans. by Benjamin Jowett. *The Great Books of the Western World.* Vol. 7. Chicago: Encyclopedia Britannica, 1952. 142–48.

Porter, Katherine Anne. "The Grave." *The Leaning Tower and Other Stories.* Boston: Houghton Mifflin Harcourt, 1944.

Postman, Neil. *Amusing Ourselves to Death: Public Discourse in the Age of Show Business.* New York: Penguin Books, 1985.

———. *The Disappearance of Childhood.* New York: Random House, 1982.

Price, Reynolds. *A Palpable God: Thirty Stories Translated from the Bible with an Essay on the Origins and Life of Narrative.* 1978. San Francisco: North Point Press, 1985.

Proulx, E. Annie. *The Shipping News.* New York: Simon & Schuster, 1993.

Proust, Marcel. *Remembrance of Things Past.* 1913. Trans. C. K. Scott Moncrieff. Vol. 1. New York: Random House, 1934.

Quindlen, Anna. *How Reading Changed My Life.* The Library of Contemporary Thought. New York: Ballantine, 1998.

Redfield, James. "The Aims of Education." 1974. *The Aims of Education: The College of the University of Chicago.* Ed. John W. Boyer. Chicago: University of Chicago Press, 1997. 169–90.

Ricoeur, Paul. *Oneself as Another.* Trans. Kathleen Blamey. Chicago: University of Chicago Press, 1992.

Rudman, Mark. "Disorder, Sorrow, and Early Reading." *The Most Wonderful Books: Writers on Discovering the Pleasures of Reading.* Ed. Michael Dorris and Emilie Buchwald. Minneapolis: Milkweed Editions, 1997. 211–17.

Sanders, Scott Russell. *Secrets of the Universe: Scenes from the Journey Home.* Boston: Beacon Press, 1991.

Santayana, George. *The Sense of Beauty.* 1896. New York: Dover Publications, 1955.

Searle, Leroy. "Literature Departments and the Practice of Theory." *MLN* (2006): 1237–61.

Shakespeare, William. *Hamlet.* 1623. *The Norton Shakespeare.* Ed. Stephen Greenblatt. New York: W. W. Norton, 1997. 1659–759.

———. *Julius Caesar.* 1623. *The Norton Shakespeare.* Ed. Stephen Greenblatt. New York: W. W. Norton, 1997. 1525–89.

———. *The Merchant of Venice.* 1623. *The Norton Shakespeare.* Ed. Stephen Greenblatt. New York: W. W. Norton, 1997. 1081–146.

———. *The Tempest.* 1623. *The Norton Shakespeare.* Ed. Stephen Greenblatt. New York: W. W. Norton, 1997. 3047–108.

Shapiro, Alan. *The Last Happy Occasion.* Chicago: University of Chicago Press, 1996.

Shelley, Mary. *Frankenstein.* 1818. London: J. M. Dent & Sons, 1963.

Shelley, Percy. *A Defence of Poetry.* 1839. *A Defence of Poetry* and *The Four Ages of Poetry.* Indianapolis: Bobbs-Merrill, 1965.

Shklovsky, Viktor. *Theory of Prose.* 1929. Trans. Benjamin Sher. Elmwood Park, IL: Dalkey Archive Press, 1990.

Sidney, Philip. "An Apology for Poetry." 1595. *Critical Theory Since Plato.* Ed. Hazard Adams. New York: Harcourt Brace Jovanovich, 1971. 154–77.

Thurber, James. "The Catbird Seat." *The Thurber Carnival.* New York: Harper & Row, 1945.

Weldon, Fay. *Letters to Alice on First Reading Jane Austen.* New York: Carroll & Graf, 1984.

Wilde, Oscar. "The Decay of Lying." *Critical Theory Since Plato.* Ed. Hazard Adams. New York: Harcourt Brace Jovanovich, 1971. 673–86.

Willard, Nancy. "The Well-Tempered Falsehood: The Art of Storytelling." *ALA Magazine* (Fall 1982): 104–12.

Wilson, E. O. *Consilience: The Unity of Knowledge.* New York: Alfred A. Knopf, 1998.

———. *On Human Nature.* Cambridge, MA: Harvard University Press, 1978.

Wilson, James Q. *The Moral Sense.* New York: Free Press, 1993.

Woods, James. *The Broken Estate: Essays on Literature and Belief.* New York: Random House, 1999.

Wordsworth, William. "Composed a Few Miles Above Tintern Abbey on Re-visiting the Banks of the Wye During a Tour, July 13, 1798." Bartleby.com, http://www.bartleby.com/145/ww138.html.

———. Preface to *Lyrical Ballads. The Critical Tradition: Classic Texts and Contemporary Trends.* Ed. David H. Richter. New York: St. Martin's Press, 1989. 285–98.

Wrangham, Richard, and Dale Peterson. *Demonic Males: Apes and Origins of Human Violence.* Boston: Houghton Mifflin, 1996.

INDEX

❧❦✻❧❦

MARSHALL W. GREGORY

is Ice Professor of English, Liberal Education, and Pedagogy at Butler University. He is co-author with Wayne Booth of *The Harper and Row Rhetoric: Writing as Thinking, Thinking as Writing* and *The Harper and Row Reader: Liberal Education through Reading and Writing;* and co-author with Ellie Chambers of *Teaching and Learning English Literature.*